Henry Wood

Verner's Pride

Vol. 2

Henry Wood

Verner's Pride
Vol. 2

ISBN/EAN: 9783337341206

Printed in Europe, USA, Canada, Australia, Japan

Cover: Foto ©Thomas Meinert / pixelio.de

More available books at **www.hansebooks.com**

VERNER'S PRIDE.

BY

MRS. HENRY WOOD,

AUTHOR OF "EAST LYNNE," "MRS. HALLIBURTON'S TROUBLES," ETC., ETC.

"Searching the window for a flint, I found
This paper, thus sealed up: and I am sure
It did not lie there when I went to bed."
Shakespeare.

IN THREE VOLUMES.

VOL. II.

LONDON:

BRADBURY & EVANS, 11, BOUVERIE STREET.

1863.

[The right of Translation is reserved.]

LONDON:
BRADBURY AND EVANS, PRINTERS, WHITEFRIARS.

CONTENTS.

iv CONTENTS.

VERNER'S PRIDE.

CHAPTER I.

BACK AGAIN!

IT was late when Lionel reached Verner's Pride. Night had set in, and his dinner was waiting.

He ate it hurriedly—he mostly did eat hurriedly when he was alone, as if he were glad to get it over—Tynn waiting on him. Tynn liked to wait upon his young master. Tynn had been in a state of glowing delight since the accession of Lionel. Attached to the old family, Tynn had felt it almost as keenly as Lionel himself, when the estate had lapsed to the Massingbirds. Mrs. Tynn was in a glow of delight also. There was no mistress, and she ruled the household, including Tynn.

The dinner gone away and the wine on the table, Lionel drew his chair in front of the fire, and fell into a train of thought, leaving the wine untouched. Full half-an-hour had he thus sat, when the entrance of Tynn aroused him. He poured out a glass, and raised it to his lips. Tynn bore a note on his silver waiter.

"Matiss's boy has just brought it, sir. He is waiting to know whether there's any answer."

Lionel opened the note, and was reading it, when a sound of carriage wheels came rattling on to the terrace, passed the windows, and stopped at the hall door. "Who can be paying me a visit to-night, I wonder?" cried he. "Go and see, Tynn."

"It sounded like one of them rattling one-horse flies from the railway station," was Tynn's comment to his master, as he left the room.

Whoever it might be, they appeared pretty long in entering, and Lionel, very greatly to his surprise, heard a sound as of much luggage being deposited in the hall. He was on the point of going out to see, when the door opened, and a lovely vision glided forward. A young, fair face and form, clothed in deep mourning, with a shower of golden curls shading her damask cheeks. For one single moment, Lionel was lost in the beauty of the vista. Then he recognised her, before Tynn's announcement was heard; and his heart leaped as if it would burst its bounds.

"Mrs. Massingbird, sir."

Leaped within him fast and furiously. His pulses throbbed, his blood coursed on, and his face went hot and cold with its emotion. Had, he been fondly persuading himself, during the past months, that she was forgotten? Truly the present moment rudely undeceived him.

Tynn shut the door, leaving them alone. Lionel was not so agitated as to forget the courtesies of

life. He shook hands with her, and, in the impulse
of the moment, called her Sibylla : and then bit his
tongue for doing it.

She burst into tears. There, as he held her
hand. She lifted her lovely face to him with a
yearning, pleading look. " Oh, Lionel!—you will
give me a home, won't you ? "

What was he to say ? He could not, in that
first instant, abruptly say to her—No, you cannot
have a home here. Lionel could not hurt the feelings of any one. " Sit down, Mrs. Massingbird,"
he gently said, drawing an easy chair to the fire.
"You have taken me quite by surprise. When did
you land ? "

She threw off her bonnet, shook back those
golden curls, and sat down in the chair, a large
heavy shawl on her shoulders. " I will not take it
off yet," she said in a plaintive voice. " I am very
cold."

She shivered slightly. Lionel drew her chair yet
nearer the fire, and brought a footstool for her feet.
Repeating his question as he did so.

" We reached Liverpool late yesterday, and I
started for home this morning," she answered, her
eyelashes wet still, as she gazed into the fire.
" What a miserable journey it has been ! " she
added, turning to Lionel. " A miserable voyage
out ; a miserable ending ! "

" Are you aware of the changes that have taken
place since you left ? " he asked. " Your aunt is
dead."

"Yes, I know it," she answered. "They told me at the station just now. That lame porter came up and knew me; and his first news to me was, that Mrs. Verner was dead. What a greeting! I was coming home here to live with her."

"You could not have received my letter. One which I wrote at the request of Mrs. Verner in answer to yours."

"What news was in it?" she asked. "I received no letter from you."

"It contained remittances. It was sent, I say, in answer to yours, in which you requested money should be forwarded for your home passage. You did not wait for it?"

"I was tired of waiting. I was sick for home. And one day, when I had been crying more than usual, Mrs. Eyre said to me, that if I were so anxious to go, there need be no difficulty about the passage-money. That they would advance me any amount I might require. Oh, I was so glad! I came away by the next ship."

"Why did you not write, saying that you were coming?"

"I did not think it mattered—and I knew I had this home to come to. If I had had to go to my old home again at papa's, then I should have written. I should have seemed like an intruder arriving at their house, and have deemed it necessary to warn them of it."

"You heard in Australia of Mr. Verner's death, I presume?"

"I heard of that, and that my husband had inherited Verner's Pride. The news came out just before I sailed for home. Of course I thought I had a right to come to this home, though he was dead. I suppose it is yours now?"

"Yes."

"Who lives here?"

"Only myself."

"Have I a right to live here—as Frederick's widow?" she continued, lifting her large blue eyes anxiously at Lionel. "I mean would the law give it me?"

"No," he replied, in a low tone. He felt that the truth must be told to her without disguise. She was placing both him and herself in an embarrassing situation.

"Was there any money left to me?—or to Frederick?"

"None to you. Verner's Pride was left to your husband. But at his demise it came to me."

"Did my aunt leave me nothing?"

"She had nothing to leave, Mrs. Massingbird. The settlement which Mr. Verner executed on her, when they married, was only for her life. It lapsed back to the Verner's Pride revenues when she died."

"Then I am left without a shilling, to the mercy of the world!"

Lionel felt for her—felt for her rather more than was safe. He began planning in his own mind how he could secure to her an income from the Verner's Pride estate, without her knowing whence it came.

Frederick Massingbird had been its inheritor for a
short three or four months, and Lionel's sense of
justice revolted against his widow being thrown on
the world, as she expressed it, without a shilling.

"The revenues of the estate, during the short
time that elapsed between Mr. Verner's death and
your husband's, are undoubtedly yours, Mrs. Massingbird," he said. "I will see Matiss about it,
and they shall be paid over."

"How long will it be first?"

"A few days, possibly. In a note which I
received but now from Matiss, he tells me he is
starting for London, but will be home the beginning
of the week. It shall be arranged on his return."

"Thank you. And, until then, I may stay
here?"

Lionel was at a nonplus. It is not a pleasing
thing to tell a lady that she must quit your house,
in which, like a stray lamb, she has taken refuge.
Even though it be, for her own fair sake, expedient
that she should go.

"I am here alone," said Lionel, after a pause.
"Your temporary home had better be with your
sisters."

"No, that it never shall," returned Sibylla, in a
hasty tone of fear. "I will never go home to them
now papa's away. Why did he leave Deerham?
They told me at the station that he was gone, and
Jan was doctor."

"Dr. West is travelling on the Continent, as
medical attendant and companion to a nobleman,

At least—I think I heard it was a nobleman," continued Lionel. " I am really not sure."

" And you would like me to go home to those two cross, fault-finding sisters!" she resumed. " They might reproach me all day long with coming home to be kept. As if it were my fault that I am left without anything. Oh, Lionel! don't turn me out! Let me stay until I can see what is to be done for myself. I shall not hurt you. It would have been all mine had Frederick lived."

He did not know what to do. Every moment there seemed to grow less chance that she would leave the house. A bright thought darted into his mind. It was, that he would get his mother or Decima to come and stay with him for a time.

, " What would you like to take ? " he inquired. " Mrs. Tynn will get you anything you wish. I——"

" Nothing yet," she interrupted. " I could not eat; I am too unhappy. I will take some tea presently, but not until I am warmer. I am very cold."

She cowered over the fire again, shivering much. Lionel, saying he had a note to write, sat down to a distant table. He penned a few hasty lines to his mother, telling her that Mrs. Massingbird had arrived, under the impression that she was coming to Mrs. Verner, and that he could not well turn her out again that night, fatigued and poorly as she appeared to him to be. He begged his mother to come to him for a day or two, in the emergency; or to send Decima.

An under-current of conviction ran in Lionel's mind, during the time of writing it, that his mother would not come: he doubted even whether she would allow Decima to come. He drove the thought away from him; but the impression remained. Carrying the note out of the room when written, he despatched it to Deerham Court by a mounted groom. As he was returning to the dining-room, he encountered Mrs. Tynn.

"I hear Mrs. Massingbird has arrived, sir," cried she.

"Yes," replied Lionel. "She will like some tea presently. She appears very much fatigued."

"Is the luggage to be taken up-stairs, sir?" she continued, pointing to the pile in the hall. "Is she going to stay here?"

Lionel really did not know what answer to make.

"She came, expecting to stay," he said, after a pause. "She did not know but your mistress was still here. Should she remain, I dare say Lady Verner, or my sister, will join her. You have beds ready?"

"Plenty of them, sir, at five minutes' notice."

When Lionel entered the room, Sibylla was in the same attitude, shivering over the fire. Unnaturally cold she appeared to be, and yet her cheeks were brilliantly bright, as if with a touch of fever.

"I fear you have caught cold on the journey to-day," he said.

"I don't think so," she answered. "I am cold

from nervousness. I went cold at the station when they told me that my aunt was dead, and I have been shivering ever since. Never mind me: it will go off presently."

Lionel drew a chair to the other side of the fire, compassionately regarding her. He could have found in his heart to take her in his arms, and warm her there.

" What was that, about a codicil?" she suddenly asked him. " When my aunt wrote to me upon Mr. Verner's death, she said that a codicil had been lost: or that, otherwise, the estate would have been yours."

Lionel explained it to her. Concealing nothing.

" Then—if that codicil had been forthcoming, Frederick's share would have been but five hundred pounds ? "

" That is all."

" It was very little to leave him," she musingly rejoined.

" And still less to leave me, considering my nearer relationship—my nearer claims. When the codicil could not be found, the will had to be acted upon : and five hundred pounds was all the sum it gave me."

" Has the codicil never been found ? "

" Never."

" How very strange ! What became of it, do you think ? "

" I wish I could think what," replied Lionel. " Although Verner's Pride has come to me without it, it would be satisfactory to solve the mystery."

Sibylla looked round cautiously, and sunk her voice. "Could Tynn or his wife have done any-thing with it? You say they were present when it was signed."

"Most decidedly they did not. Both of them were anxious that I should succeed."

"It is so strange! To lock a paper up in a desk, and for it to disappear of its own accord! The moths could not have got in and eaten it?"

"Scarcely," smiled Lionel. "The day before your aunt died, she ——"

"Don't talk of that," interrupted Mrs. Massing-bird. "I will hear about her death to-morrow. I shall be ill if I cry much to-night."

She sank into silence, and Lionel did not interrupt it. It continued, until his quick ears caught the sound of the groom's return. The man rode his horse round to the stables at once. Presently Tynn came in with a note. It was from Lady Verner. A few lines, written hastily with a pencil:

"I do not understand your request, Lionel, or why you make it. Whatever may be my opinion of Frederick Massingbird's widow, I will not insult her sense of propriety by supposing that she would attempt to remain at Verner's Pride now her aunt is dead. It is absurd of you to ask me to come: neither shall I send Decima. Were I and Decima re-siding with you, it would not be the place for Sibylla Massingbird. She has her own home to go to."

There was no signature. Lionel knew his mother's handwriting too well to require the addition. It was just the note that he might have expected her to write.

What was he to do? In the midst of his ruminations, Sibylla rose.

"I am warm now," she said. "I should like to go up-stairs and take this heavy shawl off."

Lionel rang the bell for Mrs. Tynn. And Sibylla left the room with her.

"I'll get her sisters here!" he suddenly exclaimed, the thought of them darting into his mind. "They will be the proper persons to explain to her the inexpediency of her remaining here. Poor girl! she is unable to think of it in her fatigue and grief."

He did not give it a second thought, but snatched his hat, and went down himself to Dr. West's with strides as long as Jan's. Entering the general sitting-room without ceremony, his eyes fell upon a supper-table and Master Cheese; the latter regaling himself upon apple-puffs to his heart's content.

"Where are the Miss Wests?" asked Lionel.

"Gone to a party," responded the young gentleman, as soon as he could get his mouth sufficiently empty to speak.

"Where to?"

"To Heartburg, sir. It's a ball at old Thingumtight's, the doctor's. They are gone off in grey gauze, with branches of white flowers hanging to their curls, and they call that mourning. The fly is to bring them back at two in the morning. They left these apple-puffs for me and Jan. Jan said he should not want any ; he'd eat meat; so I have got his share and mine !"

And Master Cheese appeared to be enjoying the shares excessively. Lionel left him to it, and went thoughtfully back to Verner's Pride.

CHAPTER II.

A MOMENT OF DELIRIUM.

THE dining-room looked a picture of comfort: and Lionel thought so as he entered. A blaze of light and warmth burst upon him. A well-spread tea-table was there, with cold meat, game and else, at one end of it. Standing before the fire, her young, slender form habited in its black robes, was Sibylla. No one, looking at her, would have believed her to be a widow: partly from her youth, partly that she did not wear the widow's dress. Her head was uncovered, and her fair curls fell, shading her brilliant cheeks. It has been mentioned that her chief beauty lay in her complexion: seen by candle-light, flushed as she was now, she was inexpressibly beautiful. A dangerous hour, a perilous situation for the yet unhealed heart of Lionel Verner.

The bright flush was the result of excitement, of some degree of inward fever. Let us allow that it was a trying time for her. She had arrived to find Mrs. Verner dead, her father absent: she had arrived to find that no provision had been made for her by Mr. Verner's will, as the widow of Frederick Massingbird. Frederick's having succeeded to the inheritance debarred her even of the five hundred pounds. It is true there would be the rents, received for the short time it had been his. There was no doubt that Sibylla, throughout the long voyage, had cherished the prospect of finding a home at Verner's Pride. If her husband had lived, it would have been wholly hers; she appeared still to possess a right in it; and she never gave a thought to the possibility that her aunt would not welcome her to it. Whether she cast a reflection to Lionel Verner in the matter, she best knew: had she reflected pro- perly, she might have surmised that Lionel would be living at it, its master. But—the voyage ended, the home gained—what did she find? That Mrs. Verner was no longer at Verner's Pride, to press the kiss of welcome upon her lips; a few feet of earth was all her home now.

It was a terrible disappointment. There could be no doubt of that. And another disappointment was. to find Dr. West away. Sibylla's sisters had been at times over-strict with her, much as they loved her, and the vision of returning to her old home, to them, was one of bitterness. So bitter, in fact, that she would not glance at its possibility.

Fatigued, low-spirited, feverishly perplexed, Sibylla did not know what she could do. She was not in a state that night to give much care to the future. All she hoped was, to stay in that haven until some- thing else could be arranged for her. Let us give her her due. Somewhat careless, naturally, of the punctilios of life, it never occurred to her that it might not be the precise thing for her to remain,

young as she was, the sole guest of Lionel Verner.
Her voyage out, her residence in that very uncon-
ventional place, Melbourne, the waves and storms
which had gone over her there in more ways than
one, the voyage back again alone, all had tended to
give Sibylla Massingbird an independence of thought;
a contempt for the rules and regulations, the little
points of etiquette obtaining in civilised society.
She really thought no more harm of staying at
Verner's Pride with Lionel, than she would have
thought it had old Mr. Verner been its master.
The eyelashes, resting on her hot cheeks, were wet,
as she turned round when Lionel entered.

"Have you taken anything, Mrs. Massingbird?"

"No."

"But you should have done so," he remonstrated,
his tone one of the most considerate kindness.

"I did not observe that tea waited," she replied,
the covered table catching her eye for the first time.
"I have been thinking."

He placed a chair for her before the tea-tray,
and she sat down. "Am I to preside?" she
asked.

"If you will. If you are not too tired."

"Who makes tea for you in general?" she continued.

"They send it in, made."

Sibylla busied herself with the tea, in a languid
sort of manner. In vain Lionel pressed her to eat.
She could touch nothing. She took a piece of rolled
bread-and-butter, but left it.

" You must have dined on the road, Mrs. Massing-bird ? " he said with a smile.

" I ? I have not taken anything all day. I kept thinking 'I shall get to Verner's Pride in time for my aunt's dinner.' But the train arrived later than I anticipated; and when I got here she was gone."

Sibylla bent her head, as if playing with her tea-spoon. Lionel detected the dropping tears.

" Did you wonder where I was going just now, when I went out ? "

" I did not know you had been out," replied Sibylla.

" I went to your sisters'. I thought it would be better for them to come here. Unfortunately, I found them gone out: and young Cheese says they will not be home until two in the morning."

" Why, where can they be gone ? " cried Sibylla, aroused to interest. It was so unusual for the Miss Wests to be out late.

" To some gathering at Heartburg. Cheese was eating apple-puffs with unlimited satisfaction."

The connection of apple-puffs with Master Cheese called up a faint smile into Sibylla's face. She pushed her chair away from the table, turning it towards the fire.

" But you surely have not finished, Mrs. Massing-bird ? "

" Yes, thank you. I have drunk my tea. I cannot eat anything."

Lionel rang, and the things were removed. Sibylla

was standing before the mantel-piece when they were left alone, unconsciously looking at herself in the glass. Lionel stood near her.

"I have not got a widow's cap," she exclaimed, turning to him, the thought appearing suddenly to strike her. "I had two or three curious things made, that they called widow's caps in Melbourne, but they were spoilt on the voyage."

"You have seen some trouble since you went out," Lionel observed.

"Yes, I have. It was an ill-starred voyage. It has been ill-starred from the beginning to the end ; all of it together."

"The voyage has, you mean ? "

"I mean more than the voyage," she replied. But her tone did not invite further question.

"Did you succeed in getting particulars of the fate of John ? "

"No. Captain Cannonby promised to make inquiries, but we had not heard from him before I came away. I wish we could have found Luke Roy."

"Did you not find him ? "

"We heard of him from the Eyres—the friends I was staying with. It was so singular," she continued, with some animation in her tone. "Luke Roy came to Melbourne after John was killed, and fell in with the Eyres. He told them about John : little thinking that I and Frederick should meet the Eyres afterwards. John died from a shot."

"From a shot ! " involuntarily exclaimed Lionel.

"He and Luke were coming down to Melbourne from—where was it?—the Bendigo Diggings, I think; but I heard so much of the different names, that I am apt to confound one with another. John had a great deal of gold on him, in a belt round his waist. and Luke supposes that it got known. John was attacked as they were sleeping by night in the open air, beaten, and shot. It was the shot that killed him."

"Poor fellow!" exclaimed Lionel, his eyes fixed on vacancy, mentally beholding John Massingbird. "And they robbed him!"

"They had robbed him of all. Not a particle of gold was left upon him. And the report sent home by Luke, that the gold and men were taken, proved to be a mistaken one. Luke came on afterwards to Melbourne, and tried to discover the men; but he could not. It was this striving at discovery which brought him in contact with Mr. Eyre. After we reached Melbourne and I became acquainted with the Eyres, they did all they could to find out Luke. but they were unsuccessful."

"What had become of him?"

"They could not think. The last time Mr. Eyre saw him, Luke said he thought he had obtained a clue to the men who killed John. He promised to go back the following day and tell Mr. Eyre more about it. But he did not. And they never saw him afterwards. Mrs. Eyre used to say to me that she sincerely trusted no harm had come to Luke."

" Harm in what way?" asked Lionel.

" She thought—but she would say that it was a foolish thought—if Luke should have found the men, and been sufficiently imprudent to allow them to know that he recognised them, they might have worked him some ill. Perhaps killed him."

Sibylla spoke the last words in a low tone. She was standing very still; her hands lightly resting before her, one upon another. How Lionel's heart was beating as he gazed on her, he alone knew. She was once again the Sibylla of past days. He forgot that she was the widow of another; that she had left him for that other of her own free will. All his past resentment faded in that moment: nothing was present to him but his love; and Sibylla with her fascinating beauty.

" You are thinner than when you left home," he remarked.

" I grew thin with vexation; with grief. He ought not to have taken me."

The concluding sentence was spoken in a strangely resentful tone. It surprised Lionel. " Who ought not to have taken you?—taken you where?" he asked, really not understanding her.

" He. Frederick Massingbird. He might have known what a place that Melbourne was. It is not fit for a lady. We had lodgings in a wooden house, near a spot that had used to be called Canvas Town. The place was crowded with people."

" But surely there are decent hotels at Melbourne?"

c 2

"All I know is, he did not take me to one. He inquired at one or two, but they were full; and then somebody recommended him to get a lodging. It was not right. He might have gone to it himself, but he had me with him. He lost his desk, you know."

"I heard that he did," replied Lionel.

"And I suppose that frightened him. Everything was in the desk: money and letters of credit. He had a few bank-notes, only, left in his pocket-book. It never was recovered. I owe my passage-money home, and I believe Captain Cannonby supplied him with some funds—which of course ought to be repaid. He took to drink brandy," she continued.

"I am much surprised to hear it."

"Some fever came on. I don't know whether he caught it, or whether it came to him naturally. It was a sort of intermittent fever. At times he was very low with it, and then it was that he would drink the brandy. Only fancy what my position was!" she added, her face and voice alike full of pain. "He, not always himself; and I, out there in that wretched place alone. I went down on my knees to him one day, and begged him to send me back to England."

"Sibylla!"

He was unconscious that he called her by the familiar name. He was wishing he could have shielded her from all this. Painful as the retrospect might be to her, the recital was far more painful to him.

"After that, we met Captain Cannonby. I did not much like him, but he was kind to us. He got us to change to an hotel, made them find room for us, and then introduced me to the Eyres. Afterwards, he and Fred started from Melbourne, and I went to stay at the Eyres'."

Lionel did not interrupt her. She had made a pause, her eyes fixed on the fire.

"A day or two, and Captain Cannonby came back, and said that my husband was dead. I was not very much surprised. I thought he would not live when he left me: he had death written in his face. And so, I am alone in the world."

She raised her large blue eyes, swimming in tears, to Lionel. It completely disarmed him. He forgot all his prudence, all his caution; he forgot things that it was incumbent upon him to remember; and, like many another has done before him, older and wiser than Lionel Verner, he suffered a moment's impassioned impulse to fix the destiny of a life.

"Not alone from henceforth, Sibylla," he murmured, bending towards her in agitation, his lips apart, his breath coming fast and loud, his cheeks scarlet. "Let me be your protector. I love you more fondly than I have ever done."

She was entirely unprepared for the avowal. It may be, that she did not know what to make of it—how to understand it. She stepped back, her eyes strained on him inquiringly, her face turning to pallor. Lionel threw his arms round her, drew her to him, and sheltered her on his breast: as if he would ward off ill from her for ever.

"Be my wife," he fondly cried, his voice trembling with its own tenderness. "My darling, let this home be yours! Nothing shall part us more."

She burst into tears, raised herself, and looked at him. "You cannot mean it! After behaving to you as I did, can you love me still?"

"I love you far better than ever," he answered, his voice becoming hoarse with emotion. "I have been striving to forget you ever since that cruel time; and not until to-night did I know how utterly futile has been the strife. You will let me love you! you will help me to blot out its remembrance!"

She drew a long deep sigh, like one who is relieved from some wearing pain, and laid her head down again as he had placed it. "I can love you better than I loved him," she breathed, in a low whisper.

"Sibylla, why did you leave me? Why did you marry him?"

"O Lionel, don't reproach me!—don't reproach me!" she answered, bursting into tears. "Papa made me. He did, indeed."

"*He* made you! Dr. West?"

"I liked Frederick a little. Yes, I did; I will not deny it. And oh, how he loved me! All the while, Lionel, that you hovered near me—never speaking, never saying that you loved—he told me of it incessantly."

" Stay, Sibylla. You could not have mistaken me."

" 'True. Yours was silent love; his was urgent. When it came to the decision, and he asked me to marry him, and to go out to Australia, then papa interfered. He suspected that I cared for you—that you cared for me; and he—he —— "

Sibylla stopped and hesitated.

" Must I tell you all?" she asked. " Will you never, never repeat it to papa, or reproach him? Will you let it remain a secret between us?"

" I will, Sibylla. I will never speak upon the point to Dr. West."

"'Papa said that I must choose Frederick Massingbird. He told me that Verner's Pride was left to Frederick, and he ordered me to marry him. He did not say how he knew it—how he heard it; he only said that it was so. He affirmed that you were cut off with nothing, or next to nothing; that you would not be able to take a wife for years—perhaps never. And I weakly yielded."

A strangely stern expression had darkened Lionel's face. Sibylla saw it, and wrung her hands.

" Oh, don't blame me!—don't blame me more than you can help! I know how weak, how wrong it was; but you cannot tell how entirely obedient we have always been to papa."

" Dr. West became accidentally acquainted with the fact that the property was left away from me," returned Lionel, in a tone of scorn he could not entirely suppress. " He made good use, it seems, of his knowledge."

"Do not blame *me!*" she reiterated. . " It was not my fault."

" I do not blame you, my dearest."

" I have been rightly served," she said, the tears streaming down. " I married him, pressed to it by my father, that I might share in Verner's Pride ; and, before the news came out that Verner's Pride was ours, he was dead. It had lapsed to you, whom I rejected! Lionel, I never supposed that you would cast another thought to me; but, many a time have I felt that I should like to kneel and, ask your forgiveness."

He bent his head, fondly kissing her. " We will forget it together, Sibylla."

A sudden thought appeared to strike her, called forth, no doubt, by this new state of things, and her face turned crimson as she looked at Lionel.

" Ought I to remain here now ?"

" You cannot well do anything else, as it is so late," he answered. " Allow Verner's Pride to afford you an asylum for the present, until you can make arrangements to remove to some temporary home. Mrs. Tynn will make you comfortable. I shall be, during the time, my mother's guest."

" What is the time now ?" asked Sibylla.

" Nearly ten. And, I dare say you are tired. I will not be selfish enough to keep you up," he added, preparing to depart. " Good-night, my dearest."

She burst into fresh tears, and clung to his hand. "I shall be thinking it must be a dream as soon as you leave me. You will be sure to come back and see me to-morrow?"

"Come back—ay!" he said, with a smile; "Verner's Pride never contained the magnet for me that it contains now."

He gave a few brief orders to Mrs. Tynn and to his own servant, and quitted the house. Neither afraid of ghosts nor thieves, he took the field way, the road which led by the Willow-pond. It was a fine, cold night, his mind was unsettled, his blood was heated, and the lonely route appeared to him preferable to the one through the village.

As he passed the Willow-pond with a quick step, he caught a glimpse of some figure bending over it, as if it were looking for something in the water, or else about to take a leap in. Remembering the fate of Rachel, and not wishing to have a second catastrophe of the same nature happen on his estate, Lionel strode towards the figure and caught it by the arm. The head was flung upwards at the touch, and Lionel recognised Robin Frost.

"Robin! what do you do here?" he questioned, his tone somewhat severe in spite of its kindness.

"No harm," answered the man. "There be times, Mr. Lionel, when I am forced to come. If I am in my bed, and the thought comes over me that

I may see her if I only stay long enough upon the brink of this here water, which was her ending, I'm obliged to get up and come here. There be nights, sir, when I have stood here from sunset to sunrise."

"But you never have seen her, Robin?" returned Lionel, humouring his grief.

"No; never. But it's no reason why I never may. Folks say there be some of the dead that comes again, sir—not all."

"And if you did see her, what end would it answer?"

"She'd tell me who the wicked one was that put her into it," returned Robin, in a low whisper; and there was something so wild in the man's tone as to make Lionel doubt his perfect sanity. "Many a time do I hear her voice a-calling to me. It comes at all hours, abroad and at home; in the full sunshine, and in the dark night. 'Robin!' it says, 'Robin!' But it never says nothing more."

Lionel laid his hand on the man's shoulder, and drew him with him. "I am going your way, Robin: let us walk together."

Robin made no resistance; he went along with his head down.

"I heard a word said to-night, sir, as Miss Sibylla had come back;" he resumed, more calmly, "Mrs. Massingbird, that is. Somebody said they saw her at the station. Have you seen her, sir?"

"Yes; I have," replied Lionel.

" Does she say anything about John Massingbird?" continued the man with feverish eagerness.
" Is he dead ? or is he alive ? "

" He is dead, Robin. There has never been a
doubt upon the point since the news first came. He
died by violence."

" Then he got his deserts," returned Robin, lifting his hand in the air, as he had done once before
when speaking upon the same subject. " And
Luke Roy, sir ? Is he coming ? I'm a-waiting
for him."

" Of Luke, Mrs. Massingbird knows nothing. For
myself, I think he is sure to come home, sooner or
later."

" Heaven send him ! " aspirated Robin.

Lionel saw the man turn to his home, and very
soon afterwards he was at his mother's. Lady
Verner had retired for the night. Decima and
Lucy were about retiring. They had risen from
their seats, and Decima—who was too cautious to
trust it to servants—was taking the fire off the
grate. They looked inexpressibly surprised at the
entrance of Lionel.

" I have come on a visit, Decima," began he,
speaking in a gay tone. " Can you take me in ? "

She did not understand him, and Lionel saw by
the questioning expression of her face that Lady
Verner had not made public the contents of his
note to her: he saw that they were ignorant of
the return of Sibylla. The fact that they were
so, seemed to rush over his spirit as a refreshing

dew. Why it should do so, he did not seek to analyse : and he was all too self-conscious that he dared not.

"A friend has come unexpectedly on a visit, and taken possession of Verner's Pride," he pursued. "I have lent it for a time."

"Lent it all ?" exclaimed the wondering Decima.

"Lent it all. You will make room for me, won't you ?"

"To be sure," said Decima, puzzled more than she could express. "But was there no room left for you ?"

"No," answered Lionel.

"What very unconscionable people they must be, to invade you in such numbers as that! You can have your old chamber, Lionel. But I will just go and speak to Catherine."

She hastened from the room. Lionel stood before the fire, positively turning his back upon Lucy Tempest. Was his conscience already smiting him ? Lucy, who had stood by the table, her bed candle in her hand, stepped forward and held out the other hand to Lionel.

"May I wish you good-night ?" she said.

"Good-night," he answered, shaking her hand. "How is your cold ?"

"Oh! it is so much better!" she replied, with animation. "All the threatened soreness of the chest is gone. I shall be well by to-morrow. Lady Verner said I ought to have gone to bed early, but I felt too well. I knew Jan's advice would be good."

She left him, and Lionel leaned his elbow on the mantel-piece, his brow contracting as does that of one in unpleasant thought. Was he recalling the mode in which he had taken leave of Lucy earlier in the day?

CHAPTER III.

IF he did not recal it then, he recalled it later :
when he was upon his bed, turning and tossing from
side to side. His conscience was smiting him :
smiting him from more points than one. Carried
away by the impulse of the moment, he had spoken
words that night, in his hot passion, which might
not be redeemed; and now that the leisure for reflection was come, he could not conceal from himself that he had been too hasty. Lionel Verner
was one who possessed excessive conscientiousness :
even as a boy, had impetuosity led him into a fault—
as it often did—his silent, inward repentance would
be always keenly real, more so than the case deserved. It was so now. He loved Sibylla: there
had been no mistake there : but it is certain that
the unexpected delight of meeting her, her presence
palpably before him in all its beauty, her manifested
sorrow and grief, her lonely, unprotected position,
all had worked their effect upon his heart and mind,
had imparted to his love a false intensity. However
the agitation of the moment may have caused him
to fancy it, he did *not* love Sibylla as he had loved
her of old: else why should the image of Lucy

Tempest present itself to him surrounded by a halo
of regret? The point is as unpleasant for us to
touch upon, as it was to Lionel to think of: but
the fact was all too palpable, and cannot be suppressed. He did love Sibylla: nevertheless there
obtruded the unwelcome reflection that, in asking
her to be his wife, he had been hasty; that it had
been better had he taken time for consideration. He
almost doubted whether Lucy would not have been
more acceptable to him: not loved *yet* so much as
Sibylla, but better suited to him in all other ways:
worse than this, he doubted whether he had not in
honour bound himself tacitly to Lucy that very day.

The fit of repentance was upon him, and he
tossed and turned from side to side upon his uneasy
bed. But, toss and turn as he would, he could not
undo his night's work. There remained nothing
for him but to carry it out, and make the best of
it; and he strove to deceive his conscience with the
hope that Lucy Tempest, in her girlish innocence,
had not understood his hinted allusions to her
becoming his wife: that she had looked upon his
snatched caresses as but trifling pastime, such as
he might offer to a child. Most unjustifiable he
now felt those hints, those acts to have been, and
his brow grew red with shame at their recollection.
One thing he did hope, hope sincerely—that Lucy
did not care for him. That she liked him very
much, and had been on most confidential terms
with him he knew: but he did hope her liking went
no deeper. Strange sophistry! how it will deceive

the human heart! how prone we are to admit it!
Lionel was honest enough in his hope now: but,
not many hours before, he had been hugging his
heart with the delusion that Lucy did love him.

Towards morning he dropped into an uneasy sleep.
He awoke later than his usual hour from a dream
of Frederick Massingbird. Dreams play us strange
fantasies. Lionel's had taken him to that past
evening, prior to Frederick Massingbird's marriage,
when he had sought him in his chamber, to offer a
word of warning against the union. He seemed to be
living the interview over again, and the first words
when he awoke, rushing over his brain with minute
and unpleasant reality, were those he had himself
spoken in reference to Sibylla:—"Were she free
as air this moment, were she to come to my feet, and
say 'Let me be your wife,' I should tell her that
the whole world was before her to choose from, save
myself. She can never again be anything to me."

Brave words: fully believed in when they were
spoken: but what did Lionel think of them now?

He went down to breakfast. He was rather late,
and found they had assembled. Lady Verner, who
had just heard for the first time of Lionel's presence
in the house, made no secret now of Lionel's note
to her. Therefore Decima and Lucy knew that the
"invasion" of Verner's Pride had been caused by
Mrs. Massingbird.

She—Lady Verner—scarcely gave herself time to
greet Lionel before she commenced upon it. She
did not conceal, or seek to conceal, her sentiments—

either of Sibylla herself, or of the step she had taken. And Lionel had the pleasure of hearing his intended bride alluded to, in a manner that was not altogether complimentary.

He could not stop it. He could not take upon himself the defence of Sibylla, and say, "Do you know that you are speaking of my future wife?" No, for Lucy Tempest was there. Not in her presence had he the courage to bring home to himself his own dishonour: to avow that, after wooing her (it was very like it), he had turned round and asked another to marry him. The morning sun shone into the room upon the snowy cloth, upon the silver breakfast service, upon the exquisite cups of painted porcelain, upon those seated round the table. Decima sat opposite to Lady Verner, Lionel and Lucy were face to face on either side. The walls exhibited a few choice paintings; the room and its appurtenances were in excellent taste. Lady Verner liked things that pleased the eye. That silver service had been a recent present of Lionel's, who had delighted in showering elegancies and comforts upon his mother since his accession.

"What could have induced her ever to think of taking up her residence at Verner's Pride on her return?" reiterated Lady Verner to Lionel.

" She believed she was coming to her aunt. It was only at the station, here, that she learnt Mrs. Verner was dead."

" She did learn it there? "

" Yes. She learnt it there."

"And she could come to Verner's Pride *after*
that? knowing that you, and you alone, were its
master?"

Lionel toyed with his coffee-cup. He wished his
mother would spare her remarks.

"She was so fatigued, so low-spirited, that I
believed she was scarcely conscious where she
drove," he returned. "I am certain that the idea
of there being any impropriety in it never once
crossed her mind."

Lady Verner drew her shawl around her with a
peculiar movement. If ever action expressed scorn,
that one did;—scorn of Sibylla, scorn of her conduct, scorn of Lionel's credulity in believing in her.
Lionel read it all. Happening to glance across the
table, he caught the eyes of Lucy Tempest fixed
upon him with an open expression of wonder.
Wonder at what? At his believing in Sibylla? It
might be. With all Lucy's straightforward plainness, she would have been one of the last to storm
Lionel's abode, and take refuge in it. A retort,
defending Sibylla, had been upon Lionel's tongue,
but that gaze stopped it.

"How long does she purpose honouring Verner's
Pride with her presence, and keeping you out of it?"
resumed Lady Verner.

"I do not know what her plans for the present may
be," he answered, his cheek burning at the thought
of the avowal he had to make—that her future plans
would be contingent upon his. Not the least painful of the results which Lionel's haste had brought

in its train, was the knowledge of the shock it would prove to his mother, whom he so loved and reverenced. Why had he not thought of it at the time?

Breakfast over, Lionel went out, a very coward. A coward, in so far as that he had shrunk from making yet the confession. He was aware that it ought to be done. The presence of Decima and Lucy Tempest had been his mental excuse for putting off the unwelcome task.

But a better frame of mind came over him ere he had gone many paces from the door; better, at any rate, as regarded the cowardice.

"A Verner never shrank yet from his duty," was his comment, as he bent his steps back again. "Am I turning renegade?"

He went straight up to Lady Verner, and asked her, in a low tone, to grant him a minute's private interview. They had breakfasted in the room which made the ante-room to the drawing-room: it was their usual morning-room. Lady Verner answered her son by stepping into the drawing-room.

He followed her and closed the door. The fire was but just lighted, scarcely giving out any heat. She slightly shivered, and requested him to stir it. He did so mechanically; wholly absorbed by the revelation he had to impart. He remembered how she had once fainted at nearly the same revelation.

"Mother, I have a communication to make to you," he began with desperate energy. "And I don't know how to do it. It will pain you greatly.

Nothing, that I can think of, or imagine, would cause you so much pain."

Lady Verner seated herself in her low violet-velvet chair, and looked composedly at Lionel. She did not dread the communication very much. He was secure in Verner's Pride; what could there be that she need fear? She no more cast a glance to the possibility of his marrying the widow of Frederick Massingbird, than she would have done to his marrying that gentleman's wife. Buried in this semi-security, the shock must be all the greater.

"I am about to marry," said Lionel, plunging into the news headlong. "And I fear that you will not approve my choice. Nay, I know you will not."

A foreshadowing of the truth came across her then. She grew deadly pale, and put up her hands, as if to ward off the blow. "Oh, Lionel! don't say it! don't say it!" she implored. "I never can receive her."

"Yes you will, mother," he whispered, his own face pale too, his tone one of painful entreaty. "You will receive her for my sake."

"Is it—*she*?"

The aversion with which the name was avoided was unmistakable. Lionel only nodded a grave affirmative.

"Have you engaged yourself to her?"

"I have. Last night."

"Were you mad?" she asked in a whisper.

"Stay, mother. When you were speaking against Sibylla at breakfast, I refrained from interference, for you did not then know that defence of her was my duty. Will you forgive me for reminding you that I cannot permit it to be continued, even by you?"

"But, do you forget that it is not a respectable alliance for you?" resumed Lady Verner. "No, not a respectable—"

"I cannot listen to this; I pray you cease!" he broke forth, a blaze of anger lighting his face. "Have you forgotten of whom you are speaking, mother? Not respectable!"

"I say that it is not a respectable alliance for you—Lionel Verner," she persisted. "An obscure surgeon's daughter, he of not too good repute, who has been out to the end of the world, and found her way back alone, a widow, is *not* a desirable alliance for a Verner. It would not be desirable for Jan; it is terrible for you?"

"We shall not agree upon this," said Lionel, preparing to take his departure. "I have acquainted you, mother, and I have no more to say. Except to urge —if I may do so—that you will learn to speak of Sibylla with courtesy, remembering that she will shortly be my wife."

Lady Verner caught his hand as he was retreating.

"Lionel, my son, tell me how you came to do it," she wailed. "You cannot *love* her! the wife, the widow of another man! It must have been the work of a moment of folly. Perhaps she drew you into it!"

The suggestion, " the work of a moment of folly,"
was so very close a representation of what it had
been, of what Lionel was beginning to see it to have
been now, that the rest of the speech was lost to him
in the echo of that one sentence. Somehow, he did
not care to refute it.

"She will be my wife, respected and honoured,"
was all he answered, as he quitted the room.

Lady Verner followed him. He went straight
out, and she saw him walk hastily across the court-
yard, putting on his hat as he traversed it. She
wrung her hands, and broke into a storm of wailing
despair, ignoring the presence of Decima and Lucy
Tempest.

"I had far rather that she had stabbed him!"

The words excited their amazement. They turned
to Lady Verner, and were struck with the marks of
agitation on her countenance.

"Mamma, what are you speaking of?" asked
Decima.

Lady Verner pointed to Lionel, who was then
passing through the front gates. "I speak of _him_,"
she answered: "my darling; my pride; my much-
loved son. That woman has worked his ruin."

Decima verily thought her mother must be wan-
·dering in her intellect. Lucy could only gaze at
Lady Verner in consternation.

"What woman?" repeated Decima.

"_She._ She who has been Lionel's bane. She
who came and thrust herself into his home last
night in her unseemly conduct. What passed be-

tween them, Heaven knows; but she has contrived
to cajole him out of a promise to marry her."

Decima's pale cheek turned to a burning red.
She was afraid to ask questions.

" Oh, mamma ! it cannot be !" was all she uttered.

" It *is*, Decima.   I told Lionel that he could not
love *her*, who had been the wife of another man : and
he did not refute it.   I told him she must have
drawn him into it ; and that he left unanswered.
He replied that she would be his wife, and must be
honoured as such.   Drawn in to marry her ! one
who is so utterly unworthy of him ! whom he does
not even love !   Oh, Lionel, my son, my son !"

In their own grievous sorrow they noticed not the
face of Lucy Tempest, or what they might have
read there.

CHAPTER IV.

LIONEL went direct to the house of Dr. West. It was early; and the Miss Wests, fatigued with their night's pleasure, had risen in a scuffle, barely getting down at the breakfast hour. Jan was in the country attending on a patient, and, not anticipating the advent of visitors, they had honoured Master Cheese with hair *en papillotes.* Master Cheese had divided his breakfast hour between eating and star-ing. The meal had been sometime over, and the young gentleman had retired, but the ladies sat over the fire in unusual idleness, discussing the dis-sipation they had participated in. A scream from the two arose upon the entrance of Lionel, and Miss Amilly flung her pocket-handkerchief over her head.

" Never mind," said Lionel, laughing good-naturedly. " I have seen curl-papers before, in my life. Your sitting here quietly, tells me that you do not know what has occurred."

" What *has* occurred ? " interrupted Deborah, before he could continue. " It—it—" her voice grew suddenly timid—" is nothing bad about papa ? "

" No, no. Your sister has arrived from Australia.

In this place of gossip, I wonder the news has not travelled to Jan or to Cheese."

They had started up, poor things, their faces flushed, their eyelashes glistening, forgetting the little episode of the mortified vanity, eager to embrace Sibylla.

" Come back from Australia!" uttered Deborah in wild astonishment. " Then where is she, that she is not here, in her own home?"

" She came to mine," replied Lionel. " She supposed Mrs. Verner to be its mistress still. I made my way here last night to ask you to come up, and found you were gone to Heartburg."

" But—she—is not remaining at it?" exclaimed Deborah, speaking with hesitation, in her doubt, the flush on her face deepening.

"I placed it at her disposal until other arrangements could be made," replied Lionel. "I am at present the guest of Lady Verner. You will go to Sibylla, will you not?"

Go to her? Ay! They tore the curl-papers out of their hair, and flung on bonnets and shawls, and hastened to Verner's Pride.

" Say that I will call upon her in the course of the morning, and see how she is after her journey," said Lionel.

In hurrying out, they encountered Jan. Deborah stopped to say a word about his breakfast: it was ready, she said, and she thought he must want it.

"I do," responded Jan. "I shall have to get an assistant, after all, Miss Deb. I find it doesn't answer to go quite without meals and sleep; and that's what I have done lately."

"So you have, Mr. Jan. I say every day to Amilly that it can't go on, for you to be walked off your legs in this way. Have you heard the cheering news, Mr. Jan? Sibylla's come home. We are going to her now, at Verner's Pride."

"I have heard it," responded Jan. "What took her to Verner's Pride?"

"We have yet to learn all that. You know, Mr. Jan, she never was given to consider a step much, before she took it."

They tripped away, and Jan, in turning from them, met his brother. Jan was one utterly incapable of finesse: if he wanted to say a thing, he said it out plainly. What havoc Jan would have made, enrolled in the corps of diplomatists!

"I say, Lionel," began he, "is it true that you are going to marry Sibylla West?"

Lionel did not like the plain question, so abruptly put. He answered curtly:

"I am going to marry Sibylla Massingbird."

"The old name comes the readiest," said Jan. "How did it come about, Lionel?"

"May I ask whence you derived your information, Jan?" returned Lionel, who was marvelling where Jan could have heard this.

"At Deerham Court. I have been calling in, as I passed it, to see Miss Lucy. The mother is going wild, I think. Lionel, if it is as she says, that Sibylla drew you into it against your will, don't you carry it out. *I'd* not. Nobody should hook me into anything."

"My mother said that, did she? Be so kind as not to repeat it, Jan. I am marrying Sibylla because I love her; I am marrying her of my own free will. If anybody—save my mother—has aught of objection to make to it, let them make it to me."

"Oh! that's it, is it?" returned Jan. "You need not be up, Lionel, it is no business of mine. I'm sure you are free to marry her for me. I'll be groomsman, if you like."

"Lady Verner has always been prejudiced against Sibylla," observed Lionel. "You might have remembered that, Jan."

"So I did," said Jan; "though I assumed that what she said was sure to be true. You see, I have been on the wrong scent lately. I thought you were getting fond of Lucy Tempest. It has looked like it."

Lionel murmured some unintelligible answer, and turned away, a hot flush dyeing his brow.

Meanwhile Sibylla was already up, but not down. Breakfast she would have carried up to her room, she told Mrs. Tynn. She stood at the window, looking forth; not so much at the extensive prospect that swept the horizon in the distance, as at the fair lands immediately around. "All his," she murmured, "and I shall be his wife at last!"

She turned languidly round at the opening of the door, expecting to see her breakfast. Instead of

which, two frantic little bodies burst in and seized
upon her. Sibylla shrieked.

"Don't, Deb! don't, Amilly! Are you going to
hug me to death?"

Their kisses of welcome over, they went round
about her, fondly surveying her from all points with
their tearful eyes. She was thinner: but she was
more lovely. Amilly expressed an opinion that the
bloom on her delicate wax face was even brighter
than of yore.

"Of course it is, at the present moment," answered Sibylla, "when you have been kissing me
into a fever."

"She is not tanned a bit with her voyage, that I
see," cried Deborah, with undisguised admiration.
"But Sibylla's skin never did tan. Child," she
added, bending towards her, and allowing her voice
to become grave, "how could you think of coming to
Verner's Pride? It was not right. You should
have come home."

"I thought Mrs. Verner was living still."

"And if she had been?—This is Mr. Lionel's
house now; not hers. You ought to have come
home, my dear. You will come with us now, will
you not?"

"I suppose you'll allow me to have some breakfast first," was Sibylla's answer. Secure in her
future position, she was willing to go home to them
temporarily now. "Why is papa gone away,
Deborah?"

"He will be coming back some time, dear," was

Deborah's evasive answer, spoken soothingly. "But
tell us a little about yourself, Sibylla. When poor
Frederick—"

"Not this morning, Deborah," she interrupted,
putting up her hand. "I will tell you all another
time. It was an unlucky voyage."

"Have you realised John's money that he left?
That he lost, I should rather say."

"I have realised nothing," replied Sibylla.
"Nothing but ill luck. We never got tidings of
John in any way, beyond the details of his death :
we never saw a particle of the gold belonging to him,
or could hear of it. And my husband lost his desk
the day we landed—as I sent you word ; and I had
no money out there, and I have only a few shillings
in my pocket."

This catalogue of ills nearly stunned Deborah and
Amilly West. They had none too much of life's
great need, gold, for themselves ; and the burden of
keeping Sibylla would be sensibly felt. A tolerably
good table it was indispensable to maintain, on
account of Jan, and that choice eater, Master Cheese:
but how they had to pinch in the matter of dress,
they alone knew. Sibylla also knew, and she read
arightly the drooping of their faces.

"Never mind, Deborah ; cheer up, Amilly. It is
only for a time. Ere very long I shall be leaving
you again."

"Surely not for Australia!" returned Deborah,
the hint startling her.

"Australia ? Well, I am not sure that it will be

quite so far," answered Sibylla, in a little spirit of mischief. And, in the bright prospect of the future, she forgot past and present grievances, turned her laughing blue eyes upon her sisters, and, to their great scandal, began to waltz round and round the room.

CHAPTER V.

By the light of a single tallow candle which flared aloft on a shelf in Peckaby's shop, consecrated in more prosperous days to wares, but bare now, a large collected assemblage was regarding each other with looks of eager interest. There could not have been less than thirty present, all crammed together in that little space of a few feet square. The first comers had taken their seats on the counters; the others stood as they could. Two or three men, just returned from their day's labour, were there; but the crowd was chiefly composed of the weaker sex.

The attention of these people was concentrated on a little man who faced them, leaning against the wall at the back of the shop, and holding forth in a loud, persuasive tone. If you object to the term "holding forth," you must blame Mrs. Duff: it is borrowed from her. She informed us, you may remember, that the stranger who met, and appeared to avoid Lionel Verner, was no other than a "missionary from Jerusalem," taken with an anxiety for the souls of Deerham, and about to do what he could to convert them—" Brother Jarrum."

Brother Jarrum had entered upon his work, con-

jointly with his entry upon Peckaby's spare bedroom.
He held nightly meetings in Peckaby's shop, and
the news of his fame was spreading. Women of all
ages flocked in to hear him—you know how im-
pressionable they have the character of being. A
sprinkling of men followed out of curiosity, of idleness, or from propensity to ridicule. Had Brother
Jarrum proved to be a real missionary from Jerusalem—though, so far as my knowledge goes, such
messengers from that city are not common—
genuinely desirous of converting them from wrath
to grace, I fear his audience would, after the first
night or two, have fallen off considerably. *This*
missionary, however, contrived both to keep his
audience and to increase it; his promises partaking
more of the mundane nature than do such promises
in general. In point of fact, Brother Jarrum was
an Elder from a place that he was pleased to term
"New Jerusalem:" in other words, from the Salt
Lake city.

It has been the fate of certain spots of England,
more so than of most other parts of the European
world, to be favoured by periodical visits from these
gentry. Deerham was now suffering under the inflic-
tion, and Brother Jarrum was doing all that lay in
his power to convert half its female population into
Mormon proselytes. His peculiar doctrines it is of
no consequence to transcribe; but some of his promises were so rich that it is a pity you should lose
the treat of hearing them. They commenced with—
husbands to all. Old or young, married or single,

each was safe to be made the wife of one of these favoured prophets the instant she set foot in the new city. This of course was a very grand thing for the women—as you may know if you have any experience with them—especially for those who were getting on the shady side of forty, and had not changed their name. They, the women, gathered together and pressed into Peckaby's shop, and stared at Brother Jarrum with eager eyes, and listened with strained ears, only looking off him to cast admiring glances one to another.

" Stars and snakes ! " said Brother Jarrum, whose style of oratory was more peculiar than elegant, " what flounders me is, that the whole lot of you Britishers don't migrate of yourselves to the desired city—the promised land—the Zion on the mountains. You stop here to pinch and toil and care, and quarrel one of another, and starve your children through having nothing to give 'em, when you might go out there to ease, to love, to peace, to plenty. It's a charming city ; what else should it be called the City of the Saints for ? The houses have shady veranders round 'em, with sweet shrubs a-creeping up, and white posts and pillows to lean against. The bigger a household is, the more rooms it have got ; not a lady there, if there was a hundred of 'em in family, but what's got her own parlour and bed-room to herself, which no stranger thinks of going in at without knocking for leaf. All round and about these houses is productive gardens, trees and flowers for ornament, and fruits and green stuff to eat. There's trees that they call cotton wood, and firs, and locusts, and balsams, and poplars, and pines, and acacias, some of 'em in blossom. A family may live for nothing upon the produce of their own ground. Vegetables is to be had for the cutting; their own cows gives the milk—such milk and butter as this poor place, Deerham, never saw—but the rich flavour's imparted to 'em from the fine quality of the grass; and fruit you might feed upon till you got a surfeit. Grapes and peaches is all a hanging in clusters to the hand, only waiting to be plucked! Stars! my mouth's watering now at the thoughts of 'em! I—"

"Please, sir, what did you say the name of the place was again?" interrupted a female voice.

"New Jerusalem," replied Brother Jarrum. "It's in the territory of Utah. On the maps and on the roads, and for them that have not awoke to the new light, it's called the Great Salt Lake City; but for us favoured saints, it's New Jerusalem. It's Zion—it's Paradise—it's anything beautiful you may like to call it. There's a ball-room in it."

This abrupt wind-up rather took some of the audience aback. "A ball-room!"

"A ball-room," gravely repeated Brother Jarrum. "A public ball-room not far from a hundred feet long; and we have got a theatre for the acting of plays; and we go for rides in winter in sleighs. Ah! did you think it was with us, out there, as it is with you in the old country?—one's days to be made up of labour, labour, labour; no interlude to it but starvation and the crying of children as can't get nursed or fed! We like amusement; and we have it; dancing in particular. Our great prophet himself dances; and all the apostles and bishops dance. They dance themselves down."

The assemblage sat with open eyes. New wonders were revealed to them every moment. Some of the younger legs grew restless at the mental vision conjured up.

"It's part of our faith to dance," continued Brother Jarrum. "Why shouldn't we? Didn't David dance? Didn't Jephthah dance? Didn't the prodigal son dance? You'll all dance on to the last if you come to us. Such a thing as old legs is hardly known among us. As the favoured climate makes the women's faces beautiful, so it keeps the limbs from growing old. The ball-room is hung with green branches and flags: you might think it was a scene of trees lit with lamps; and you'd never tire of listening to the music, or of looking at the supper-table. If you could only see the suppers given, in a picture to-night, it 'ud spoil your sleep, and you'd not rest till you had started to partake of 'em. Ducks and turkeys, and oysters, and fowls, and fish, and meats, and custards, and pies, and potatoes, and greens, and jellies, and coffee, and tea, and cake, and drinks, and so many more things that you'd be tired only of hearing me say the names. There's abundance for all."

Some commotion amid Brother Jarrum's hearers, and a sound as of licking of lips. That supper

account was a great temptation. Had Brother
Jarrum started then, straight off for the Salt Lake,
the probability is that three-parts of the room would
have formed a tail after him.

"What's the drinks?" inquired Jim Clark, the
supper items imparting to his inside a curious feeling of emptiness.

"There's no lack of drinks in the City of the
Saints," returned Brother Jarrum. "Whiskey's
plentiful. Have you heard of mint julep? That *is*
delicious. Mint is one of the few productions not
common out there, and we are learning to make the
julep with sage instead. You should see the plains
of sage! It grows wild."

"And there's ducks, you say?" observed Susan
Peckaby. "It's convenient to have sage in plenty
where there's ducks," added she to the assembly in
general. "What a land it must be!"

"A land that's not to be ekalled! A land flowing with milk and honey!" rapturously echoed
Brother Jarrum. "Ducks is in plenty, and sage
grows as thick as nettles do here; you can't
go out to the open country but you put your
foot upon it. Nature's generally in accordance
with herself. What should she give all them
bushes of wild sage for, unless she gave ducks to
match?"

A problem that appeared indisputable to the
minds of Brother Jarrum's listeners. They sincerely wished themselves in New Jerusalem.

"Through the streets runs a stream of sparkling

water, clear as crystal," continued Brother Jarrum.
"You have only got to stoop down with a can on a
hot summer's day, and take a drink of it. It runs
on both sides the streets for convenience; folks step
out of their houses, and draw it up with no trouble.
You have not got to toil half-a-mile to a spring of
fresh water there! You'd never forget the silver
lake at the base of Antelope Island, once you set
eyes on it."

Several haggard eyes were lifted at this. "Do
silver grow there, like the sage?"

"I spoke metaphorical," explained Brother
Jarrum. "Would I deceive you? No. It's the
Great Salt Lake, that shines out like burnished
silver, and bursts on the sight of the new pilgrims
when they arrive in bands at the holy city—the
emigrants from this land."

"Some do arrive then, sir?" timidly questioned
Dinah Roy.

"Some!" indignantly responded Brother Jarrum.
"They are arriving continual. The very evening
before I left, a numerous company arrived. It was
just upon sunset. The clouds was all of rose colour,
tipped with purple and gold, and there lay the holy
city at their feet, in the lovely valley I told you of
last night, with the lake of glittering silver in the
distance. It is a sight for 'em, I can tell you! The
regular-built houses, enclosed in their gardens and
buildings, like farm homesteads, and the inhabitants
turning out with fiddles, to meet and welcome the
travellers. Some of the pilgrims fainted with joy;

some shouted; lots danced; and sobs and tears of delight burst from all. If the journey had been a little fatiguing—what of that, with that glorious scene at the end of it?"

"And you see this?" cried a man, Davies, in a somewhat doubtful tone.

"I see it with my two eyes," answered Brother Jarrum. "I often see it. We had had news in the city that a train of new-comers was approaching, mostly English, and we went out to meet 'em. Not one of us saints, hardly, but was expecting some friend by it: a sister, or a father, or a sweetheart, may-be: and away we hurried outside the city. Presently the train came in sight."

"They have railroads there, then?" spoke a man, who was listening with eager interest. It was decent, civil Grind.

"Not yet: we shall have 'em shortly," said Brother Jarrum. "The train consisted of carts, carriages, vehicles of all sorts ; and some rode mules, and some were walking on their legs. They were all habited nicely, and singing hymns. A short way afore they arrive at the holy city, it's the custom for the emigrants to make a halt, and wash and dress themselves, so as to enter proper. Such a meeting! the kissing and the greeting drownding the noise of the music, and the old men and the little children dancing. The prophet himself came out, and shook hands with 'em all, his brass band blowing in front of him, and he standing up in his carriage. Where else would you travel to, I'd like to know, and find such

a welcome at the end of your journey? Houses,
and friends, and plenty, all got ready aforehand;
and gentlemen waiting to marry the ladies that may
wish to enter the holy state!"

"There *is* a plenty?" questioned again that unbelieving man, Davies.

"There's such a plenty that the new arrivals are
advised to eat, for a week or two, only half their
fill," returned Brother Jarrum. "Of fruits in partic'lar. Some, that have gone right in at the good
things without mercy, have been laid up through it,
and had to fine themselves down upon physic for a
week after. No; it's best to be a little sparing at
the beginning."

"What did he say just now about all the Mormons
being beautiful?" questioned a pretty looking girl
of her neighbours. And Brother Jarrum caught the
words, although they were spoken in an undertone.

"And so they are," said he. "The climate's of
a nature that softens the faces, keeps folks in health,
and stops 'em from growing old. If you see two
females in the street, one a saint's wife, the t'other
a new arrival, you can always tell which is which.
The wife's got a slender waist, like a lady, with a
delicate colour in her face, and silky hair: the new-
comer's tanned, and fat, and freckled, and clumsy.
If you don't believe me, you can ask them as have
been there. There's something in the dress they
wear, too, that sets 'em off. No female goes out
without a veil, which hangs down behind. They
don't want to hide their pretty faces, not they."

Mary Green, a damsel of twenty, she who had previously spoken, really did possess a pretty face: and a rapturous vision came over her at this juncture, of beholding it shaded and set off by a white lace veil, as she had often seen Miss Decima Verner's.

"Now, I can't explain to you why it is that the women in the city should be fair to the eye, or why the men don't seem to grow old," resumed Brother Jarrum. "It is so, and that's enough. People, learned in such things, might tell the cause; but I'm not learned in 'em. Some says it's the effect of the New Jerusalem climate; some thinks it's the fruits of the happy and plentiful life we lead: my opinion is, it's a mixture of both. A man of sixty hardly looks forty, out there. It's a great favour!"

One of the ill-doing Dawsons, who had pushed his way in at the shop-door in time to hear part of the lavished praise on New Jerusalem, interrupted at this juncture.

"I say, master, if this is as you're a-telling us, how is it that folks talk so again the Mormons? I met a man in Heartburg once, who had been out there, and he couldn't say bad enough of 'em."

"Snakes! but that's a natural question of yours, and I'm glad to answer it," replied Brother Jarrum, with a taking air of candour. "Those evil reports come from our enemies. There's another tribe living in the Great Salt Lake City besides ours; and that's the Gentiles. Gentiles is our name for 'em. It's this set that spreads about uncredible reports, and we'd like to sew their mouths up—"

Brother Jarrum probably intended to say " unac-
credited." He continued, somewhat vehemently:

" —To sew their mouths up with a needle and
thread, and let 'em be sewed up for ever. They
are jealous of us; that's what it is. Some of their
wives, too, have left 'em to espouse our saints, at
which they nagger greatly. The outrageousest
things that enemies' tongues can be laid to, they
say. Don't you ever believe 'em; it flounders me
to think as anybody can. Whoever wants to see
my credentials, they are at their beck and call. Call
to-morrow morning—in my room up-stairs—call any
other morning, and my certificates is open to be
looked at, with spectacles or without 'em, signed in
full, at the Great Salt Lake City, territory of Utah,
by our prophet, Mr. Brigham Young, and two of
his councillors, testifying that I am Elder Silas
Jarrum, and that my mission over here is to preach
the light to them as are at present asleep in dark-
ness, and bring 'em to the community of the Latter
Day Saints. *I'm* no imposter, I'm not; and I
tell you that the false reports come from them
unbelieving Gentiles. Instead of minding their
own affairs, they pass their days nagging at the
saints."

" Why don't they turn saints theirselves ? " cried
a voice, sensibly.

" Because Satan stops 'em. You have heard of
him, you know. He's busy everywhere, as you've
been taught by your parsons. I put my head inside
of your church-door, last Sunday night, while the

sermon was going on, and I heard your parson tell you as Satan was the foundation of all the ill that was in you. He was right there : though I'm no friend to parsons in general. Satan is the head and tail of bad things, and he fills up the Gentiles with proud notions, and blinds their eyes against us. No wonder! If every soul in the world turned Latter Day Saint, and come over to us at New Jerusalem, where 'ud Satan's work be ? We are striving to get you out of the clutches of Satan, my friends, and you must strive for yourselves also. Where's the use of us elders coming among you to preach and convert, unless you meet us half-way ? Where's the good of keeping up that 'Perpetual Emigration Fund Company,' if you don't reap its benefit and make a start to emigrate ? These things is being done for you, not for us. The Latter Day Saints have got nothing mean nor selfish about 'em. They are the richest people in the world—in generosity and good works."

" Is servants allowed to dress in veils, out there ? " demanded Mary Green, during a pause of Brother Jarrum's, afforded to the audience that they might sufficiently revolve the disinterested generosity of the Latter Day Saint community.

"Veils ! Veils, and feathers, too, if they are so minded," was Brother Jarrum's answer ; and it fell like a soothing sound on Mary Green's vain ear, " It's not many servants, though, that you'd find in New Jerusalem."

" Ain't servants let go out to New Jerusalem ? "

quickly returned Mary Green. She was a servant herself, just now out of place, given to spend all her wages upon finery, and coming to grief perpetually with her mistresses upon the score.

"Many of 'em goes out," was the satisfactory reply of Brother Jarrum. "But servants here are not servants there. Who'd be a servant if she could be a missis? Wouldn't a handsome young female prefer to be her master's wife than to be his servant?"

Mary Green giggled; the question had been pointedly put to her.

"If a female servant *chooses* to remain a servant, in course she can," Brother Jarrum resumed. "And precious long wages she'd get; eighty pound a-year—good."

A movement of intense surprise amid the audience. Brother Jarrum went on:

"I can't say I have knowed many as have stopped servants, even at that high rate of pay. My memory won't charge me with one. They have married and settled, and so have secured for themselves paradise."

This might be taken as a delicate hint that the married state, generally, deserved that happy title. Some of the experiences of those present, however, rather tended to accord it a less satisfactory one, and there arose some murmuring. Brother Jarrum explained:

"Women is not married with us for time, but

for eternity — as I tried to beat into you last
night. Once the wife of a saint, their entrance
into paradise is safe and certain. We have not
got a old maid among us — not a single old
maid!"

The sensation that this information caused, I'll
leave you to judge; considering that Deerham
was famous for old maids, and that several were
present.

"No old maids, and no widders," continued
Brother Jarrum, wiping his forehead, which was
becoming moist with the heat of argument. "We
have respect to our women, we have, and like to
make 'em comfortable."

"But if their husbands die off?" suggested a
puzzled listener.

"The husband's successor marries his widders,"
explained Brother Jarrum. "Look at our late head
and prophet, Mr. Joe Smith,—him that appeared in
a vision to our present prophet, and pointed out the
spot for the new temple. He died a martyr, Mr.
Joe Smith did,—a prey to wicked murderers. Were
his widders left to grieve and die out after him?
No. Mr. Brigham Young, he succeeded to his
honours, and he married the widders."

This was received somewhat dubiously: the assemblage not clear whether to approve it or to cavil
at it.

"Not so much to be his wives, you know, as to
be a kind of ruling matrons in his household," went
on Brother Jarrum. "To have their own places

apart, their own rooms in the house, and to be as happy as the day's long. They don't—"

" How they must quarrel, a lot of wives together!" interrupted a discontented voice.

Brother Jarrum set himself energetically to disprove this supposition. He succeeded. Belief is easy to willing minds.

" Which is best?" asked he. " To be one of the wives of a rich saint, where all the wives is happy, and honoured, and well dressed; or to toil and starve, and go next door to naked, as a poor man's solitary wife does here? I know which *I* should choose if the two chances was offered me. A woman can't put her foot inside the heavenly kingdom, I tell you, unless she has got a husband to lay hold of her hand and draw her in. The wives of a saint are safe; paradise is in store for 'em; and that's why the Gentiles' wives—them folks that's for ever riling at us—leave their husbands to marry the saints."

" Does the saints' wives ever leave 'em to marry them others—the Gentiles?" asked that troublesome Davies.

" Such cases have been heered of," responded Brother Jarrum, shaking his head with a grave solemnity of manner. " They have braved the punishment and done it. But the act has been rare."

" What is the punishment?" inquired somebody's wife.

" When a female belonging to the Latter Day

Saints—whether she's married or single—falls off
from grace and goes over to them Gentiles, and
marries one of 'em, she's condemned to be buffeted
by Satan for a thousand years."

A pause of consternation.

"Who condemns her?" a voice, more venture-
some than the rest, was heard to ask.

"There's mysteries in our faith which can't be
disclosed even to you," was the reply of Brother
Jarrum. "Them apostate women are condemned
to it; and that's enough. It's not everybody as can
see the truth. Ninety-nine may see it, and the
hundredth mayn't."

"Very true, very true," was murmured around.

"I think I see the waggins and the other vehicles
arriving now!" rapturously exclaimed Brother
Jarrum, turning his eyes right up into his head,
the better to take in the mental vision. "The
travellers, tired with their journey, washed and
shaved, and dressed, and the women's hair anointed,
all flagrant with oil and frantic with joy,—shouting,
singing, and dancing to the tune of the advancing
fiddles! I think I see the great prophet himself,
with his brass-band in front and his body-guard
around him, meeting the travellers and shaking their
hands individ'ally! I think I see the joy of the
women, and the nice young girls, when they are led
to the hyminial halter in our temple by the saints
that have fixed on 'em, to be inducted into the
safety of paradise! Happy those that the prophet
chooses for himself! While them other poor mis-

taken backsliders shall be undergoing their thou-
sand years of buffetings, they'll reign triumphant,
the saved saints of the Mil——"

How long Brother Jarrum's harangue might have
rung on the wide ears of his delighted listeners, it
is not easy to say. But an interruption occurred
to the proceedings. It was caused by the entrance
of Peckaby; and the meeting was terminated somewhat abruptly. While Susan Peckaby sat at the
feet of the saint, a willing disciple of his doctrine,
her lord and master, however disheartening it may
be to record it, could not, by any means, be induced
to open his heart and receive the grace. He
remained obdurate. Passively obdurate during the
day; but rather demonstratively obdurate towards
night. Peckaby, a quiet, civil man enough when
sober, was just the contrary when *ivre*; and since
he had joined the blacksmith's shop, his evening
visits to a noted public-house — the Plough and
Harrow—had become frequent. On his return
home from these visits, his mind had once or twice
been spoken out pretty freely as to the Latter Day
Saint doctrine : once he had gone the length of
clearing the shop of guests, and marshalling the
saint himself to the retirement of his own apartment. However contrite he may have shown
himself for this the next morning, nobody desired
to have the scene repeated. Consequently, when
Peckaby now entered, defiance in his face and un-
steadiness in his legs, the guests filed out of their
own accord ; and Brother Jarrum, taking the flaring

candle from the shelf, disappeared with it up the stairs.

This has been a very fair specimen of Brother Jarrum's representations and eloquence. It was only one meeting out of a great many. As I said before, the precise tenets of his religious faith need not be enlarged upon : it is enough to say that they were quite equal to his temporal promises. You will, therefore, scarcely wonder that he made disciples. But the mischief, as yet, had only begun to brew.

CHAPTER VI.

WHATEVER may have been Lionel Verner's private sentiments, with regard to his choice of a wife,— whether he repented his hasty bargain or whether he did not, no shade of dissatisfaction escaped him. Sibylla took up her abode with her sisters, and Lionel visited her, just as other men visit the young ladies they may be going to marry. The servants at Verner's Pride were informed that a mistress for them was in contemplation, and preparations for the marriage were begun. Not until summer would it take place, when twelve months should have elapsed from the demise of Frederick Massingbird.

Deerham was, of course, free in its comments, differing in no wise on that score from other places. Lionel Verner was pitied, and Sibylla abused. The heir of Verner's Pride, with his good looks, his manifold attractions, his somewhat cold impassibility as to the tempting snares laid out for him in the way of matrimony, had been a beacon for many a young lady to steer towards. Had he married Lucy Tempest, had he married Lady Mary Elmsley, had he married a royal princess, he and she would both have been equally cavilled at. He, for placing himself beyond the pale of competition; she, for securing the prize. It always was so, and it always will be.

His choice of Mrs. Massingbird, however, really did afford some grounds for grumbling. She was not worthy of Lionel Verner. So Deerham thought; so Deerham said. He was throwing himself away; he would live to repent it; she must have been the most crafty of women, so to have secured him! Free words enough, and harshly spoken: but they were as water by the side of those uttered by Lady Verner.

In the first bitter hour of disappointment, Lady Verner gave free speech to harsh things. It was in her love for Lionel that she so grieved. Setting aside the facts that Sibylla had been the wife of another man, that she was, in position, beneath Lionel—which facts, however, Lady Verner could not set aside, for they were ever present to her— her great objection lay in the conviction that Sibylla would prove entirely unsuited to him; that it would turn out an unhappy union. Short and sharp was the storm with Lady Verner: but in a week or two she subsided into quietness, buried her grief and resentment within her, and made no further outward demonstration.

"Mother, you will call upon Sibylla?" Lionel said to her one day that he had gone to Deerham Court. He spoke in a low deprecating tone, and his face flushed: he anticipated he knew not what torrent of objection.

Lady Verner met the request differently.

"I suppose it will be expected of me, that I should do so," she replied, strangely calm. "How I dislike this artificial state of things! Where the customs of society must be bowed to, by those who live in it: their actions, good or bad, commented upon and judged! You have been expecting that I should call before this, I suppose, Lionel?"

"I have been hoping, from day to day, that you would call."

"I will call—for your sake. Lionel," she passionately added, turning to him, and seizing his hands between hers, "what I do now, I do for your sake. It has been a cruel blow to me: but I will try to make the best of it, for you, my best-loved son."

He bent down to his mother, and kissed her tenderly. It was his mode of showing her his thanks.

"Do not mistake me, Lionel. I will go just so far in this matter as may be necessary to avoid open disapproval. If I appear to approve it, that the world may not cavil and you complain, it will be little more than an appearance. I will call upon your intended wife, but the call will be one of etiquette, of formal ceremony: you must not expect me to get into the habit of repeating it. I shall never become intimate with her."

"You do not know what the future may bring forth," returned Lionel, looking at his mother with a smile. "I trust the time will come when you shall have learnt to love Sibylla."

"I do not think that time will ever arrive," was the frigid reply of Lady Verner. "Oh, Lionel!" she added, in an impulse of sorrow, "what a barrier this has raised between us—what a severing for the future!"

"The barrier exists in your own mind only, mother," was his answer, spoken sadly. "Sibylla would be a loving daughter to you, if you would allow her so to be."

A slight, haughty shake of the head, suppressed at once, was the reply of Lady Verner. "I had looked for a different daughter," she continued. "I had hoped for Mary Elmsley."

"Upon this point, at any rate, there need be no misunderstanding," returned Lionel. "Believe me once for all, mother: I should never have married Mary Elmsley. Had I and Sibylla remained apart for life, separated as wide as the two poles, it is not Mary Elmsley whom I should have made my wife. It is more than probable that my choice would have pleased you only in a degree more than it does now."

The jealous ears of Lady Verner detected an under-current of meaning in the words.

"You speak just as though you had some one in particular in your thoughts!" she uttered.

It recalled Lucy, it recalled the past connected with her, all too plainly to his mind; and he returned an evasive answer. He never willingly recalled her: or it: if they obtruded themselves on his memory— as they very often did—he drove them away, as he was driving them now.

He quitted the house, and Lady Verner proceeded up-stairs to Decima's room. That pretty room, with its blue panels and hangings, where Lionel used to be when he was growing convalescent. Decima and Lucy were in it now. "I wish you to go out with me to make a call," she said to them.

"Both of us, mamma?" inquired Decima.

"Both," repeated Lady Verner. "It is a call of etiquette," she added, a sound of irony mixing in the tone, "and therefore you must both make it. It is to Lionel's chosen wife."

A hot flush passed into the face of Lucy Tempest: hot words rose to her lips. Hasty, thoughtless, impulsive words, to the effect that *she* could not pay a visit to the chosen wife of Lionel Verner.

But she checked them ere they were spoken. She turned to the window, which had been opened to the early spring day, and suffered the cool air to blow on her flushed face, and calmed down her impetuous thoughts. Was *this* the course of conduct that she had marked out for herself? She looked round at Lady Verner and said, in a gentle tone, that she would be ready at any hour named.

"We will go at once," replied Lady Verner. "I have ordered the carriage. The sooner we make it —as we have to make it—the better."

There was no mistake about it. Lucy had grown to love Lionel Verner. *How* she loved him, esteemed him, venerated him, none, save her own heart, could tell. Her days had been as one long dream of Eden. The very aspect of the world had changed: the blue sky, the soft breathing wind, the scent of the budding flowers, had spoken a language to her, never before learned: "Rejoice in us, for we are lovely!" It was the strange bliss in her own heart that threw its rose hues over the face of nature, the sweet, mysterious rapture arising from love's first dream: which can never be described by mortal pen; and never while it lasts, can be spoken of by living tongue. *While it lasts.* It never does last. It is the one sole ecstatic phase of life, the solitary romance stealing in once, and but once, amidst the world's hard realities; the "fire filched for us from heaven." Has it to arise yet for you—you, who read this? Do not trust it when it comes, for it will be fleeting as a summer cloud. Enjoy it, revel in it while you hold it; it will lift you out of earth's clay and earth's evil, with its angel wings; but trust not to its remaining: even while you are saying, "I will make it mine for ever," it is gone. It had gone for Lucy Tempest. And, oh! better for her, perhaps, that it should go: better, perhaps, for all: for if that sweet glimpse of paradise could take up its abode permanently in the heart, we should never look, or wish, or pray for that better Paradise which has to come hereafter.

But who can see this in the sharp flood tide of despair? Not Lucy. In losing Lionel she had lost all: and nothing remained for her but to do battle with her trouble alone. Passionately and truly as

Lionel had loved Sibylla; so, in her turn, did Lucy love him.

It is not the fashion now for young ladies to die of broken hearts—as it was in the old days. A little while given to " the grief that kills," and then Lucy strove to arouse herself to better things. She would go upon her way, burying all feelings within her; she would meet him and others with a calm exterior and placid smile; none should seè that she suffered : no, though her heart were breaking.

" I will forget him," she murmured to herself ten times in the day. " What a mercy that I did not let him see I loved him ! I never should have loved him, but that I thought he—Psha! why do I recal it ? I was mistaken; I was stupid—and all that's left to me is, to make the best of it."

So she drove her thoughts away, as Lionel did. She set out on her course bravely, with the determination to forget him. She schooled her heart, and schooled her face, and believed she was doing great things. To Lionel she cast no blame—and that was unfortunate for the forgetting scheme. She blamed herself; not Lionel. Remarkably simple and humble-minded, Lucy Tempest was accustomed to think of every one before herself. Who was she, that she should have assumed Lionel Verner was growing to love her ? Sometimes she would glance at another phase of the picture : That Lionel *had* been growing to love her; but that Sibylla Massingbird had, in some weak moment, by some sleight of hand, drawn him to her again, extracted from him a promise that he could not retract. She did not dwell upon this; she drove it from her, as she drove away, or strove to drive away, the other thoughts: although the theory, regarding the night of Sibylla's return, was the favourite theory of Lady Verner. Altogether, I say, circumstances were not very favourable towards Lucy's plan of forgetting him.

Lady Verner's carriage — the most fascinating carriage in all Deerham, with its blue and silver appointments, its fine horses, all the present of Lionel—conveyed them to the house of Dr. West. Lady Verner would not have gone otherwise than in state, for untold gold. Distance allowing her, for she was not a good walker, she would have gone on foot, without attendants, to visit the Countess of Elmsley and Lady Mary; but not Sibylla. You can understand the distinction.

They arrived at an inopportune moment, for Lionel was there. At least, Lionel thought it in-opportune. On leaving his mother's house he had gone to Sibylla's. And, however gratified he may have been by the speedy compliance of his mother with his request, he had very much preferred not to be present himself, if the call comprised, as he saw it did comprise, Lucy Tempest.

Sibylla was at home alone; her sisters were out. She had been leaning back in an invalid chair, listening to the words of Lionel, when a servant opened the door and announced Lady Verner. Neither had observed the stopping of the carriage. Carriages often stopped at the house, and visitors entered it: but they were most frequently professional visits, concerning nobody but Jan. Lady Verner swept in. For her very life she could not avoid showing hauteur in that moment. Sibylla sprung from her chair, and stood with a changing face.

Lionel's countenance, too, was changing. It was the first time he had met Lucy face to face in the close proximity necessitated by a room. He had studiously striven not to meet her, and had contrived to succeed. Did he call himself a coward for it? But where was the help?

A few moments given to greeting, to the assuming of seats, and they were settled down. Lady Verner and Decima on a sofa opposite Sibylla; Lucy in a low chair—what she was sure to look out for; Lionel leaning against the mantelpiece—as favourite a position of his, as a low seat was of Lucy's. Sibylla had been startled by their entrance, and her chest was beating. Her brilliant colour went and came, her hand was pressed upon her bosom, as if to still it, and she lay rather back in her chair for support. She had not assumed a widow's cap since her arrival, and her pretty hair fell around her in a shower of gold. In spite of Lady Verner's prejudices, she could not help thinking her very beautiful; but she looked suspiciously delicate.

" It is very kind of you to come to see me," said Sibylla, speaking timidly across to Lady Verner.

Lady Verner slightly bowed. " You do not look

strong," she observed to Sibylla, speaking in the moment's impulse. " Are you well ? "

" I am pretty well. I am not strong. Since I returned home, a little thing seems to flutter me, as your entrance has done now. Lionel had just told me you would call upon me, he thought. I was so glad to hear it! Somehow I had feared you would not."

Candid, at any rate ; and Lady Verner did not disapprove the apparent feeling that prompted it : but how her heart revolted at hearing those lips pronounce "Lionel" familiarly, she alone could tell. Again came the offence.

" Lionel tells me sometimes I am so changed since I went out, that even he would scarcely have known me. I do not think I am so changed as all that. I had a great deal of vexation and trouble, and I grew thin. But I shall soon be well again now."

A pause.

" You ascertained no certain news of John Massingbird, I hear," observed Lady Verner.

" Not any. A gentleman there is endeavouring to trace out more particulars. I heard—did Lionel mention to you—that I heard, strange to say, of Luke Roy, from the family I was visiting—the Eyres ? Lionel,"—turning to him, — "did you repeat it to Lady Verner ? "

" I believe not," replied Lionel. He could not say to Sibylla, " My mother would tolerate no conversation on any topic connected with you."

Another flagging pause.

Lionel, to create a divertissement, raised a remarkably fine specimen of coral from the table, and carried it to his mother.

"It is beautiful," he remarked. "Sibylla brought it home with her."

Lady Verner allowed that it was beautiful.

"Show it to Lucy," she said, when she had examined it with interest. "Lucy, my dear, do you remember what I was telling you the other evening, about the black coral?"

Sibylla rose and approached Lucy with Lionel.

"I am so pleased to make your acquaintance," she said, warmly. "You only came to Deerham a short while before I was leaving it, and I saw scarcely anything of you. Lionel has seen a great deal of you, I fancy, though he will not speak of you. I told him one day it looked suspicious; that I should be jealous of you, if he did not mind."

It was a foolish speech, foolish of Sibylla to give utterance to it; but she did so in all singleness of heart, meaning nothing. Lucy was bending over the coral, held by Lionel. She felt her own cheeks flush, and she saw by chance, not by direct look, that Lionel's face had turned a deep scarlet. Jealous of her! She continued to admire the coral some little time longer, and then resigned it to him with a smile.

"Thank you, Mr. Verner. I am fond of these marine curiosities. We had a good many of them at the Rectory. Mr. Cust's brother was a sailor."

Lionel could not remember the time when she had called him "Mr. Verner." It was right, however, that she should do so; but in his heart he felt thankful for that sweet smile. It seemed to tell him that she, at any rate, was heart whole, that she certainly bore him no resentment. He spoke freely now.

"You are not looking well, Lucy—as we have been upon the subject of looks."

"I? Oh, I have had another cold since the one Jan cured. I did not try his remedies in time, and it fastened upon me. I don't know which barked the most—I, or Growler."

"Jan says he shall have Growler here," remarked Sibylla.

"No, Sibylla," interposed Lionel: "Jan said he should like to have Growler here if it were convenient to do so, and my mother would spare him. A medical man's is not the place for a barking dog: he might attack the night applicants."

"Is it Jan's dog?" inquired Lucy.

"Yes," said Lionel. "I thought you knew it. Why, don't you remember, Lucy, the day I—"

Whatever reminiscence Lionel may have been about to recal, he cut it short midway, and subsided into silence. What was his motive? Did Lucy know? She did not ask for the ending, and the rest were then occupied, and had not heard.

More awkward pauses—as in these visits where

the parties do not amalgamate, is sure to be the case, and then Lady Verner slightly bowed to Lucy, as she might have done on their retiring from table, and rose. Extending the tips of her delicately-gloved fingers to Sibylla, she swept out of the room. Decima shook hands with her more cordially, although she had not spoken half-a-dozen words during the interview, and Sibylla turned and put her hand into Lucy's.

"I hope we shall be intimate friends," she said. "I hope you will be our frequent guest at Verner's Pride."

"Thank you," replied Lucy. And perhaps the sudden flush on her face might have been less vivid, had Lionel not been standing there.

He attended them to the carriage, taking up his hat as he passed through the vestibule : for really the confined space that did duty for hall in Dr. West's house, did not deserve the name. Lady Verner sat on one side the carriage, Decima and Lucy on the seat opposite. Lionel stood a moment after handing them in.

"If you can tear yourself away from the house for half-an-hour, I wish you would take a drive with us," said Lady Verner, her tone of voice no more pleasant than her words. Try as she would, she could not help her jealous resentment, against Sibylla, from peeping out.

Lionel smiled, and took his seat by his mother, opposite to Lucy. He was resolved to foster no ill-feeling by his own conduct, but to do all that

lay in his power to subdue it in Lady Verner.
He had not taken leave of Sibylla; and it may
have been this, the proof that he was about to
return to her, which had excited the ire of my
lady. She, his mother, nothing to him; Sibylla
all in all. Sibylla stood at the window, and
Lionel bent forward, nodded his adieu, and raised
his hat.

The footman ascended to his place, and the
carriage went on. All in silence for some minutes.
A silence which Lady Verner suddenly broke.

"What have you been doing to your cheeks,
Lucy? You look as if you had caught a fever."

Lucy laughed. "Do I, Lady Verner? I hope it
is not a third cold coming on, or Jan will grumble
that I take them on purpose. As he did the last
time."

She caught the eyes of Lionel riveted on her
with a strangely perplexed expression. It did not
tend to subdue the excitement of her cheeks.

Another moment, and Decima's cheeks appeared
to have caught the infection. They had suddenly
become one glowing crimson; a strange sight on
her delicately pale face. What could have caused
it? Surely not the quiet riding up to the carriage
of a stately old gentleman who was passing, wearing
a white frilled shirt and hessian boots. He looked
as if he had come out of a picture-frame, as he sat
there, his hat off and his white hair flowing, courte-
ously but not cordially, inquiring after the health of
my Lady Verner.

"Pretty well, Sir Rufus. I have had a great deal of vexation to try me lately."

"As we all have, my dear lady. Vexation has formed a large portion of my life. I have been calling at Verner's Pride, Mr. Verner."

"Have you, Sir Rufus? I am sorry I was not at home."

"These fine spring days tempt me out. Miss Tempest, you are looking remarkably well. Good morning, Lady Verner. Good morning."

A bow to Lady Verner, a sweeping bow to the rest collectively, and Sir Rufus rode away at a trot, putting on his hat as he went. His groom trotted after him, touching his hat as he passed the carriage.

But not a word had he spoken to Decima Verner, not a look had he given her. The omission was unnoticed by the others; not by Decima. The crimson of her cheeks had faded to an ashy paleness, and she silently let fall her veil to hide it.

What secret understanding could there be between herself and Sir Rufus Hautley?

CHAPTER VII.

Not until summer, when the days were long and the nights short, did the marriage of Lionel Verner take place. Lady Verner declined to be present at it: Decima and Lucy *were*. It was a grand ceremony, of course : that is, it would have been grand, but for an ignominious interruption which occurred to mar it. At the very moment they were at the altar, Lionel placing the ring on his bride's finger, and all around wrapt in breathless silence, in a transport of enthusiasm, the bridesmaids uncertain whether they must go off in hysterics or not, there tore into the church Master Dan Duff, in a state of extreme terror and ragged shirt sleeves, fighting his way against those who would have impeded him, and shouting out at the top of his voice : "Mother was took with the cholic, and she'd die right off if Mr. Jan didn't make haste to her." Upon which Jan, who had positively no more sense of what was due to society than Dan Duff himself had, went flying away there and then, muttering something about "those poisonous mushrooms." And so, they were made man and wife ; Lionel, in his heart of hearts, doubting if he did not best love Lucy Tempest.

A breakfast at Dr. West's : Miss Deborah and Miss Amilly not in the least knowing (as they said afterwards) how they comported themselves at it ; and then Lionel and his bride departed. He was taking her to Paris, which Sibylla had never seen.

Leaving them to enjoy its attractions — and Sibylla, at any rate, would not fail to do so—we must give another word to that zealous missionary, Brother Jarrum.

The seed, scattered broadcast by Brother Jarrum, had had time to fructify. He had left the glowing promises of all that awaited them, did they decide to voyage out to New Jerusalem, to take root in the imaginations of his listeners, and absented himself for a time from Deerham. This may have been crafty policy on Brother Jarrum's part; or may have resulted from necessity. It was hardly likely that so talented and enlightened an apostle as Brother Jarrum, should confine his labours to the limited sphere of Deerham : in all probability, they had to be put in requisition elsewhere. However it may have been, for several weeks towards the end of spring, Brother Jarrum was away from Deerham. Mr. Bitterworth, and one or two more influential people, of whom Lionel was one, had very strongly objected to Brother Jarrum's presence in it at all ; and, again, this may have been the reason of his quitting it. However it was, he did quit it ; though not without establishing a secret understanding with the more faithful of his converts. With the exception of these converts, Deerham thought he had left

it for good ; that it was, as they not at all politely
expressed it, "shut of him." .In this Deerham
was mistaken.

On the very day of Lionel Verner's marriage,
Brother Jarrum reappeared in the place. He took
up his abode, as before, in Mrs. Peckaby's spare
room. Peckaby, this time, held out against it.
However welcome the four shillings rent, weekly,
was from Brother Jarrum, Peckaby assumed a
lordly indifferenee to it, and protested he'd rather
starve, nor have pison like him in the house.
Peckaby, however, possessed a wife, who on occasion wore, metaphorically speaking, his nether
garments, and it was her will and pleasure to
countenance the expected guest. Brother Jarrum,
therefore, was received and welcomed.

He did not hold forth this time in Peckaby's
shop. He did not in public urge the delights of
New Jerusalem, or the expediency of departure for
it. He kept himself quiet and retired, receiving
visits in the privacy of his chamber. After dark,
especially, friends would drop in ; admitted without
noise or bustle by Mrs. Peckaby ; parties of ones, of
twos, of threes, until there would be quite an assembly collected up-stairs : why should not Brother
Jarrum hold his levees as well as his betters?

That something unusual was in the wind, was
very evident; some scheme, or project, which it
appeared expedient to keep a secret. Had Peckaby
been a little less fond of the seductions of the
Plough and Harrow, his suspicions must have been

aroused. Unfortunately, Peckaby yielded unremit-
tingly to that renowned inn's temptations, and spent
every evening there, leaving full sway to his wife
and Brother Jarrum.

About a month thus passed on, and Lionel Verner
and his wife were expected home, when Deerham
woke up one morning to a commotion. A flitting
had taken place from it in the night. Brother
Jarrum had departed, conveying with him a train of
followers.

One of the first to hear of it was Jan Verner; and,
curious to say, he heard it from Mrs. Baynton, the
lady at Chalk Cottage. Jan, who, let him be called
abroad in the night as he would, was always up with
the sun, stood one morning in his surgery, between
seven and eight o'clock, when he was surprised by
the entrance of Mrs. Baynton; a little woman, with
a meek, pinched face, and grey hair. Since Dr.
West's departure, Jan had attended the sickly
daughter, therefore he knew Mrs. Baynton, but he
had never seen her abroad in his life. Her bonnet
looked ten years old. Her daughters were named—
at least, they were called—Flore and Kitty; Kitty
being the sickly one. To see Mrs. Baynton arrive
thus, Jan jumped to the conclusion that Kitty must
be dying."

"Is she ill again?" he hastily asked, with his
usual absence of ceremony, giving the lady no time
to speak.

"She's gone," gasped Mrs. Baynton.

"Gone—dead?" asked Jan, with wondering **eyes**.

" She's gone off with the Mormons."

Jan stood upright against the counter, and stared at the old lady. He could not understand. " Who is gone off with the Mormons ? " was his rejoinder.

" Kitty is. Oh, Mr. Jan, think of her sufferings ! A journey, like that, before her ! All the way to that dreadful place ! I have heard that even strong women die on the road of the hardships."

Jan had stood with open mouth. " Is she mad ? " he questioned.

" She has not been much better than mad since— since—But I don't wish to go into family troubles. Can you give me Dr. West's address ? She might come back for him."

Now Jan had received positive commands from that wandering physician not to give his address to chance applicants : the inmates of Chalk Cottage having come in for a special interdiction. Therefore Jan could only decline.

" He is moving about from one place to another," said Jan. " To-day in Switzerland, to-morrow in France ; the next day in the moon, for what we can tell. You can give me a letter, and I'll try and get it conveyed to him somehow."

Mrs. Baynton shook her head.

" It would be too late. I thought if I could telegraph to him, he might have got to Liverpool in time to stop Kitty. There's a large migration of Mormons to take place in a day or two, and they are collecting at Liverpool."

" Go and stop her yourself," said Jan, sensibly.

" She'd not come back for me," replied Mrs. Baynton, in a depressed tone. " What with her delicate health, and what with her wilfulness, I have always had trouble with her. Dr. West was the only one—but I can't refer to those matters. Flore is broken-hearted. Poor Flore ! she has never given me an hour's grief in her life. Kitty has given me little else. And now to go off with the Mormons ! "

" Who has she gone with ? "

" With the rest from Deerham. They have gone off in the night. That Brother Jarrum and a company of about five-and-twenty, they say."

Jan could scarcely keep from exploding into laughter. Part of Deerham gone off to join the Mormons ! " Is it a fact ? " cried he.

" It is a fact that they are gone," replied Mrs. Baynton. " She has been out several times in an evening to hear that Brother Jarrum, and had be-come infected with the Mormon doctrine. In spite of what I or Flore could say, she would go to listen to the man, and she grew to believe the foolish things he uttered. And you can't give me Dr. West's address ? "

" No, I can't," replied Jan. " And I see no good that it would be to you, if I could. He could not get to Liverpool in time, from wherever he may be, if the flight is to take place in a day or two."

" Perhaps not," sighed Mrs. Baynton. " I was un-willing to come, but it seemed like a forlorn hope."

She let down her old crape veil as she went out at the door: and Jan, all curious for particulars, went abroad to pick up anything he could learn.

About fifteen had gone off, exclusive of children. Grind's lot, as it was called, meaning Grind, his wife, and their young ones; Davies had gone, Mary Green had gone, Nancy from Verner's Pride had gone, and sundry others whom it is not necessary to enumerate. It was said that Dinah Roy made preparations to go, but her heart failed her at the last. Some accounts ran that she did start, but was summarily brought up by the appearance of her husband, who went after her. At his sight she turned without a word, and walked home again, meekly submitting to the correction he saw fit to inflict. Jan did not believe this. His private opinion was, that had Dinah Roy started, her husband would have deemed it a red-letter day, and never have sought to bring her back more.

Last, but not least, Mrs. Peckaby had *not* gone. No: for Brother Jarrum had stolen a march upon her. What his motive in doing this might be, was best known to himself. Of all the converts, none had been so eager for the emigration, so fondly anticipative of the promised delights, as Susan Peckaby; and she had made her own private arrangements to steal off secretly, leaving her un-believing husband to his solitary fate. As it turned out, however, she was herself left: the happy company stole off, and abandoned her.

Brother Jarrum so contrived it, that the night

fixed for the exodus was kept secret from Mrs. Peckaby. She did not know that he had even gone out of the house, until she got 'up in the morning and found him absent. Brother Jarrum's personal luggage was not of an extensive character. It was contained in a blue bag: and this bag was likewise missing. Not, even then, did a shadow of the cruel treachery played her, darken the spirit of Mrs. Peckaby. Her faith in Brother Jarrum was of an unlimited extent: she would as soon have thought of deceiving her own self, as that he could deceive. The rumour that the migration had taken place, the company off, awoke her from her happy security to a state of raving torture. Peckaby dodged out of her way, afraid. There is no knowing but Peckaby himself may have been the stumbling block in the mind of Brother Jarrum. A man so dead against the Latter Day Saints as Peckaby had shown himself, would be a difficult customer to deal with. He might be capable of following them and upsetting the minds of all the Deerham converts, did his wife start with them for New Jerusalem.

All this information was gathered by Jan. Jan had heard nothing for many a day that so tickled his fancy. He bent his steps to Peckaby's, and went in. Jan, you know, was troubled neither with pride nor ceremony: nobody less so in all Deerham. Where inclination took him, there went Jan.

Peckaby, all black, with a bar of iron in his hand, a leather apron on, and a broad grin upon his countenance, was coming out of the door as Jan entered. The affair seemed to tickle Peckaby's fancy as much as it tickled Jan's. He touched his hair. "Please, sir, couldn't you give her a dose of jalap, or something comforting o' that sort, to bring her to?" asked he, pointing with his thumb indoors, as he stamped across the road to the forge.

Mrs. Peckaby had calmed down from the rampant state to one of prostration. She sat in her kitchen behind the shop, nursing her knees, and moaning. Mrs. Duff, who, by Jan's help, had survived the threatened death from "cholic," and was herself again, stood near the sufferer, in company with one or two more cronies. All the particulars, Susan Peckaby's contemplated journey, with the deceitful trick played her, had got wind; and the Deerham ladies were in consequence flocking in.

"You didn't mean going, did you?" began Jan.

"Not mean going!" sobbed Susan Peckaby, rocking herself to and fro. "I did mean going, sir, and I'm not ashamed to own to it. If folks is in the luck to be offered a chance of Paradise, I dun know many as ud say they wouldn't catch at it."

"Paradise, was it?" said Jan. "What was it chiefly to consist of?"

"Of everything," moaned Susan Peckaby. "There isn't a thing you could wish for under the sun, but what's to be had in plenty at New Jerusalem. Dinners and teas, and your own cows, and big houses and parlours, and gardens loaded

with fruit, and garden stuff as decays for want o'
cutting, and veils when you go out, and evening
dances, like the grand folks here has, and new caps
perpetual! And I have lost it! They be gone
and have left me!—oh, o-o-o-h!"

"And husbands, besides; one for everybody!"
spoke up a girl. "You forgot that, Mrs. Peckaby."

"Husbands besides," acquiesced Susan Peckaby,
aroused from her moaning. "Every woman's sure
to be chose by a saint as soon as she gets out.
There's not such a thing as a old maid there, and
there needn't be no widders."

Mrs. Duff turned up her nose, and turned it
wrathfully on the girl who had spoken.

"If they call husbands their paradise, keep me
away from 'em, say I. You girls be like young
bears—all your troubles have got to come. You
just try a husband, Bess Dawson; whether he's a
saint, or whether he's a sinner, let him be of a
cranky temper, thwarting you at every trick and
turn, and you'll see what sort of a paradise marriage
is! Don't you think I'm right, sir?"

Jan's mouth was extended from ear to ear,
laughing.

"I never tried it," said he. "Were you to have
been espoused by Brother Jarrum?" he asked, of
Susan Peckaby.

"No, sir, I was not," she answered, in much
anger. "I did not favour Brother Jarrum. I'd
prefer to pick and choose when I got there. But
I had a great amount of respect for Brother Jarrum,

sir, which I'm proud to speak to. And I don't believe that he has served me this shameful trick of his own knowledge," she added, with emphasis. " I believe there has been some unfortinate mistake, and that when he finds I'm not among the company, he'll come back for me. I'd go after them, only that Peckaby's on the watch. I never see such a altered man as Peckaby: it had used to be as I could just turn him round my little finger, but he won't be turned now."

She finished up with a storm of sobs. Jan, in an ecstacy of mirth yet, offered to send her some cordials from the surgery, by way of consolation : not, however, the precise one suggested by Peckaby. But cordials had no charm in that unhappy moment for Mrs. Peckaby's ear.

Jan departed. In quitting the door he encountered a stranger, who inquired if that was Peckaby's shop. Jan fancied the man looked something the cut of Brother Jarrum, and sent him in. His coat and boots were white with dust. Looking round on the assembled women when he reached the kitchen, the stranger asked which was Mrs. Peckaby. Mrs. Peckaby looked up, and signified that she was.

"I have a message from the saint and elder, Brother Jarrum," he mysteriously whispered in her ear. " It must be give to you in private."

Mrs. Peckaby, in a tremble of delight, led the stranger to a small shed in the yard, which she used for washing purposes, and called the back 'us.

It was the most private place she could think of,
in her fluster. The stranger, propping himself
against a broken tub, proceeded, with some circumlocution and not remarkable perspicuity of speech,
to deliver the message with which he was charged.
It was to the effect that a vision had revealed to
Brother Jarrum the startling fact, that Susan
Peckaby was *not* to go out with the crowd at
present on the wing. A higher destiny awaited
her. She would be sent for in a different manner
—in a more important form ; sent for special,
on a quadruped. That is to say, on a white
donkey.*

"On a white donkey?" echoed the trembling and
joyful woman.

"On a white donkey," gravely repeated the
brother — for that he was another brother of the
community, there could be little doubt. "What
the special honour intended for you may be, me
and Brother Jarrum don't pertend to guess at. It's
above us. May be you are fated to be chose by
our great prophet hisself. Any how, it's something
at the top of the tree."

"When shall I be sent for, sir?" eagerly asked
Mrs. Peckaby.

"That ain't revealed neither. It may be next
week—it mayn't be for a year ; you must always
be on the look-out. One of these days or nights,
you'll see a white donkey a-standing at your door.
It'll be the messenger for you from New Jerusalem.

* A fact.

You mount him without a minute's loss of time, and come off."

But that Mrs. Peckaby's senses were exalted at that moment far above the level of ordinary mortals', it might have occurred to her to inquire whether the donkey would be endowed with the miraculous power of bearing her over the sea. No such common question presented itself. She asked another.

"Why couldn't Brother Jarrum have told me this hisself, sir? I have been a'most mad this morning, ever since I found as they had gone."

The brother—this brother—turned up the whites of his eyes. "When unknown things is revealed to us, and mysterious orders give, they never come to us a minute afore the time," he replied. "Not till Brother Jarrum was fixing the night of departure, did the vision come to him. It was commanded him that it should be kept from you till the rest were off, and then he were to send back a messenger to tell you—and many a mile I've come! Brother Jarrum and me has no doubt that it is meant as a trial of your faith."

Nothing could be more satisfactory to the mind of Mrs. Peckaby than this explanation. Had any mysterious vision appeared to herself, showing her that it was false, commanding her to disbelieve it, it could not have shaken her faith. If the white donkey arrived at her door that very night, she would be sure to mount him.

"Do you think it'll be very long, sir, that I shall

have to wait?" she resumed, feverishly listening for the answer.

"My impression is, that it'll be very short," was the reply. "And it's Brother Jarrum's also. Any way, you be on the look-out—always prepared. Have a best robe at hand continual, ready to clap on the instant the quadruped appears, and come right away to New Jerusalem."

In the openness of her heart, Mrs. Peckaby offered refreshment to the brother. The best her house afforded: which was not much. Peckaby should be condemned to go foodless for a week, rather than that *he* should depart fasting. The brother, however, declined: he appeared to be in a hurry to leave Deerham behind him.

"I'd not disclose this to anybody if I was you," was his parting salutation. "Leastways, not for a day or two. Let the ruck of 'em embark first at Liverpool. If it gets wind, some of them may be for turning crusty, because they are not favoured with special animals, too."

Had the brother recommended Susan Peckaby to fill the tub with water, and stand head down-wards in it for a day or two, she was in the mood to obey him. Accordingly, when questioned by Mrs. Duff, and the other curious ones, what had been the business of the stranger, she' made a great mystery over it, and declined to answer.

"It's good news, by the signs of your face," remarked Mrs. Duff.

"Good news!" rapturously repeated Susan

Peckaby, "it's heaven. I say, Mother Duff, I want
a new gownd : something of the very best. I'll pay
for it by degrees. There ain't no time to be lost,
neither; so I'll come down at once and choose it."

"What *has* happened?" was the wondering
rejoinder of Mother Duff.

"Never you mind, just yet. I'll tell you about it
afore the week's out."

And accordingly, before the week was out, all
Deerham was regaled with the news; full particulars.
And Susan Peckaby, a robe of purple, of the stuff
called lustre, laid up in state, to be donned when
the occasion came, passed her time, night and day,
at her door and windows, looking out for the white
donkey that was to bear her in triumph to New
Jerusalem. .

CHAPTER VIII.

IN the commodious dressing-room at Verner's Pride, appropriated to its new mistress, Mrs. Verner, stood the housekeeper, Tynn, lifting her hands and her eyes. You once saw the chamber of John Massingbird, in this same house, in a tolerable litter: but that was as nothing, compared with the litter in this dressing-room, piles and piles of it, one heap by the side of another. Mary Tynn stood screwed against the wainscoting of the wall : she had got in, but to get out was another matter : there was not a free place where she could put her foot. Strictly speaking, perhaps, it could not be called litter, and Mrs. Verner and her French maid would have been alike indignant at hearing it so classed. Robes of rich and rare texture; silks standing on end with magnificence; dinner attire, than which nothing could be more exquisite; ball dresses in all sorts of gossamer fabrics; under-skirts, glistening with their soft lustre; morning costumes, pure and costly; shawls of Cashmere and other *recherché* stuffs, enough to stock a shop; mantles of every known make; bonnets that would send an English milliner crazy: veils charming to look upon; laces that might rival Lady

Verner's embroideries, their price fabulous; hand-
kerchiefs that surely never were made for use;
dozens of delicately-tinted gloves, cased in orna-
mental boxes, costing as much as they did; every
description of expensive *chaussure;* and trinkets,
the drawn cheques for which must have caused
Lionel Verner's sober bankers to stare. Tynn might
well heave her hands and eyes in dismay. On the
chairs, on the tables, on the drawers, on the floor,
on every conceivable place and space, they lay; a
goodly mass of vanity, just unpacked from their
cases.

Flitting about amidst them was a damsel of
coquettish appearance, with a fair skin, light hair,
and her nose a turn-up. Her grey gown was flounced
to the waist, her small cap of lace, its pink strings
flying, was lodged on the back of her head. It was
Mademoiselle Benoite, Mrs. Verner's French maid,
one she had picked up in Paris. Whatever other
qualities the damsel might lack, she had enough of
confidence. Not many hours yet in the house, and
she was assuming more authority in it than her
mistress did.

Mr. and Mrs. Verner had returned the night before,
Mademoiselle Benoite and her packages making part
of their train. A whole *fourgon* could not have been
sufficient to convey these packages from the French
capital to the frontier. Phœby, the simple country
maid whom Sibylla had taken to Paris with her,
found her place a sinecure since the engagement of
Mademoiselle Benoite. She stood now on the oppo-

site side of the room to Tynn, humbly waiting Mademoiselle Benoite's imperious commands.

" Where on earth will you stow 'em away ? " cried Tynn, in her wonder. " You'll want a length of rooms to do it in."

" Where I stow 'em away ! " retorted Mademoiselle Benoite, in her fluent speech, but broken English. " I stow 'em where I please. Note you that, Madame Teen. Par exemple! The château is grand enough."

" What has its grandeur got to do with it ? " was Mary Tynn's answer. She knew but little of French phrases.

" Now, then, what for you stand there, with your eyes staring and your hands idle ? " demanded Mademoiselle Benoite sharply, turning her attack on Phœby.

" If you'll tell me what to do, I'll do it," replied the girl. " I could help to put the things up, if you'd show me where to begin."

" I like to see you dare to put a finger on one of these things ! " returned Mademoiselle Benoite. " You can confine your services to sewing, and to waiting upon me ; but not you dare to interfere with my lady's toilette. Tiens, I am capable, I hope ! I'd give up the best service to-morrow where I had not sole power ! Go you down to the of-fice, and order me a cup of chocolate, and wait you and bring it up to me. That maudite drogue, that coffee, this morning, has made me as thirsty as a panthère."

Phœby, glancing across at Mrs. Tynn, turned

somewhat hesitatingly to pick her way out of the
room. The housekeeper, though not half understanding, contrived to make out that the morning
coffee was not approved of. The French mademoiselle had breakfasted with her, and, in Mrs.
Tynn's opinion, the coffee had been perfect, fit for
the table of her betters.

"Is it the coffee that you are abusing?" asked
she. "What was the matter with it?"

"Ciel! You ask what the matter with it!" returned Mademoiselle Benoite, in her rapid tongue.
"It was everything the matter with it. It was all
bad. It was drogue, I say; médecine. There!"

"Well, I'm sure!" resentfully returned the housekeeper. "Now, I happened to make that coffee myself this morning—Tynn, he's particular in his coffee,
he is—and I put in—"

"I not care if you put in the whole canastre,"
vehemently interrupted Mademoiselle Benoite.
"You English know not to make coffee. All the
two years I lived in London with Madame la
Duchesse, I never got one cup of coffee that was
not enough to choke me. And they used pounds of
it in the house, where they might have used ounces.
Bah! You can make tea, I not say no; but you
cannot make coffee. Now, then! I want a great
number sheets of silk paper."

"Silk paper?" repeated Tynn, whom the item
puzzled. "What's that?"

"You know not what silk paper is!" angrily
returned Mademoiselle Benoite. "*Quelle ignorance!*"

she apostrophised, not caring whether she was understood or not. "*Ellé ne connait pas ce que c'est, papier-de-soie!* I must have it, and a great deal of it, do you hear? It is as common as anything— silk-paper."

"Things common in France mayn't be common with us," retorted Mrs. Tynn. "What is it for?"

"It is for some of these articles. If I put them by without the paper-silk round them in the cartons, they'll not keep their colour."

"Perhaps you mean silver-paper," said Mary Tynn. "Tissue-paper, I have heard my Lady Verner call it. There's none in the house, Madmisel Bennot."

"Madmisel Bennot" stamped her foot. "A house without silk-paper in it! When you knew my lady was coming home!"

"I didn't know she'd bring—a host of things with her that she has brought," was the answering shaft lanced by Mrs. Tynn.

"Don't you see that I am waiting? Will you send out for some?"

"It's not to be had in Deerham," said Mrs. Tynn. "If it must be had, one of the men must go to Heartburg. Why won't the paper do that was over 'em before?"

"There not enough of that. And I choose to have fresh, I do."

"Well, you had better give your own orders about it," said Mary Tynn. "And then if there's any mistake, it'll be nobody's fault, you know."

Mademoiselle Benoite did not on the instant reply. She had her hands full just then. In reaching over for a particular bonnet, she managed to turn a dozen or two on to the floor. Tynn watched the picking up process, and listened to the various ejaculations that accompanied it, in much grimness.

"What a sight of money those things must have cost!" cried she.

"What that matter?" returned the lady's-maid. "The purse of a milor Anglais can stand anything."

"What did she buy them for?" went on Tynn. "For what purpose?"

"*Bon!*" ejaculated Mademoiselle. "She buy them to wear. What else you suppose she buy them for?"

"Why! she would never wear out the half of them in all her whole life!" uttered Tynn, speaking the true sentiments of her heart. "She could not."

"Much you know of things, Madame Teen!" was the answer, delivered in undisguised contempt for Tynn's primitive ignorance. "They'll not last her six months."

"Six months!" shrieked Tynn. "She couldn't come to an end of them dresses in six months, if she wore three a day, and never put on a dress a second time!"

"She want to wear more than three different a day sometimes. And it not the mode now to put on a robe more than once," returned Mademoiselle Benoite, carelessly.

Tynn could only open her mouth. "If they are

to be put on but once, what becomes of 'em afterwards?" questioned she, when she could find breath
to speak.

"Oh, they good for jupons—petticoats, you call
it. Some may be worn a second time ; they can be
changed by other trimmings to look like new. And
the rest will be good for me : Madame la Duchesse
gave me a great deal. ' *Tenez, ma fille,*' she would
say, ' *regardez dans ma garde-robe, et prenez autant
que vous voudrez.*' She always spoke to me in
French."

Tynn wished there had been no French invented,
so far as her comprehension was concerned. While
she stood, undecided what reply to make, wishing
very much to express her decided opinion upon the
extravagance she saw around her, yet deterred from
it by remembering that Mrs. Verner was now her
mistress, Phœby entered with the chocolate. The
girl put it down on the mantelpiece : there was
no other place : and then made a sign to Mrs.
Tynn that she wished to speak with her. They
both left the room.

"Am I to be at the beck and call of that French
madmizel?" she resentfully asked. "I was not
engaged for that, Mrs. Tynn."

"It seems we are all to be at her beck and call,
to hear her go on," was Mrs. Tynn's wrathful rejoinder. " Of course it can't be tolerated. We shall
see in a day or two. Phœby, girl, what could possess
Mrs. Verner to buy all them cart-loads of finery ?
She must have spent the money like water."

"So she did," acquiesced Phœby. "She did nothing all day long but drive about from one place to another and choose pretty things. You should see the china that's coming over!"

"I wonder Mr. Lionel let her," was the thoughtlessly-spoken remark of Tynn. And she tried, when too late, to cough it down.

"He helped her, I think," answered Phœby. "I know he bought some of that beautiful jewellery for her himself, and brought it home. I saw him kiss her, through the doorway, as he clasped that pink necklace on her neck."

"Oh well, I don't want to hear about that rubbish," tartly rejoined Tynn. "If you take to peep through doorways, girl, you won't suit Verner's Pride."

Phœby did not like the rebuff. She turned one way, and Mrs. Tynn went off another.

In the breakfast-room below, in her charming French morning costume, tasty and elegant, sat Sibylla Verner. With French dresses, she seemed to be acquiring French habits. Late as the hour was, the breakfast remained on the table. Sibylla might have sent the things away an hour ago: but she kept a little chocolate in her cup, and toyed with it. She had never tasted chocolate for breakfast in all her life, previous to this visit to Paris: now she protested she could take nothing else. Possibly she may have caught the taste for it from Mademoiselle Benoite. Her husband sat opposite to her: his chair drawn from the table, and turned to face the room. A perfectly satisfied, happy expression pervaded his face: he appeared to be fully contented with his lot and with his bride. Just now he was laughing immoderately.

Perched upon the arm of a sofa, having there come to an anchor, his legs hanging down and swaying about in their favourite fashion, was Jan Verner. Jan had come in to pay them a visit and congratulate them on their return. That is speaking somewhat figuratively, however; for Jan possessed no notion of congratulating anybody. As Lady Verner sometimes resentfully said, Jan had no more social politeness in him than a bear. Upon entering, Sibylla asked him to take some breakfast. Breakfast! echoed Jan, did she call that breakfast? He thought it was their lunch: it was getting on for his dinner-time. Jan was giving Lionel a history of the moonlight flitting, and of Susan Peckaby's expected expedition to New Jerusalem on a white donkey.

"It ought to have been stopped," said Lionel, when his laughter had subsided. "They are going out to misery, and to nothing else, poor deluded creatures!"

"Who was to stop it?" asked Jan.

"Some one might have told them the truth. If this Brother Jarrum represented things in rose-coloured hues, could nobody open to their view the other side of the picture? I should have endeavoured to do it, had I been here. If they chose to risk the venture after that, it would have been their own fault."

"You'd have done no good," said Jan. "Once

let 'em get the Mormon fever upon 'em, and it must run its course. It's like the Gold fever : nothing will convince folks they are mistaken as to that, except the going out to Australia to the Diggings. That will."

A faint tinge of brighter colour rose to Sibylla's cheeks at this allusion, and Lionel knit his brow. He would have avoided for ever any chain of thought that led his memory to Frederick Massingbird : he could not bear to think that his young bride had been another's before she was his. Jan, happily ignorant, continued.

"There's Susan Peckaby. She has got it in her head that she's going straight off to Paradise, once she is in the Salt Lake City. Well, now, Lionel, if you, and all the world to help you, set yourselves on to convince her that she's mistaken, you couldn't do it. They must go out, and find the level of things for themselves : there's no help for it."

"Jan, it is not likely that Susan Peckaby really expects a white donkey to be sent for her !" cried Sibylla.

"She as fully expects the white donkey, as I expect that I shall go from here presently, and drop in on Paynton, on my way home," earnestly said Jan. "He has had a kick from a horse on his shin, and a nasty place it is," added Jan in a parenthesis. "Nothing on earth would convince Susan Peckaby that the donkey's a myth, or will be a myth ; and she wastes all her time looking out for it. If you were opposite their place now, you'd see her head somewhere : poked out at the door, or peeping from the up-stairs window."

" I wish I could get them all back again—those who have gone from here !" warmly spoke Lionel.

" I wish sometimes I had got four legs, that I might get over double ground, when patients are wanting me on all sides," returned Jan. " The one wish is just as possible as the other, Lionel. The lot sailed from Liverpool yesterday, in the ship American Star. And I'll be bound, what with the sea-sickness, and the other discomforts, they are wishing themselves out of it already! I say, Sibylla, what did you think of Paris ?"

" Oh, Jan, it's enchanting ! And I have brought the most charming things home. You can come upstairs and see them, if you like. Benoite is unpacking them."

" Well, I don't know," mused Jan. " I don't suppose they are what I should care to see. What are the things ?"

" Dresses, and bonnets, and mantles, and lace, and coiffures," returned Sibylla. " I can't tell you half the beautiful things. One of my *cache-peignes* is of filigrane silver-work, with drops falling from it, real diamonds."

" What d'ye call a *cache-peigne* ?" asked Jan.

" Don't you know ? An ornament for the hair, that you put on to hide the comb behind. Combs are coming into fashion. Will you come up and see the things, Jan ?"

" Not I ! What do I care for lace and bonnets ?"

ungallantly answered Jan. "I didn't know but
Lionel might have brought me some anatomical
studies over. They'd be in my line."

Sibylla shrieked—a pretty little shriek of affecta-
tion. "Lionel, why do you let him say such things
to me? He means amputated arms and legs."

"I'm sure I didn't," said Jan. "I meant models.
They'd not let the other things pass the customs.
Have you brought a dress a-piece for Deb and
Amilly?"

"No," said Sibylla, looking up in some consternation. "I never thought about it."

"Won't they be disappointed, then! They have
counted upon it, I can tell you. They can't afford
to buy themselves much, you know: the doctor
keeps them so short," added Jan.

"I *would* have brought them something, if I had
thought of it; I would, indeed!" exclaimed Sibylla,
in an accent of contrition. "Is it not a pity,
Lionel?"

"I wish you had," replied Lionel. "Can you
give them nothing of what you have brought?"

"Well—I—must—consider," hesitated Sibylla,
who was essentially selfish. "The things are so
beautiful; so expensive: they are scarcely suited to
Deborah and Amilly."

"Why not?" questioned Jan.

"You have not a bit of sense, Jan," grumbled
Sibylla. "Things chosen to suit me, won't suit
them."

"Why not?" repeated Jan, obstinately.

"There never was any one like you, Jan, for stupidity," was Sibylla's retort. "I am young and pretty, and a bride; and they are two faded old maids."

"Dress 'em up young, and they'll look young," answered Jan, with composure. "Give 'em a bit of pleasure for once, Sibylla."

"I'll see," impatiently answered Sibylla. "Jan, how came Nancy to go off with the Mormons? Tynn says she packed up her things in secret, and started."

"How came the rest to go?" was Jan's answer. "She caught the fever too, I suppose."

"What Nancy are you talking of?" demanded Lionel. "Not Nancy from here!"

"Oh, Lionel, yes! I forgot to tell you," said Sibylla. "She is gone indeed. Mrs. Tynn is so indignant. She says the girl must be a fool!"

"Little short of it," returned Lionel. "To give up a good home here for the Salt Lake! She will repent it."

"Let 'em all alone for *that*," nodded Jan. "I'd like to pay an hour's visit to 'em, when they have been a month in the place—if they ever get to it."

"Tynn says she remembers, when that Brother Jarrum was here in the spring, that Nancy made frequent excuses for going to Deerham in the evening," resumed Sibylla. "She thinks it must have been to frequent those meetings in Peckaby's shop."

"I thought the man, Jarrum, had gone off, leaving the mischief to die away," observed Lionel.

" So did everybody else," said Jan. " He came
back the day that you were married. Nancy's betters
got lured into Peckaby's, as well as Nancy," he
added. " That sickly daughter at Chalk Cottage,
she's gone."

Lionel looked very much astonished.

" No !" he uttered.

" Fact," said Jan. " The mother came to me the
morning after the flitting, and said she had been
seduced away. . She wanted to telegraph to Dr.
West—"

Jan stopped dead, remembering that Sibylla was
present, as well as Lionel. He leaped off the sofa.

" Ah, we shall see them all back some day, if
they can only contrive to elude the vigilance of the
Mormons. I'm off, Lionel; old Paynton will think
I am not coming to-day. Good-bye, Sibylla."

Jan hastened from the room. Lionel stood at the
window, and watched him away. Sibylla glided up
to her husband, nestling against him.

" Lionel, tell me. Jan never would, though I
nearly teased his life out; and Deborah and Amilly
persisted that they knew nothing. *You* tell me."

" Tell you what, my dearest ? "

" After I came home in the winter, there were
strange whispers about papa and that Chalk Cottage.
People were mysterious over it, and I never could
get a word of explanation. Jan was the worst: he
was coolly tantalising, and it used to put me in a
passion. What was the tale told ? "

An involuntary darkening of Lionel's brow. He

cleared it instantly, and looked down on his wife with a smile.

"I know of no tale worth telling you, Sibylla."

"But there *was* a tale told?"

"Jan—who, being in closer proximity to Dr. West than any one, may be supposed to know best of his private affairs—tells a tale of Dr. West's having set a chimney on fire at Chalk Cottage, thereby arousing the ire of its inmates."

"Don't you repeat such nonsense to me, Lionel; you are not Jan," she returned, in a half peevish tone. "I fear papa may have borrowed money from the ladies, and did not repay them," she added, her voice sinking to a whisper. "But I would not say it to any one but you. What do you think?"

"If my wife will allow me to tell her what I think, I should say that it is her duty—and mine now—not to seek to penetrate into any affairs belonging to Dr. West which he may wish to keep to himself. Is it not so, Sibylla mine?"

Sibylla smiled, and held up her face to be kissed. "Yes, you are right, Lionel."

Swayed by impulse, more than by anything else, she thought of her treasures upstairs, in the process of disinterment from their cases by Benoite, and ran from him to inspect them. Lionel put on his hat, and strolled out of doors.

A thought came over him that he would go and pay a visit to his mother. He knew how exacting of attention from him she was, how jealous, so to speak, of Sibylla's having taken him from her.

Lionel hoped by degrees to reduce the breach narrower and narrower. Nothing should be wanting on
his part to effect it: he trusted that nothing would
be wanting on Sibylla's. He really wished to see
his mother after his month's absence: and he knew
she would be pleased at his going there on this, the
first morning of his return. As he turned into the
high road, he met the vicar of Deerham, the
Reverend James Bourne.

They shook hands. And the conversation led,
not unnaturally, on the Mormon flight. As they
were talking of it, Roy, the ex-bailiff, was observed
crossing the opposite field.

"My brother tells me the report runs that Mrs.
Roy contemplated being of the company, but was
overtaken by her husband and brought back,"
remarked Lionel.

"How it may have been, about his bringing her
back, or whether she actually started, I don't know,"
replied Mr. Bourne, who was a man with a large
pale face and iron-grey hair. "That she intended
to go, I have reason to believe."

He spoke the last words significantly, lowering
his voice. Lionel looked at him.

"She paid me a mysterious visit at the vicarage
the night before the start," continued the clergyman. "A very mysterious visit, indeed, taken in
conjunction with her words. I was in my study,
reading by candle-light, when somebody came tapping at the glass door, and stole in. It was Mrs.
Roy. She was in a state of tremor, as I have

heard it said she appeared the night the inquiry was held at Verner's Pride, touching the death of Rachel Frost. She spoke to me in ambiguous terms of a journey she was about to take—that she should probably be away for her whole life—and then she proceeded to speak of that night."

" The night of the inquiry ? " echoed Lionel.

." The night of the inquiry—that is, the night of the accident," returned Mr. Bourne. " She said she wished to confide a secret to me, which she had not liked to touch upon before, but which she could not leave the place without confiding to some one responsible, who might use it in case of need. The secret she proceeded to tell me was—that it was Frederick Massingbird who had been quarrelling with Rachel that night by the willow pool. She could swear it to me, she said, if necessary."

" But—if that were true—why did she not proclaim it at the time ? " asked Lionel, after a pause.

"It was all she said. And she would not be questioned. 'In case o' need, sir, in case anybody else should ever be brought up for it, tell 'em that Dinah Roy asserted to you with her last breath in Deerham, that Mr. Fred Massingbird was the one that was with Rachel.' Those were the words she used to me : I dotted them down after she left. As I tell you, she would not be questioned, and glided out again almost immediately."

" Was she wandering in her mind ? "

"I think not. She spoke with an air of truth. When I heard of the flight of the converts the next

morning, I could only conclude that Mrs. Roy had
intended to be amongst them. But now, understand
me, Mr. Verner, although I have told you this, I
have not mentioned it to another living soul.
Neither do I intend to do so. It can do no good to
reap up the sad tale: whether Frederick Massingbird was or was not with Rachel that night; whether
he was in any way guilty, or was purely innocent, it
boots not to inquire now."

"It does not," warmly replied Lionel. "You
have done well. Let us bury Mrs. Roy's story
between us: and forget it, so far as we can."

They parted. Lionel took his way to Deerham
Court, absorbed in thought. His own strong impression had been, that Mr. Fred Massingbird was
the black sheep, with regard to Rachel.

CHAPTER IX.

LIONEL'S PRAYER FOR FORGIVENESS.

LADY VERNER, like many more of us, found that
misfortunes do not come singly. Coeval almost
with that great misfortune, Lionel's marriage—at
any rate, coeval with his return to Verner's Pride
with his bride—another vexation befel Lady Verner.
Had Lady Verner found real misfortunes to con-
tend with, it is hard to say how she would have
borne them. Perhaps Lionel's marriage to Sibylla
was a real misfortune ; but this second vexation
assuredly was not : at any rate, to Lady Verner.

Some women—and Lady Verner was one—are
fond of scheming and planning. Whether it be the
laying out of a flower-bed, or the laying out of a
marriage, they must plan and project. Disappointment with regard to her own daughter—for Decima
most unqualifyingly disclaimed any match-making
on her own score—Lady Verner had turned her
hopes in this respect on Lucy Tempest. She
deemed that she should be ill-fulfilling the respon-
sibilities of her guardianship,. unless when Colonel
Tempest returned to England, she could present
Lucy to him, a wife : or, at least, engaged to be one.
Many a time now did she unavailingly wish that

Lionel had chosen Lucy, instead of her whom he had chosen. Although—and mark how we estimate things by comparison;—when, in the old days, Lady Verner had fancied Lionel was growing to like Lucy, she had told him emphatically it " would not do." Why would it not do? Because, in the estimation of Lady Verner, Lucy Tempest was less desirable in a social point of view than the Earl of Elmsley's daughter, and upon the latter lady had been fixed her hopes for Lionel.

All that was past and gone. Lady Verner had seen the fallacy of sublunary hopes and projects. Lady Mary Elmsley was rejected—Lionel had married in direct defiance of everybody's advice—and Lucy was open to offers. Open to offers, as Lady Verner supposed; but she was destined to find herself unpleasantly disappointed.

One came forward with an offer to her. And that was no other than the Earl of Elmsley's son, Viscount Garle. A pleasant man, of eight-and-twenty years; and he was often at Lady Verner's. He had been intimate there a long while, going in and out as unceremoniously as did Lionel or Jan. Lady Verner and Decima could tell a tale that no one else suspected. How, in the years gone by—some four or five years ago now—he had grown to love Decima with his whole heart; and Decima had rejected him. In spite of his sincere love; of the advantages of the match; of the angry indignation of Lady Verner; Decima had steadfastly rejected him. For some time Lord Garle would not take the rejection : but one day, when my lady was out, Decima spoke with him privately for five minutes, and from that hour Lord Garle had known there was no hope ; had been content to begin there and then, and strive to love her only as a sister. The little episode was never known : Decima and Lady Verner had kept counsel, and Lord Garle had not told tales of himself. Next to Lionel, Lady Verner liked Lord Garle better than any one—ten times better than she liked unvarnished Jan ; and he was allowed the run of the house as though he had been its son. The first year of Lucy's arrival—the year of Lionel's illness, Lord Garle had been away from the neighbourhood ; but somewhere about the time of Sibylla's return, he had come back to it. Seeing a great deal of Lucy, as he necessarily did, being so much at Lady Verner's, he grew to esteem and love her. Not with the same love he had borne for Decima— a love, such as that, never comes twice in a lifetime —but with a love sufficiently warm, notwithstanding. And he asked her to become his wife.

There was triumph for Lady Verner ! Next to Decima—and all hope of that was dead for ever— she would like Lord Garle to marry Lucy. A real triumph, the presenting her to Colonel Tempest on his return, my Lady Viscountess Garle ! In the delight of her heart she betrayed something of this to Lucy.

" But I am not going to marry him, Lady Verner," objected Lucy.

" You are not going to marry him, Lucy ?   He

confided to me the fact of his intention this morning before he spoke to you.   He *has* spoken to you,
has he not?"

"Yes," replied Lucy; "but I cannot accept him."

"You—cannot! What are you talking of?" cried
Lady Verner.

"Please not to be angry, Lady Verner! I could
not marry Lord Garle."

Lady Verner's lips grew pale.   "And pray why
can you not?" she demanded.

"I—don't like him," stammered Lucy.

"Not like him!" repeated Lady Verner. "Why,
what can there be about Lord Garle that you young
ladies do not like?" she wondered; her thoughts
cast back to the former rejection by Decima.   "He
is good-looking, he is sensible; there's not so
attractive a man in all the county, Lionel Verner
excepted."

Lucy's face turned to a fiery glow. "Had I
known he was going to ask me, I would have
requested him not to do so beforehand, as my
refusal has displeased you," she simply said.   "I
am sorry you should be vexed with me, Lady
Verner."

"It appears to me that nothing but vexation is
to be the portion of my life!" uttered Lady Verner.
"Thwarted—thwarted always!—on all sides.   First
from one, then the other—nothing but crosses and
vexations! What did you say to Lord Garle?"

"I told Lord Garle that I could not marry him;
that I should never like him well enough—for he

said, if I did not care for him now, I might later.
But I told him no ; it was impossible. I like him
very well as a friend, but that is all."

"*Why* don't you like him?" repeated Lady
Verner.

"I don't know," whispered Lucy, standing before
Lady Verner like a culprit, her eyes cast down, and
her eyelashes resting on her hot crimsoned face.

"Do you *both* mean to make yourselves into old
maids, you and Decima?" reiterated the angry
Lady Verner. "A pretty pair of you I shall have
on my hands! I never was so annoyed in my life."

Lucy burst into tears. "I wish I could go to
papa in India!" she said.

"Do you know what you have rejected?" asked
Lady Verner. "You would have been a peeress of
England. His father will not live for ever."

"But I should not care to be a peeress," sobbed
Lucy. "And I don't like him."

"Mamma, please do not say any more," pleaded
Decima. "Lucy is not to blame. If she does not
like Lord Garle she could not accept him."

"Of course she is not to blame—according to
you, Miss Verner! You were not to blame, were
you, when you rejected—some one we know of?
Not the least doubt that you will take her part!
Young Bitterworth wished to have proposed to you:
you sent him away—as you send all. And refuse
to tell me your motive! Very dutiful you are,
Decima!"

Decima turned away her pale face. She began

to think Lucy would do better without her advocacy
than with it.

"I cannot allow it to end thus," resumed Lady
Verner to Lucy. " You must reconsider your determination and recal Lord Garle."

The words frightened Lucy.

"I never can—I never can, Lady Verner!" she
cried. "Please not to press it; it is of no use."

"I must press it," replied Lady Verner. "I
cannot allow you to throw away your future pro-
spects in this childish manner. How should I
answer for it to Colonel Tempest?"

She swept out of the room as she concluded, and
Lucy, in an uncontrollable fit of emotion, threw
herself on the bosom of Decima, and sobbed there.
Decima hushed her to her soothingly, stroking her
hair from her forehead with a fond gesture.

" What is it that has grieved you lately, Lucy?"
she gently asked. "I am sure you have been
grieving. I have watched you. Gay as you appear
to have been, it is a false gaiety, seen only by fits
and starts."

Lucy moved her face from the view of Decima.
" Oh, Decima! if I could but go back to papa!"
was all she murmured. "If I could but go away,
and be with papa!"

This little episode had taken place the day that
Lionel Verner and his wife returned. On the following morning Lady Verner renewed the contest
with Lucy. And they were deep in it—at least my
Lady was, for Lucy's chief part was only a depre-

catory silence, when Lionel arrived at Deerham
Court, to pay that visit to his mother which you
have heard of.

"I insist upon it, Lucy, that you recal your
unqualified denial," Lady Verner was saying. "If
you will not accept Lord Garle immediately, at any
rate take time for consideration. I will inform
Lord Garle that you do it by my wish."

"I cannot," replied Lucy, in a firm, almost a vehe-
ment tone. "I—you must not be angry with me,
Lady Verner—indeed, I beg your pardon for saying
it—but I will not."

"How dare you, Lucy——"

Her ladyship stopped at the sudden opening of
the door, turning angrily to see what caused the
interruption. Her servant appeared.

"Mr. Verner, my lady."

How handsome he looked as he came forward!
Tall, noble, commanding. Never more so; never
so much so in Lucy's sight. Poor Lucy's heart was
in her mouth, as the saying runs, and her pulses
quickened to a pang. She did not know of his
return.

He bent to kiss his mother. He turned and
shook hands with Lucy. He looked gay, animated,
happy. A joyous bridegroom, beyond doubt.

"So you have reached home, Lionel?" said Lady
Verner.

"At ten last night. How well you are looking,
mother mine!"

"I am flushed just now," was the reply of Lady

Verner, her accent a somewhat sharp one from the
remembrance of the vexation which had given her
the flush. " How is Paris looking? Have you
enjoyed yourself?"

" Paris is looking hot and dusty, and we have
enjoyed ourselves much," replied Lionel. He
answered in the plural, you observe: my lady
had put the question in the singular. " Where is
Decima?"

" Decima is sure to be at some work or other for
Jan," was the answer, the asperity of Lady Verner's
tone not decreasing. " He turns the house nearly
upside down with his wants. Now a pan of broth
must be made for some wretched old creature; now
a jug of beef tea; now a bran poultice must be got;
now some linen cut up for bandages. Jan's excuse
is that he can't get anything done at Dr. West's.
If he is doctor to the parish, he need not be pur-
veyor; but you may just as well speak to a post as
speak to Jan. What do you suppose he did the
other day? Those improvident Kellys had their one
roomful of things taken from them by their landlord. Jan went there—the woman's ill with a bad
breast, or something—and found her lying on the
bare boards: nothing to cover her, not a saucepan
left to boil a drop of water. Off he comes here at
the pace of a steam-engine, got an old blanket and
pillow from Catherine, and a tea-kettle from the
kitchen. Now, Lionel, would you believe what I
am going to tell you? No! No one would. He
made the pillow and blanket into a bundle, and

walked off with it under his arm ; the kettle—never
so much as a piece of paper wrapped round it—in
his other hand! I felt ready to faint with shame
when I saw him crossing the road opposite, that
spectacle, to get to Clay Lane, the kettle held out a
yard before him to keep the black off his clothes.
He never could have been meant to be your brother
and my son ! "

Lucy laughed at the recollection. She had had
the pleasure of beholding the spectacle. Lionel
laughed now at the description. Their mirth did
not please Lady Verner. She was serious in her
complaint.

" Lionel, you would not have liked it yourself.
Fancy his turning out of Verner's Pride in that
guise, and encountering visitors ! I don't know
how it is, but there's some deficiency in Jan ; something wanting. You know he generally chooses
to come here by the back door : this day, because
he had got the black kettle in his hand like a
travelling tinker, he must go out by the front. He
did ! It saved him a few steps, and he went out
without a blush. Out of my house, Lionel ! Nobody ever lived, I am certain, who possessed so
little innate notion of the decencies of life as Jan.
Had he met a carriage full of visitors in the court-
yard, he would have swung the kettle back on his
arm, and gone up to shake hands with them. I
had the nightmare that night, Lionel. I dreamt
a tall giant was pursuing me, seeking to throw
some great machine at me, made of tea-kettles."

"Jan is an odd fellow," assented Lionel.

"The worst is, you can't bring him to see, himself, what is proper or improper," resumed Lady Verner. "He has no sense of the fitness of things. He would go as unblushingly through the village with that black ‡kettle held out before him, as he would if it were her Majesty's crown, borne on a velvet cushion."

"I am not sure but the crown would embarrass Jan more than the kettle," said Lionel, laughing still.

"Oh, I dare say: it would be just like him. Have you heard of the disgraceful flitting away of some of the inhabitants here to go after the Mormons?" added my Lady.

"Jan has been telling me of it. What with one thing and another, Deerham will rise into notoriety. Nancy has gone from Verner's Pride."

"Poor deluded woman!" ejaculated Lady Verner. "There's a story told in the village about that Peckaby's wife—Decima can tell it best, though. I wonder where she is?"

Lucy rose. "I will go and find her, Lady Verner."

No sooner had she quitted the room, than Lady Verner turned to Lionel, her manner changing. She began to speak rapidly, with some emotion.

"You observed that I looked well, Lionel. I told you I was flushed. The flush was caused by vexation, by anger. Not a week passes but something or other occurs to annoy me. I shall be worried into my grave."

"What has happened?" inquired Lionel.

"It is about Lucy Tempest. Here she is, upon my hands, and of course I am responsible. She has no mother, and I am responsible to Colonel Tempest and to my own conscience for her welfare. She will soon be twenty years of age—though I am sure nobody would believe it, to look at her—and it is time that her settlement in life should, at all events, be thought of. But now, look how things turn out! Lord Garle—than whom a better *parti* could not be wished—has fallen in love with her. He made her an offer yesterday, and she won't have him."

"Indeed!" replied Lionel, constrained to say something, but wishing Lady Verner would entertain him with any other topic.

"We had quite a scene here yesterday. Indeed, it has been renewed this morning, and your coming in interrupted it. I tell her that she must have him: at any rate, must take time to consider the advantages of the offer. She obstinately protests that she will not. I cannot think what can be her motive for rejection : almost any girl in the county would jump at Lord Garle."

"I suppose so," returned Lionel, pulling at a hole in his glove.

"I must get you to speak to her, Lionel. Ask her why she declines. Show her——"

"I speak to her!" interrupted Lionel, in a startled tone. "I cannot speak to her about it, mother. It is no business of mine."

"Good heavens, Lionel! are *you* going to turn disobedient?—And in so trifling a matter as this! —trifling so far as you are concerned. Were it of vital importance to you, you might run counter to me: it is only what I should expect."

This was a stab at his marriage. Lionel replied by disclaiming any influence over Miss Tempest. "Where your arguments have failed, mine would not be likely to succeed."

"Then you are mistaken, Lionel. I am certain that you hold a very great influence over Lucy. I observed it first when you were ill, when she and Decima were so much with you. She has betrayed it in a hundred little ways: her opinions are formed upon yours; your tastes unconsciously bias hers. It is only natural. She has no brother, and no doubt has learnt to regard you as one."

Lionel hoped in his inmost heart that she did regard him only as a brother. Lady Verner continued:

"A word from you may have great effect upon her: and I desire, Lionel, that you will, in your duty to me, undertake that word. Point out to her the advantages of the match: tell her that you speak to her as her father: urge her to accept Lord Garle: or, as I say, not to summarily reject him without consideration, upon the childish plea that she 'does not like him.' She was terribly agitated last night: nearly went into hysterics, Decima tells me, after I left her: all her burthen being that she wished she could go away to India."

"Mother—you know how pleased I should be to obey any wish of yours: but this is really not a proper business for me to interfere with," urged Lionel, a red spot upon his cheek.

"Why is it not?" pointedly asked Lady Verner, looking hard at him and waiting for an answer.

"I do not deem it to be so. Neither would Lucy consider my interference justifiable."

"But, Lionel, you take up wrong notions! I wish you to speak in my place, just as if you were her father; in short, acting for her father. As to what Lucy may consider or not consider in the matter, that is of very little consequence. Lucy is so perfectly unsophisticated, so simple in her ideas, that were I to desire my maid Thérèse to give her a lecture, she would receive it as something proper."

"I should be most unwilling to——"

"Hold your tongue, Lionel. You must do it. Here she is."

"I could not find Decima, Lady Verner," said Lucy, entering. "When I had been all over the house for her, Catherine told me Miss Decima had gone out. She has gone to Clay Lane on some errand for Jan."

"Oh, of course for Jan!" resentfully spoke Lady Verner. "Nothing else, I should think, would take her to Clay Lane. You see, Lionel!"

"There's nothing in Clay Lane that will hurt Decima, mother."

Lady Verner made no reply. She walked to the

door, and stood with the handle in her hand, turning round to speak.

"Lucy, I have been acquainting Lionel with this affair between you and Lord Garle. I have requested him to speak to you upon the point; to ascertain your precise grounds of objection, and—so far as he can—to do away with them. Try your best, Lionel."

She quitted the room, leaving them standing opposite each other. Standing like two statues. Lionel's heart smote him. She looked so innocent, so good, in her delicate morning dress, with its grey ribbons and its white lace on the sleeves, open to the small fair arms! Simple as the dress was, it looked, in its exquisite taste, worth ten of Sibylla's elaborate French costumes. Her cheeks were glowing, her hands were trembling as she stood there in her self-consciousness.

Terribly self-conscious was Lionel. He strove to say something, but in his embarrassment could not get out a single word. The conviction of the grievous fact, that she loved him, went right to his heart in that moment, and seated itself there. Another grievous fact came home to him; that she was more to him than the whole world. However he had pushed the suspicion away from his mind, refused to dwell on it, kept it down, it was all too plain to him now. He had made Sibylla his wife : and he stood there, feeling that he loved Lucy above all created things.

He crossed over to her, and laid his hand fondly

and gently on her head, as he moved to the door. "May God forgive me, Lucy!" broke from his white and trembling lips. "My own punishment is heavier than yours."

There was no need of further explanation on either side. Each knew that the love of the other was theirs, the punishment keenly bitter, as surely as if a hundred words had told it. Lucy sat down as the door closed behind him, and wondered how she should get through the long dreary life before her.

And Lionel? Lionel went out by Jan's favourite way, the back, and plunged into a dark lane where neither ear nor eye was on him. He uncovered his head, he threw back his coat, he lifted his breath to catch only a gasp of air. The sense of dishonour was stifling him.

CHAPTER X.

LIONEL VERNER was just in that frame of mind which struggles to be carried out of itself. No matter whether by pleasure or pain, so that it be not that particular pain from which it would fain escape, the mind seeks yearningly to forget itself, to be lifted out anywhere, or by any means, from its trouble. Conscience was doing heavy work with Lionel. He had destroyed his own happiness: that was nothing; he could battle it out, and nobody be the wiser or the worse, save himself: but he had blighted Lucy's. *There* was the sting that tortured him. A man of sensitively refined organisation, keenly alive to the feelings of others —full of repentant consciousness when wrong was worked through him, he would have given his whole future life and all its benefits, to undo the work of the last few months. Either that he had never met Lucy, or that he had not married Sibylla. *Which* of those two events he would have preferred to recal, he did not trust himself to think; whatever may have been his faults, he had, until now, believed himself to be a man of honour. It was too late. Give what he would, strive as he would,

repent as he would, the ill could neither be undone
nor mitigated; it was one of those unhappy things
for which there is no redress; they must be borne,
as they best can, in patience and silence.

With these thoughts and feelings full upon him,
little wonder was there that Lionel Verner, some
two hours after quitting Lucy, should turn into
Peckaby's shop. Mrs. Peckaby was seated back
from the open door, crying and moaning and swaying
herself about, apparently in terrible pain, physical
or mental. Lionel remembered the story of the
white donkey, and he stepped in to question her:
anything for a minute's divertisement; anything to
drown the care that was racking him. There was
a subject on which he wished to speak to Roy, and
that took him down Clay Lane.

"What's the matter, Mrs. Peckaby?"

Mrs. Peckaby rose from her chair, curtsied, and
sat down again. But for the state of tribulation
she was in, she would have remained standing.

"Oh, sir, I have just had a upset;" she sobbed.
"I see the white tail of a pony a-going by, and I
thought it might be some 'at else. It did give me
a turn!"

"What did you think it might be?"

"I thought it might be the tail of a different sort
of animal. I be a-going a far journey, sir, and I
thought it was, may be, the quadruple come to fetch
me. I'm a-going to New Jerusalem on a white
donkey."

"So I hear," said Lionel, suppressing a smile, in

spite of his heavy heart. " Do you go all the way
on the white donkey, Mrs. Peckaby ? "

" Sir, that's a matter that's hid from me,"
answered Mrs. Peckaby. " The gentleman that
was sent back to me by Brother Jarrum, hadn't
had particulars revealed to him. There's difficulties
in the way of a animal on four legs which can't
swim, doing it all, that I don't pertend to explain
away. I'm content, when the hour comes, sir, to
start, and trust. Peckaby, he's awful sinful, sir.
Only last evening, when I was saying the quadruple
might have mirac'lous parts give to it, like Balum's
had in the Bible, Peckaby he jeered, and said he'd
like to see Balum's or any other quadruple, set off
to swim to America—that he'd find the bottom
afore he found the land. I wonder the kitchen
ceiling don't drop down upon his head! For myself, sir, I'm rejoiced to trust, as I says; and as
soon as the white donkey do come, I shall mount
him without fear."

" What do you expect to find at New Jerusalem?"
asked Lionel.

" I could sooner tell you, sir, what I don't expect:
it 'ud take up less time. There's a'most everything
good at New Jerusalem that the world contains—
Verner's Pride's a poor place to it, sir—saving your
presence for saying so. I could have sat and
listened to Brother Jarrum in this here shop for
ever, sir, if it hadn't been that the longing was upon
me to get there. In this part o' the world we women
be poor, cast down, half-famished, miserable slaves ;

but in New Jerusalem we are the wives of saints, well cared for, and clothed and fed, happy as the day's long, and our own parlours to ourselves, and nobody to interrupt us. Yes, Peckaby, I'm a telling his honour, Mr. Verner, what's a waiting for me at New Jerusalem! And the sooner I'm on my road to it, the better."

The conclusion was addressed to Peckaby himself. Peckaby had just come in from the forge, grimed and dirty. He touched his hair to Lionel, an amused expression playing on his face. In point of fact, this New Jerusalem vision was affording the utmost merriment to Peckaby and a few more husbands. Peckaby had come home to his tea, which meal it was the custom of Deerham to enjoy about three o'clock. He saw no signs of its being in readiness; and, but for the presence of Mr. Verner, might probably have expressed his opinion demonstratively upon the point. Peckaby, of late, appeared to have changed his nature and disposition. From being a timid man, living under wife-thraldom, he had come to exercise thraldom over her. How far Mrs. Peckaby's state of low spirits, into which she was generally sunk, may have explained this, nobody knew.

"I have had a turn, Peckaby. I caught sight of a white tail a-going by, and I thought it might be the quadruple a-coming for me. I was shook, I can tell you. 'Twas more nor a hour ago, and I've been able to do nothing since, but sit here and weep: I couldn't red up after that."

"Warn't it the quadrepid?" asked Peckaby in a mocking tone.

"No, it weren't," she moaned. "It were nothing but that white pony of Farmer Blow's."

"Him, was it," said Peckaby, with affected scorn. "He is in the forge now, he is; a having his shoes changed and his tail trimmed."

"I'd give a shilling to anybody as 'ud cut his tail off;" angrily rejoined Mrs. Peckaby. "A deceiving of me, and turning my inside all of a quake! Oh, I wish it 'ud come! The white donkey as is to bear me to New Jerusalem!"

"Don't you wish her joy of her journey, sir?" cried the man, respectfully, a twinkle in his eye, while she rocked herself to and fro. "She have got a bran new gownd laid up in a old apron upstairs, ready for the start. She, and a lot more to help her, set on and made it in a afternoon, for fear the white donkey should arrive immediate. I asks her, sir, how much back the gownd 'll have left in him, by the time she have rode from here to New Jerusalem."

"Peckaby, you are a mocker!" interposed his lady, greatly exasperated. "Remember the forty-two as was eat up by bears when they mocked at Elisher!"

"Mrs. Peckaby," said Lionel, keeping his countenance, "don't you think you would have made more sure of the benefits of the New Jerusalem, had you started with the rest, instead of depending upon the arrival of the white donkey?"

"They started without her, sir," cried the man, laughing from ear to ear. "They give her the slip, while she were abed and asleep."

"It were revealed to Brother Jarrum so to do, sir," she cried eagerly. "Don't listen to *him*. Brother Jarrum as much meant me to go, sir, and I as much thought to go, as I mean to go to my bed this night—always supposing the white donkey don't come," she broke off in a different voice.

"Why did you not go, then?" demanded Lionel.

"I'll tell you about it, sir. Me and Brother Jarrum was on the best of terms—which it's a real gentleman he was, and never said a word nor gave a look as could offend me. I didn't know the night fixed for the start; and Brother Jarrum didn't know it; in spite of Peckaby's insinuations. On that last night, which it was Tuesday, not a soul came near the place but that pale lady where Dr. West attended. She stopped a minute or two, and then Brother Jarrum goes out, and says he might be away all the evening. Well, he was; but he came in again; I can be on my oath he did; and I give him his candle and wished him a good night. After that, sir, I never heard nothing till I got up in the morning. The first thing I see was his door wide open, and the bed not slept in. And the next thing I heard was, that the start had took place : they a walking to Heartburg, and taking the train there. You might just have knocked me down with a puff of wind."

"Such a howling and screeching followed on,

sir," put in Peckaby. "I were at the forge, and it reached all the way to our ears, over there. Chuff, he thought as the place had took fire and the missis was a burning."

"But it didn't last; it didn't last," repeated Mrs. Peckaby. "Thanks be offered up for it, it didn't last, or I should ha' been in my coffin afore the day were out! A gentleman came to me: a Brother he were, sent express by Brother Jarrum, and had walked afoot all the way from Heartburg. It had been revealed to Brother Jarrum, he said, that they were to start that partic'lar night, and that I was to be left behind special. A higher mission was—what was the word? resigned?—No—reserved—reserved for me, and I was to be conveyed special on a quadruple, which was a white donkey. I be to keep myself in readiness, sir, always a looking out for the quadruple's coming and stopping afore the door."

Lionel leaned against the counter, and went into a burst of laughter. The woman told it so quaintly, with such perfect good faith in the advent of the white donkey! She did not much like the mirth. As to that infidel Peckaby, he indulged in sundry mocking doubts, which were, to say the least of them, very mortifying to a believer.

"What's your opinion, sir?" she suddenly asked of Lionel.

"Well," said Lionel, "my opinion—as you wish for it—would incline to the suspicion that your friend, Brother Jarrum, deceived you. That he invented the fable of the white donkey to keep you quiet while he and the rest got clear off."

Mrs. Peckaby went into a storm of shrieking sobs. " It couldn't be! it couldn't be! Oh, sir, you be as cruel as the rest! Why should Brother Jarrum take the others, and not take me?"

" That is Brother Jarrum's affair," replied Lionel. " I only say it looks like it."

"I telled Brother Jarrum, the very day afore the start took place, that if he took off *my* wife, I'd follor him on and beat every bone to smash as he'd got in his body," interposed Peckaby, glancing at Lionel with a knowing smile. " I did, sir. Her was out" —jerking his black thumb at his wife—"and I caught Brother Jarrum in his own room and shut the door on us both, and there I telled him. He knew I meant it, too : and he didn't like the look of a iron bar I happened to have in my hand : I saw that. Other wives' husbands might do as they liked; but I warn't a going to have mine deluded off by them Latter Day Saints. Were I wrong, sir?"

" I do not think you were," answered Lionel.

" I'd Latter Day 'em! and saint 'em too, if I had my will!" continued wrathful Peckaby. " Arch-deceiving villuns!"

" Well, good day, Mrs. Peckaby," said Lionel, moving to the door. " I would not spend too much time, were I you, looking out for the white donkey."

" It'll come! it'll come!" retorted Mrs. Peckaby in an ectasy of joy, removing her hands from her ears, where she had clapped them during Peckaby's heretical speech. "I am proud, sir, to know as it'll come, in spite of opinions contrairey and Peckaby's wickedness ; and I'm proud to be always a looking out for it."

"This is never it, is it, drawing up to the door now ?" cried Lionel, with gravity.

Something undoubtedly was curvetting and prancing before the door; something with a flowing white tail. Mrs. Peckaby caught one glimpse, and bounded from her seat, her chest panting, her nostrils working. The signs betrayed how implicit was the woman's belief; how entirely it had taken hold of her.

Alas for Mrs. Peckaby! alas for her disappointment! It was nothing but that deceiving animal again, Farmer Blow's white pony. Apparently the pony had been so comfortable in the forge, that he did not care to leave it. He was dodging about and backing, wholly refusing to go forward and setting at defiance a boy who was striving to lead him onwards. Mrs. Peckaby sat down and burst into tears.

CHAPTER XI

"Now, then," began Peckaby, as Lionel departed, "what's the reason my tea ain't ready for me?"

"Be you a man to ask?" demanded she. "Could I red up and put on kettles, and see to ord'nary work, with my inside turning?"

Peckaby paused for a minute, "I've a good mind to wallop you!"

"Try it," she aggravatingly answered. "You have not kep' your hands off me yet, to be let begin now. Anybody but a brute 'ud comfort a poor woman in her distress. You'll be sorry for it when I'm gone off to New Jerusalem."

"Now look here, Suke," said he, attempting to reason with her. "It's quite time as you left off this folly: we've had enough on't. What do you suppose you'd do at Salt Lake? What sort of a life 'ud you lead?"

"A joyful life!" she responded, turning her glance sky-ward. "Brother Jarrum thinks as the head saint, the prophet hisself, has a favour to me! Wives is as happy there as the day's long."

Peckaby grinned: the reply amused him much. "You poor ignorant creatur," cried he, "you have

got your head up in a madhouse; and that's about
it.   You know Mary Green?"

"Well?" answered she, looking surprised at this
divertissement.

"And you know Nancy from Verner's Pride as is
gone off," he continued, "and you know half-a-
dozen more nice young girls about here, which you
can just set on and think of.   How 'ud you like to
see me marry the whole of 'em, and bring 'em home
here?   Would the house hold the tantrums you'd
go into, d'ye think?"

"You hold your senseless tongue, Peckaby!   A
man 'ud better try and bring home more nor one
wife here!   The law 'ud be on to him."

"In course it would," returned Peckaby.   "And
the law knowed what it was about when it made
itself into the law.   A place with more nor one wife
in it 'ud be compairable to nothing but that blazing
place you've heerd on as is under our feet, or the
Salt Lake City."

"For shame, you wicked man!"

"There ain't no shame in saying that; it's truth,"
composedly answered Peckaby.   "Brother Jarrum
said, didn't he, as the wives had a parlour a-piece.
Why do they?   'Cause they be obleeged to be kep'
apart, for fear o' damaging each other, a tearing and
biting and scratching, and a pulling of eyes out.
A nice figure you'd cut among 'em!   You'd be a
wishing yourself home again afore you'd tried it for
a day.   Don't you be a fool, Susan Peckaby."

"Don't you!" retorted she.   "I wonder you ain't

afraid o' some judgment falling on you. Lies is
sure to come home to people."

"Just take your thoughts back to the time as we
had the shop here, and plenty o' custom in it. One
day you saw me just a kissing of a girl in that there
corner—leastways you fancied as you saw me,"
corrected Peckaby, coughing down his slip. "Well,
d'ye recollect the scrimmage? Didn't you go a'most
mad, never keeping your tongue quiet for a week,
and the place hardly holding of ye? How 'ud you
like to have eight or ten more of 'em, my married
wives, like you be, brought in here?"

"You *are* a fool, Peckaby. The cases is
different."

"Where's the difference?" asked Peckaby.
"The men be men, out there; and the women be
women. I might pertend as I'd had visions and
revelations sent to me, and dress myself up in a
black coat and a white neck-an-kecher, and such like
paycock's plumes—I might tar and feather myself
if I pleased, if it come to that—and give out as I
was a prophit and a Latter Day Saint; but where
'ud be the difference, I want to know? I should
just be as good and as bad a man as I be now, only
a bit more of a hypocrite. Saints and prophits,
indeed! You just come to your senses, Susan
Peckaby."

"I haven't lost 'em yet," answered she, looking
inclined to beat him.

"You have lost 'em : to suppose as a life, out
with them reptiles, could be anything but just what

I telled you—a hell. It can't be otherways. It's
again human female natur. If you went angry mad
with jealousy, just at fancying you see a innocent
kiss give upon a girl's face, how 'ud you do, I ask,
when it come to wives? Tales runs as them
'saints' have got any number a-piece, from four or
five, up to seventy. If you don't come to your
senses, Mrs. Peckaby, you'll get a walloping, to
bring you to 'em ; and that's about it. You be the
laughing-stock o' the place as it is."

He swung out at the door, and took his way towards the nearest public-house, intending to solace
himself with a pint of ale, in lieu of tea, of which
he saw no chance. Mrs. Peckaby burst into a flood
of tears, and apostrophised the expected white
donkey in moving terms : that he would forthwith
appear and bear her off from Peckaby and trouble,
to the triumphs and delights of New Jerusalem.

Lionel, meanwhile, went to Roy's dwelling. Roy,
he found, was not in it. Mrs. Roy was : and, by
the appearance of the laid-out tea-table, she was
probably expecting Roy to enter. Mrs. Roy sat,
doing nothing : her arms hung listlessly down, her
head also ; sunk apparently in that sad state of
mind—whatever may have been its cause—which
was now habitual to her. By the start with which
she sprang from her chair, as Lionel Verner appeared at the open door, it may be inferred that she
took him for her husband. Surely nobody else
could have put her in such tremor.

"Roy's not in, sir," she said, dropping a curtsey,

in answer to Lionel's inquiry. "May be, he'll not be long. It's his time for coming home, but there's no dependence on him.''

Lionel glanced round. He saw that the woman was alone, and he deemed it a good opportunity to ask her about what had been mentioned to him, two or three hours previously, by the Vicar of Deerham. Closing the door, and advancing towards her, he began.

"I want to say a word to you, Mrs. Roy. What were your grounds for stating to Mr. Bourne that Mr. Frederick Massingbird was with Rachel Frost at the Willow-pool the evening of her death?"

Mrs. Roy gave a low shriek of terror, and flung her apron over her face. Lionel ungallantly drew it down again. Her countenance was turning livid as death.

"You will have the goodness to answer me, Mrs. Roy."

"It were just a dream, sir," she said, the words issuing in unequal jerks from her trembling lips. "I have been pretty nigh crazed lately. What with them Mormons, and the uncertainty of fixing what to do—whether to believe 'em or not—and Roy's crabbed temper, which grows upon him, and other fears and troubles, I've been a-nigh crazed. It were just a dream as I had, and nothing more; and I be vexed to my heart that I should have made such a fool of myself, as to go and say what I did to Mr. Bourne."

One word, above all others, caught the attention

of Lionel in the answer. It was "fears." He bent towards her, lowering his voice.

"What are these fears that seem to pursue you? You appear to me to have been perpetually under the influence of fear since that night. Terrified you were then; terrified you remain. What is the cause?"

. The woman trembled excessively.

"Roy keeps me in fear, sir. He's for ever a threatening. He'll shake me, or he'll pinch me, or he'll do for me, he says. I'm in fear of him always."

"That is an evasive answer," remarked Lionel. "Why should you fear to confide in me? You have never known me take an˜advantage to anybody's injury. The past is past. That unfortunate night's work appears now to belong wholly to the past. Nevertheless, if you can throw any light upon it, it is your duty to do so. I will keep the secret."

"I didn't know a thing, sir, about the night's work. I didn't," she sobbed.

"Hush!" said Lionel. "I felt sure at the time that you did know something, had you chosen to speak. I feel more sure of it now."

"No, I don't, sir; not if you pulled me in pieces for it. I had a horrid dream, and I went straight off, like a fool, to Mr. Bourne and told it, and——and—that was all, sir."

She was flinging her apron up again to hide her countenance, when, with a faint cry, she let it fall, sprung from her seat, and stood before Lionel.

"For the love of heaven, sir, say nothing to *him!*" she uttered, and disappeared within an inner door. The sight of Roy, entering, explained the enigma: she must have seen him from the window. Roy took off his cap by way of salute.

"I hope I see you well, sir, after your journey.".

"Quite well. Roy, some papers have been left at Verner's Pride for my inspection, regarding the dispute in Farmer Hartright's lease. I do not understand them. They bear your signature: not Mrs. Verner's. How is that?"

Roy stopped awhile: to collect his thoughts, possibly. "I suppose I signed it for her, sir."

"Then you did what you had no authority to do. You never received power to sign from Mrs. Verner."

"Mrs. Verner must have give me power, sir, if I *have* signed. I don't recollect signing anything. Sometimes, when she was ill, or unwilling to be disturbed, she'd say, 'Roy, do this,' or, 'Roy, do the other.' She—"

"Mrs. Verner never gave you authority to sign," impressively repeated Lionel. "She is gone, and therefore cannot be referred to; but you know as well as I do, that she never did give you such authority. Come to Verner's Pride to-morrow morning at ten, and see these papers."

Roy signified his obedience, and Lionel departed. He bent his steps towards home, taking the field way: all the bitter experiences of the day rising up within his mind. Ah! try as he would, he could not deceive himself: he could not banish or drown the one ever-present thought. The singular information imparted by Mr. Bourne; the serio-comic tribulation of Mrs. Peckaby, waiting for her white donkey; the mysterious behaviour of Dinah Roy, in which there was undoubtedly more than met the ear; all these could not cover for a moment the one burning fact—Lucy's love, and his own dishonour. In vain Lionel flung off his hat, heedless of any second sun-stroke, and pushed his hair from his heated brow. It was of no use; as he had felt when he went out from the presence of Lucy, so he felt now—*stifled* with dishonour.

Sibylla was at a table, writing notes, when he reached home. Several were on it, already written, and in their envelopes. She looked up at him.

"Oh, Lionel, what a while you have been out! I thought you were never coming home."

He leaned down and kissed her. Although his conscience had revealed to him, that day, that he loved another better, *she* should never feel the difference. Nay, the very knowledge that it was so would render him all the more careful to give her marks of love.

"I have been to my mother's, and to one or two more places. What are you so busy over, dear?"

"I am writing invitations," said Sibylla.

"Invitations! Before people have called upon you?"

"They can call all the same. I have been asking Mary Tynn how many beds she can, by dint of screwing, afford. I am going to fill them all. I shall ask them for a month. How grave you look, Lionel!"

"In this first, early sojourn together in our own house, Sibylla, I think we shall be happier alone."

"Oh, no, we should not. I love visitors. We shall be together all the same, Lionel."

"My little wife," he said, "if you cared for me as I care for you, you would not feel the want of visitors just now."

And there was no sophistry in this speech. He had come to the conviction that Lucy ought to have been his wife, but he did care for Sibylla very much. The prospect of a house full of guests at the present moment, appeared most displeasing to him, if only as a matter of taste.

"Put it off for a few weeks, Sibylla."

Sibylla pouted. "It is of no use preaching, Lionel. If you are to be a preaching husband, I shall be sorry I married you. Fred was never that."

Lionel's face turned blood-red. Sibylla put up her hand, and drew it carelessly down.

"You must let me have my own way for this once," she coaxingly said. "What's the use of my bringing all those loves of things from Paris, if we are to live in a dungeon, and nobody's to see them? I must invite them, Lionel."

"Very well," he answered, yielding the point.

Yielding it the more readily from the consciousness above spoken of.

"There's my dear Lionel! I knew you would never turn tyrant. And now I want something else."

"What's that?" asked Lionel.

"A cheque."

"A cheque? I gave you one this morning, Sibylla."

"Oh! but the one you gave me is for house-keeping—for Mary Tynn, and all that. I want one for myself. I am not going to have my expenses come out of the housekeeping."

Lionel sat down to write one, a good-natured smile on his face. "I'm sure I don't know what you will find to spend it in, after all the finery you bought in Paris," he said, in a joking tone. "How much shall I fill it in for?"

"As much as you will," replied Sibylla, too eagerly. "Couldn't you give it me in blank, and let me fill it in?"

He made no answer. He drew it for a £100, and gave it her.

"Will that do, my dear?"

She drew his face down again caressingly. But, in spite of the kisses left upon his lips, Lionel had awoke to the conviction, firm and undoubted, that his wife did not love him.

CHAPTER XII.

THE September afternoon sun streamed into the study at Verner's Pride, playing with the bright hair of Lionel Verner. His head was bending listlessly over certain letters and papers on his table, and there was a wearied look upon his face. Was it called up by the fatigue of the day? He had been out with some friends in the morning: it was the first day of partridge shoot-ing, and they had bagged well. Now Lionel was home again, had changed his attire, and was sitting down in his study—the old study of Mr. Verner. Or, was the wearied look, were the in-dented upright lines between the eyes, called forth by inward care?

Those lines were not so conspicuous when you last saw him. Twelve or fourteen months have elapsed since then. A portion of that time only had been spent at Verner's Pride. Mrs. Verner was restless; ever wishing to be on the wing; living but in gaiety. Her extravagance was something frightful, and Lionel did not know how to check it. There were no children : there had been no signs of any : and Mrs. Verner positively made the lack

into a sort of reproach, a continual cause for queru-
lousness.

She had filled Verner's Pride with guests after
their marriage—as she had coveted to do. From
that period until early spring she had kept it filled,
one succession of guests, one relay of visitors arriving after the other. Pretty, capricious, fascinating,
youthful, Mrs. Verner was of excessive popularity in
the country, and a sojourn at Verner's Pride grew
to be eagerly sought. The women liked the attractive master; the men bowed to the attractive mistress; and Verner's Pride was never free. On the
contrary, it was generally unpleasantly crammed;
and Mrs. Tynn, who was a staid, old-fashioned
housekeeper, accustomed to nothing beyond the
regular, quiet household maintained by the late Mr.
Verner, was driven to the verge of desperation.

"It would be far pleasanter if we had only half
the number of guests," Lionel had said to his
wife in the winter. He no longer remonstrated
against *any:* he had given that up as hopeless.
"Pleasanter for them, pleasanter for us, pleasanter
for the servants."

"The servants!" slightingly returned Sibylla.
"I never knew before that the pleasure of servants
was a thing to be studied."

"But their comfort is. At least, I have always
considered so, and I hope I always shall. They
complain much, Sibylla."

"Do they complain to you?"

"They do. Tynn and his wife say they are

nearly worked to death. They hint at leaving.
Mrs. Tynn is continually subjected also to what she
calls insults from your French maid. That of course
I know nothing of; but it might be as well for you
to listen to her on the subject."

"I cannot have Benoite crossed. I don't interfere in the household myself, and she does it
for me."

"But, my dear, if you would interfere a little
more, just so far as to ascertain whether these
complaints have grounds, you might apply a
remedy."

"Lionel, you are most unreasonable! As if I
could be worried with looking into things! What
are servants for? You must be a regular old
bachelor to think of my doing it."

"Well—to go to our first point," he rejoined,
"Let us try half the number of guests, and see
how it works. If you do not find it better,
more agreeable in all ways, I will say no more
about it."

He need not have said anything, then. Sibylla
would not listen to it. At any rate, would not act
upon it. She conceded so far as to promise that she
would not invite so many next time. But, when
that next time came, and the new sojourners arrived,
they turned out to be more. Beds had to be im-
provised in all sorts of impossible places; the old
servants were turned out of their chambers and
huddled into corners; nothing but confusion and
extravagance reigned. Against some of the latter,

Mrs. Tynn ventured to remonstrate to her mistress. Fruits and vegetables out of season; luxuries in the shape of rare dishes, many of which Verner's Pride had never heard of, and did not know how to cook, and all of the most costly nature, were daily sent down from London purveyors. Against this expense Mary Tynn spoke. Mrs. Verner laughed good-naturedly at her, and told her it was not her pocket that would be troubled to pay the bills. Additional servants were obliged to be had; and, in short, to use an expression that was much in vogue at Deerham about that time, Verner's Pride was going the pace.

This continued until early spring. In February Sibylla fixed her heart upon a visit to London; "of course," she told Lionel, "he would treat her to a season in town." She had never been to London in her life to stay. For Sibylla to fix her heart upon a thing, was to have it: Lionel was an indulgent husband.

To London they proceeded in February. And there the cost was great. Sibylla was not one to go to work sparingly in any way; neither, in point of fact, was Lionel. Lionel would never have been unduly extravagant; but, on the other hand, he was not accustomed to spare. A furnished house in a good position was taken; servants were imported to it from Verner's Pride; and there Sibylla launched into all the follies of the day. At Easter she "set her heart" upon a visit to Paris, and Lionel acquiesced. They remained there three weeks;

Sibylla laying in a second stock of *toilettes* for
Mademoiselle Benoite to rule over; and then they
went back to London.

The season was prolonged that year. The
house sat until August, and it was not until the
latter end of that month that Mr. and Mrs.
Verner returned to Verner's Pride. Though
scarcely home a week yet, the house was filled
again — filled to overflowing : Lionel can hear
sounds of talking and laughter from the various
rooms, as he bends over his table. He was opening his letters, three or four of which lay in a
stack. He had gone out in the morning before
the post was in.

Tynn knocked at the door and entered, bringing
a note.

"Where's this from ?" asked Lionel, taking it
from the salver. Another moment, and he had
recognised the hand-writing of his mother.

"From Deerham Court, sir. My lady's footman brought it. He asks whether there is any
answer."

Lionel opened the note, and read as follows :

"MY DEAR LIONEL,—I am obliged to be a beggar
again. My expenses seem to outrun my means in
a most extraordinary sort of way. Sometimes I
think it must be Decima's fault, and tell her she
does not properly look after the household. In
spite of my own income, your ample allowance, and
the handsome remuneration received for Lucy, I

cannot make both ends meet. Will you let me
have two or three hundred pounds ?

"Ever your affectionate mother,

"LOUISA VERNER."

"I will call on Lady Verner this afternoon,
Tynn."

Tynn withdrew with the answer. Lionel leaned
his brow upon his hand; the weary expression
terribly plain just then.

"My mother shall have it at once—no matter what
my own calls may be," was his soliloquy. "Let me
never forget that Verner's Pride might have been
hers all these years. Looking at it from our own
point of view, my father's branch in contradistinction to my uncle's, it ought to have been hers. It
might have been her jointure-house now, had my
father lived, and so willed it. I am *glad* to help my
mother," he continued, an earnest glow lighting his
face. "If I get embarrassed, why I must get embarrassed ; but she shall not suffer."

That embarrassment would inevitably come, if he
went on at his present rate of living, he had the
satisfaction of knowing beyond all doubt. That
was not the worst point upon his conscience. Of
the plans and projects that Lionel had so eagerly
formed when he came into the estate, some were
set afloat, some were not. Those that were most
wanted—that were calculated to do the most real
good—lay in abeyance ; others, that might have
waited, were in full work. Costly alterations were

making in the stables at Verner's Pride, and the
working man's institute at Deerham, reading-room,
club—whatever it was to be—was progressing swim-
mingly. But the draining of the land near the poor
dwellings was not begun, and the families, many of
them, still herded in consort—father and mother,
sons and daughters, sleeping in one room—compelled to it by the wretched accommodation of the
tenements. It was on this last score that Lionel
was feeling a pricking of conscience. And how
to find the money to make these improvements now,
he knew not. Between the building in progress
and Sibylla, he was drained.

A circumstance had occurred that day to bring
the latter neglect forcibly to his mind. Alice Hook
—Hook the labourer's eldest daughter—had, as the
Deerham phrase ran, got herself into trouble. A
pretty child she had grown up amongst them—she
was little more than a child now—good-tempered,
gay-hearted. Lionel had heard the ill news the
previous week on his return from London. When
he was out shooting that morning he saw the girl at
a distance, and made some observation to his gamekeeper, Broom, to the effect that it had vexed him.

"Ay, sir, it's a sad pity," was Broom's answer;
"but what else can be expected of poor folks
that's brought up to live as they do—like pigs in a
sty?"

Broom had intended no reproach to his master;
such an impertinence would not have crossed his
mind; but the words carried a sting to Lionel.

He knew how many, besides Alice Hook, had had their good conduct undermined through the living "like pigs in a sty." Lionel had, as you know, a lively conscience; and his brow reddened with self-reproach as he sat and thought these things over. He could not help comparing the contrast: Verner's Pride, with its spacious bed-rooms, one of which was not deemed sufficient for the purposes of retire-ment, where two people slept together, but a dress-ing-closet must be attached; and those poor Hooks, with their growing-up sons and daughters, and but one room, save the kitchen, in their whole dwelling!

"I will put things on a better footing," impul-sively exclaimed Lionel. "I care not what the cost may be, or how it may fall upon my comforts, do it I will. I declare I feel as if the girl's blight lay at my own door!"

Again he and his reflections were interrupted by Tynn.

"Roy has come up, sir, and is asking to see you."

"Roy! Let him come in," replied Lionel. "I want to see him."

It frequently happened, when agreements, leases, and other deeds were examined, that Roy had to be referred to. Things would turn out to have been drawn up, agreements made, in precisely the oppo-site manner to that expected by Lionel. For some of these Roy might have received sanction; but, for many, Lionel felt sure Roy had acted on his own responsibility. This chiefly applied to the short period of the management of Mrs. Verner: a little,

very little, to the latter year of her husband's life.
Matiss was Lionel's agent during his absences:
when at home, he took all management into his
own hands.

Roy came in. The same ill-favoured, hard-look-
ing man as ever. The ostensible business which
had brought him up to Verner's Pride, proved to be
of a very trivial nature, and was soon settled. It is
well to say " ostensible," because a conviction arose
in Lionel's mind afterwards that it was but an
excuse: that Roy made it a pretext for the purpose of obtaining an interview. Though why, or
wherefore, or what he gained by it, Lionel could
not imagine. Roy merely wanted to know if he
might be allowed to put a fresh paper on the walls
of one of his two upper rooms. He'd get the paper
at his own cost, and hang it at his own leisure, if
Mr. Verner had no objection.

"Of course I can have no objection to it," replied
Lionel. " You need not have lost an afternoon's
work, Roy, to come here to inquire that. You
might have asked me when I saw you by the brickfield this morning. In fact, there was no necessity
to mention it at all."

" So I might, sir. But it didn't come into my
mind at the moment to do so. It's poor Luke's
room, and the missis, she goes on continual about
the state it's in, if he should come home. The
paper's all hanging off it in patches, sir, as big as
my two hands. It have got damp through not
being used."

"If it is in that state, and you like to find the time to hang the paper, you may purchase it at my cost," said Lionel, who was of too just a nature to be a hard landlord.

"Thank ye, sir," replied Roy, ducking his head. "It's well for us, as I often says, that you be our master at last, instead of the Mr. Massingbirds."

"There was a time when you did not think so, Roy, if my memory serves me rightly," was the rebuke of Lionel.

"Ah, sir, there's a old saying, 'Live and learn.' That was in the days when I thought you'd be a over strict master: we have got to know better now, taught from experience. It was a lucky day for the Verner Pride estate when that lost codicil was brought to light! The Mr. Massingbirds be dead, it's true, but there's no knowing what might have happened: the law's full of quips and turns. With the codicil found, you can hold your own again the world."

"Who told you anything about the codicil being found?" demanded Lionel.

"Why, sir, it was the talk of the place just about the time we heard of Mr. Fred Massingbird's death. Folks said, whether he had died, or whether he had not, you'd have come in all the same. T'other day, too, I was talking of it to Lawyer Matiss, and he said what a good thing it was, that that there codicil was found."

Lionel knew that a report of the turning up of the codicil had travelled to Deerham. It had never

been contradicted. But he wondered to hear Roy
say that Matiss had spoken of it. Matiss, himself,
Tynn, and Mrs. Tynn, were the only persons who
could have testified that the supposed codicil was
nothing but a glove. From the finding of that, the
story had originally got wind.

"I don't know why Matiss should have spoken to
you on the subject of the codicil," he remarked to
Roy.

"It's not much that Matiss talks, sir," was the
man's answer. "All he said was as he had got the
codicil in safe keeping under lock and key. Just
put to Matiss the simplest question, and he'll turn
round and ask what business it is of yours."

"Quite right of him, too," said Lionel. "Have
you any news of your son yet, Roy?"

Roy shook his head. "No, sir. I'm a beginning
to wonder now whether there ever will be news of
him."

After the man had departed, Lionel looked at his
watch. There was just time for a ride to Deerham
Court before dinner. He ordered his horse, and
mounted it, a cheque for three hundred pounds in
his pocket.

He rode quickly, musing upon what Matiss had
said about the codicil—as stated by Roy. Could
the deed have been found?—and Matiss forgotten
to acquaint him with it. He turned his horse down
the Belvedere Road, telling his groom to wait at the
corner; and stopped before the lawyer's door. The
latter came out.

"Matiss, is that codicil found?" demanded Lionel, bending down his head to speak.

"What codicil, Mr. Verner?" returned Matiss, looking surprised.

"*The* codicil. The one that gave me the estate. Roy was with me just now, and he said you stated to him that the codicil was found—that it was safe under lock and key."

The lawyer's countenance lighted up with a smile. "What a meddler the fellow is! To tell you the truth, sir, it rather pleases me to mislead Roy, and put him on the wrong scent. He comes here, pumping, trying to get what he can out of me: asking this, asking that, fishing out anything there is to fish. I recollect, he did say something about the codicil, and I replied 'Ay, it was a good thing it was found, and safe under lock and key.' He tries at the wrong handle when he pumps at me."

"What is his motive for pumping at all?" returned Lionel.

"There's no difficulty in guessing at that, sir. Roy would give his two ears to get into place again: he'd like to fill the same post to you that he did to the late Mr. Verner. He thinks if he can hang about here and pick up any little bit of information, that may be let drop, and carry it to you, that it might tell in his favour. He would like you to discover how useful he could be. That is the construction I put upon it."

"Then he wastes his time," remarked Lionel, as he turned his horse. "I would not put power of any sort into Roy's hands, if he paid me in diamonds to do it. You can tell him so, if you like, Matiss."

Arrived at Deerham Court, Lionel left his horse with his groom, and entered. The first person to greet his sight in the hall was Lucy Tempest. She was in white silk: a low dress, somewhat richly trimmed with lace, and pearls in her hair. It was the first time that Lionel had seen her since his return from London. He had been at his mother's once or twice, but Lucy did not appear. They met face to face. Lucy's turned crimson, in spite of herself.

" Are you quite well ? " asked Lionel, shaking hands, his own pulses beating. " You are going out this evening, I see ? "

He made the remark as a question, noticing her dress ; and Lucy, gathering her senses about her, and relapsing into her calm composure, looked somewhat surprised.

" We are going to dinner to Verner's Pride ; I and Decima. Did you not expect us ? "

" I—did not know it," he was obliged to answer. " Mrs. Verner mentioned that some friends would dine with us this evening, but I was not aware that you and Decima were part of them. I am glad to hear it."

Lucy continued her way, wondering what sort of a household it could be where the husband remained in ignorance of his wife's expected guests. Lionel passed on to the drawing-room.

Lady Verner sat in it. Her white gloves on her

delicate hands as usual, her essence bottle and laced handkerchief beside her. Lionel offered her his customary fond greeting, and placed the cheque in her hands.

"Will that do, mother mine?"

"Admirably, Lionel. I am so much obliged to you. Things get behind-hand in the most unaccountable manner, and then Decima comes to me with a long face, and says here's this debt and that debt. It is quite a marvel to me how the money goes. Decima would like to put her accounts into my hands that I may look over them. The idea of my taking upon myself to examine accounts! But how it is she gets into such debt, I cannot think."

Poor Decima knew only too well. Lionel knew it also; though, in his fond reverence, he would not hint at such a thing to his mother. Lady Verner's style of living was too expensive, and that was the cause.

"I met Lucy in the hall, dressed. She and Decima are coming to dine at Verner's Pride, she tells me."

"Did you not know it?"

"No. I have been out shooting all day. If Sibylla mentioned it to me, I forgot it."

Sibylla had not mentioned it. But Lionel would rather take any blame to himself than suffer a shade of it to rest upon her.

"Mrs. Verner called yesterday, and invited us. I declined for myself. I should have declined for

Decima, but I did not think it right to deprive Lucy of the pleasure, and she could not go alone. Ungrateful child!" apostrophised Lady Verner. " When I told her this morning I had accepted an invitation for her to Verner's Pride, she turned the colour of scarlet, and said she would rather remain at home. I never saw so unsociable a girl; she does not care to go out, as it seems to me. I insisted upon it for this evening."

"Mother, why don't *you* come?"

Lady Verner half turned from him.

"Lionel, you must not forget our compact. If I visit your wife now and then, just to keep gossiping tongues quiet, from saying that Lady Verner and her son are estranged, I cannot do it often."

" Were there any cause why you should show this disfavour to Sibylla—"

"Our compact, our compact, my son! You are not to urge me upon this point, do you remember? I rarely break my resolutions, Lionel."

" Or your prejudices either, mother."

"Very true," was the equable answer of Lady Verner.

Little more was said. Lionel found the time drawing on, and left. Lady Verner's carriage was already at the door, waiting to convey Decima and Lucy Tempest to the dinner at Verner's Pride. As he was about to mount his horse, Peckaby passed by, rolling a wheel before him. He touched his cap.

"Well," said Lionel, "has the white donkey arrived yet?"

A contraction of anger, not, however, unmixed with mirth, crossed the man's face.

"I wish it would come, sir, and bear her off on't!" was his hearty response. "She's more a fool nor ever over it, a whining and a pining all day long, 'cause she ain't at New Jerusalem. She wants to be in Bedlam, sir; that's what she do! it'ud do her more good nor t'other."

Lionel laughed, and Peckaby struck his wheel with such impetus that it went off at a tangent, and he had to follow it on the run.

CHAPTER XIII.

THE rooms were lighted at Verner's Pride: the blaze from the chandeliers fell on gay faces and graceful forms. The dinner was over, its scene "a banquet hall deserted;" and the guests were filling the drawing-rooms.

The centre of an admiring group, its chief attraction, sat Sibylla, her dress some shining material that glimmered in the light, and her hair confined with a band of diamonds. Inexpressibly beautiful by this light she undoubtedly was, but she would have been more charming had she less laid herself out for attraction. Lionel, Lord Garle, Decima, and young Bitterworth,—he was generally called young Bitterworth, in contradistinction to his father, who was "old Bitterworth"—formed another group; Sir Rufus Hautley was talking to the Countess of Elmsley: and Lucy Tempest sat apart near the window.

Sir Rufus had but just moved away from Lucy, and for the moment she was alone. She sat within the embrasure of the window, and was looking on the calm scene outside. How different from the garish scene within! See the pure moonlight, side by side with the most brilliant light we earthly inventors can produce, and contrast them! Pure and fair as the moonlight looked Lucy, her white robes falling softly round her, and her girlish face wearing a thoughtful expression. It was a remarkably light night: the terrace, the green slopes beyond it, and the clustering trees far away, all standing out clear and distinct in the moon's rays. Suddenly her eye rested on a particular spot: she possessed a very clear sight, and it appeared to detect something dark there; which dark something had not been there a few moments before.

Lucy strained her eyes, and shaded them, and gazed again. Presently she turned her head, and glanced at Lionel. An expression in her eyes seemed to call him, and he advanced.

"What is it, Lucy? We must have a set of gallant men here to-night, to leave you alone like this!"

The compliment fell unheeded on her ear. Compliments from *him!* Lionel only so spoke to hide his real feelings.

"Look on the lawn, right before us," said Lucy to him, in a low tone. " Underneath the spreading yew-tree. Do you not fancy the trunk looks remarkably dark and thick?"

" The trunk remarkably dark and thick!" echoed Lionel. "What do you mean, Lucy?" For he judged by her tone that she had some hidden meaning.

" I believe that some man is standing there. He must be watching this room."

Lionel could not see it. His eyes had not been watching so long as Lucy's, consequently objects were less distinct. " I think you must be mistaken, Lucy," he said. " No one would be at the trouble of standing there to watch the room. It is too far off to see much, whatever may be their curiosity."

Lucy held her hands over her eyes, gazing attentively from beneath them. " I feel convinced of it now," she presently said. " There is some one, and it looks like a man, standing behind the trunk, as if hiding himself. His head is pushed out on this side, certainly, as though he were watching these windows. I have seen the head move twice."

Lionel placed his hands in the same position, and took a long gaze. " I do think you are right, Lucy!" he suddenly exclaimed. " I saw something move then. What business has anyone to plant himself there ? "

He stepped impulsively out as he spoke: the windows opened to the ground : crossed the terrace, descended the steps, and turned on the lawn, to the left hand. A minute, and he was up at the tree.

But he gained no satisfaction. The spreading tree, with its imposing trunk—which trunk was nearly as thick as a man's body—stood all solitary on the smooth grass, no living thing being near it.

" We must have been mistaken, after all," thought Lionel.

Nevertheless, he stood under the tree, and cast his keen glances around. Nothing could he see; nothing but what ought to be there. The wide

lawn, the sweet flowers closed to the night, the
remoter parts where the trees were thick, all stood
cold and still in the white moonlight. But of human
disturber there was none.

Lionel went back again, plucking a white geranium
blossom and a sprig of sweet verbena on his way.
Lucy was sitting alone, as he had left her.

"It was a false alarm," he whispered. "Nothing's
there, except the tree."

"It was not a false alarm," she answered. I saw
him move away as you went on to the lawn. He
drew back towards the thicket."

"Are you sure?" questioned Lionel, his tone
betraying that he doubted whether she was not
mistaken.

"Oh, yes, I am sure," said Lucy. "Do you
know what my old nurse used to tell me when I was
a child?" she asked, lifting her face to his. "She
said I had the Indian sight, because I could see so
far and so distinctly. Some of the Indians have
the gift greatly, you know. I am quite certain that
I saw the object—and it looked like the figure of a
man—go swiftly away from the tree across the grass.
I could not see him to the end of the lawn, but he
must have gone into the plantation. I daresay he
saw you coming towards him."

Lionel smiled. "I wish I had caught the spy.
He should have answered to me for being there.
Do you like verbena, Lucy?"

He laid the verbena and geranium on her lap, and
she took them up mechanically.

"I do not like spies," she said, in a dreamy tone. "In India they have been known to watch the inmates of a house in the evening, and to bowstring one of those they were watching before the morning. You are laughing! Indeed, my nurse used to tell me tales of it."

"We have no spies in England—in that sense, Lucy. When I used the word spy, it was with no meaning attached to it. It is not impossible but it may be a sweetheart of one of the maid-servants, come up from Deerham for a rendezvous. Be under no apprehension."

At that moment, the voice of his wife came ringing through the room. "Mr. Verner!"

He turned to the call. Waiting to say another word to Lucy, as a thought struck him. "You would prefer not to remain at the window, perhaps. Let me take you to a more sheltered seat."

"Oh, no, thank you," she answered impulsively. "I like being at the window. It is not of myself that I am thinking." And Lionel moved away.

"Is it not true that the fountains at Versailles played expressly for me?" eagerly asked Sibylla, as he approached her. "Sir Rufus won't believe that they did. The first time we were in Paris, you know."

Sir Rufus Hautley was by her side then. He looked at Lionel. "They never play for private individuals, Mr. Verner. At least, if they do, things have changed."

"My wife thought they did," returned Lionel, with a smile. "It was all the same."

"They did, Lionel; you know they did," vehemently asserted Sibylla. "De Coigny told me so: and he held authority in the Government."

"I know that De Coigny told you so, and that you believed him," answered Lionel, still smiling. "I did not believe him."

"Sibylla turned her head away petulantly from her husband. "You are saying it to annoy me. I'll never appeal to you again. Sir Rufus, they did play expressly for me."

"It may be bad taste, but I'd rather see the waterworks at St. Cloud than at Versailles," observed a Mr. Gordon, some acquaintance that they had picked up in town, and to whom it had been Sibylla's pleasure to give an invitation. "Cannonby wrote me word last week from Paris—"

"Who?" sharply interrupted Sibylla.

Mr. Gordon looked surprised. Her tone had betrayed something of eager alarm, not to say terror.

"Captain Cannonby, Mrs. Verner. A friend of mine just returned from Australia. Business took him to Paris as soon as he landed."

"Is he from the Melbourne port? Is his Christian name Lawrence?" she reiterated, breathlessly.

"Yes—to both questions," replied Mr. Gordon.

Sibylla shrieked, and lifted her handkerchief to her face. They gathered round her in consternation. One offering smelling-salts, one running for water. Lionel gently drew the handkerchief from her face. It was white as death.

"What ails you, my dear?" he whispered.

She seemed to recover her equanimity as suddenly as she had lost it, and the colour began to appear in her cheeks again.

"His name—Cannonby's—puts me in mind of those unhappy days," she said, not in the low tone used by her husband, but aloud—speaking, in fact, to all around her. "I did not know Captain Cannonby had returned. When did he come, Mr. Gordon?"

"About eight or nine days ago."

"Has he made his fortune?"

Mr. Gordon laughed. "I fancy not. Cannonby was always of a roving nature. I expect he got tired of the Australian world before fortune had time to find him out."

Sibylla was soon deep in her flirtations again. It is not erroneous to call them so. But they were innocent flirtations—the result of vanity. Lionel moved away.

Another commotion. Some great long-legged fellow, without ceremony or warning, came striding in at the window close to Lucy Tempest. Lucy's thoughts had been buried—it is hard to say where, and her eyes were strained to the large yew-tree upon the grass. The sudden entrance startled her, albeit she was not of a startlish temperament. With Indian bow-strings in the mind, and fancied moonlight spies before the sight, a scream was inevitable.

Whom should it be but Jan! Jan, of course. What other guest would be likely to enter in that

unceremonious fashion ?   Strictly speaking, Jan was
not a guest—at any rate, not an invited one.

"I had got a minute to spare this evening, so
thought I'd come up and have a look at you," pro-
claimed unfashionable Jan to the room, but prin-
cipally addressing Lionel and Sibylla.

And so Jan had come, and stood there without
the least shame, in drab trousers and a loose, airy
coat, shaking hands with Sir Rufus, shaking hands
with anybody who would shake hands with him.
Sibylla looked daggers at Jan, and Lionel cross.
Not from the same cause. Sibylla's displeasure
was directed to Jan's style of evening costume;
Lionel felt vexed with him for alarming Lucy. But
Lionel never very long retained displeasure, and
his sweet smile stole over his lips as he spoke.

"Jan, I shall be endorsing Lady Verner's request
—that you come into a house like a Christian—if
you are to startle ladies in this fashion."

"Whom did I startle ?" asked Jan.

"You startled Lucy."

"Nonsense ! Did I, Miss Lucy ?"

"Yes, you did a little, Jan," she replied.

"What a stupid you must be !" retorted gallant
Jan. "I should say you want doctoring, if your
nerves are in that state. You take—"

"Oh, Jan, that will do," laughed Lucy. "I am
sure I don't want medicine. You know how I dislike it."

They were standing together within the large
window, Jan and Lionel, Lucy sitting close to them.

She sat with her head a little bent, scenting her verbena.

"The truth is, Jan, I and Lucy have been watching some intruder who had taken up his station on the lawn, underneath the yew-tree," whispered Lionel. "I suppose Lucy thought he was bursting in upon us."

"Yes, I did really think he was," said Lucy, looking up with a smile.

"Who was it?" asked Jan.

"He did not give us the opportunity of ascertaining," replied Lionel. "I am not quite sure, mind, that I did see him ; but Lucy is positive upon the point. I went to the tree, but he had disappeared. It is rather strange why he should be watching."

"He was watching this room attentively," said Lucy, " and I saw him move away when Mr. Verner went on the lawn. I am sure he was a spy of some sort."

"I can tell you who it was," said Jan. "It was Roy."

"Roy!" repeated Lionel. "Why do you say this?"

"Well," said Jan, " as I turned in here, I saw Roy cross the road to the opposite gate. I don't know where he could have sprung from, except from these grounds. That he was neither behind me nor before me as I came up the road, I can declare."

"Then it was Roy!" exclaimed Lionel. "He

would have had about time to get into the road,
from the time we saw him under the tree. That
the fellow is prying into my affairs and movements,
I was made aware of to-day: but why he should
watch my house I cannot imagine. We shall have
an account to settle, Mr. Roy!"

Decima came up, asking what private matter they
were discussing, and Lionel and Lucy went over the
ground again, acquainting her with what had been
seen. They stood together in a group, conversing
in an under-tone. By and by, Mrs. Verner passed,
moving from one part of the room to another, on
the arm of Sir Rufus Hautley.

"Quite a family conclave," she exclaimed with
a laugh. "Decima, however much you may wish
for attention, it is scarcely fair to monopolise that
of Mr. Verner in his own house. If he forgets that
he has guests present, you should not help him in
the forgetfulness."

"It would be well if all wished for attention as
little as does Miss Verner," exclaimed Lord Garle.
His voice rung out to the ends of the room, and a
sudden stillness fell upon it: his words may have
been taken as a covert reproof to Mrs. Verner.
They were not meant as such. There was no living
woman of whom Lord Garle thought so highly as
he thought of Decima Verner; and he had spoken
in his mind's impulse.

Sibylla believed he had purposely flung a shaft at
her. And she flung one again—not at him, but at
Decima. She was of a terribly jealous nature, and

could bear any reproach to herself, better than that
another woman should be praised beside her.

"When young ladies find themselves neglected,
their charms wasted on the desert air, they naturally
do covet attention, although it be but a brother's."

Perhaps the first truly severe glance that Lionel
Verner ever gave his wife he gave her then. Dis-
daining any defence of his sister, he stood, haughty,
impassive, his lips drawn in, his eyes fixed sternly
on Sibylla. Decima remained quiet under the
insult, save that she flushed scarlet. Lord Garle
did not. Lord Garle spoke up again, in the impetuosity of his open, honest nature.

"I can testify that if Miss Verner is neglected, it
is her own fault alone. You are mistaken in your
premises, Mrs. Verner."

The tone was pointedly significant, the words
were unmistakably clear, and the room could not
but become enlightened to the fact that Miss Verner
might have been Lady Garle. Sibylla laughed a
little laugh of disbelief, as she went onwards with
Sir Rufus Hautley; and Lionel remained enshrined
in his terrible mortification. That his wife should
so have forgotten herself!

"I must be going off," cried Jan, good-naturedly
interrupting the unpleasant silence.

"You have not long come," said Lucy.

"I didn't leave word where I was coming, and
somebody may be going dead while they are scour-
ing the parish for me. Good-night to you all; good-
night, Miss Lucy."

With a nod to the room, away went Jan as unceremoniously as he had come; and, not very long afterwards, the first carriage drew up. It was Lady Verner's. Lord Garle hastened to Decima, and Lionel took out Lucy Tempest.

"Will you think me very foolish, if I say a word of warning to you?" asked Lucy in a low tone to Lionel, as they reached the terrace.

"A word of warning to me, Lucy!" he repeated. "Of what nature?"

"That Roy is not a good man. He was greatly incensed at your putting him out of his place when you succeeded to Verner's Pride, and it is said that he cherishes vengeance. He may have been watching to-night for an opportunity to injure you. Take care of him."

Lionel smiled as he looked at her. Her upturned face looked pale and anxious in the moonlight. Lionel could not receive the fear at all: he would as soon have thought to dread the most improbable thing imaginable, as to dread this sort of violence, whether from Roy, or from any one else.

"There's no fear whatever, Lucy."

"I know you will not see it for yourself, and that is the reason why I am presumptive enough to suggest the idea to you. Pray be cautious! pray take care of yourself!"

He shook his head laughingly as he looked down upon her. "Thank you heartily all the same for your consideration, Lucy," said he, and for the very life of him he could not help pressing her hand warmer than was needful as he placed her in the carriage.

They drove away. Lord Garle returned to the room; Lionel stood against one of the outer pillars, looking forth on the lovely moonlight scene. The part played by Roy—if it was Roy—in the night's doings disturbed him not; but that his wife had shown herself so entirely unlike a lady did disturb him. In bitter contrast to Lucy did she stand out to his mind that night. He turned away, after some minutes, with an impatient movement, as if he would fain throw remembrance and vexation from him. Lionel had himself chosen his companion in life, and none knew better than he that he must abide by it: none could be more firmly resolved to do his full duty by her in love. Sibylla was standing outside the window alone. Lionel approached her, and gently laid his hand upon her shoulder.

"Sibylla, what caused you to show agitation when Cannonby's name was mentioned?"

"I told you," answered Sibylla. "It is dreadful to be reminded of that miserable time. It was Cannonby, you know, who buried my husband."

And before Lionel could say more, she had shaken his hand from her shoulder, and was back amidst her guests.

CHAPTER XIV.

JAN had said somebody might be going dead while the parish was being scoured for him : and, in point of fact, Jan found, on reaching home, that that undesirable consummation was not unlikely to occur. As you will find also, if you will make an evening call upon Mrs. Duff.

Mrs. Duff stood behind her counter, sorting silks. Not rich piece silks that are made into gowns ; Mrs. Duff's shop did not aspire to that luxurious class of goods; but humble skeins of mixed sewing-silks, that were kept tied up in a piece of wash-leather. Mrs. Duff's head and a customer's head were brought together over the bundle, endeavouring to fix upon a skein of a particular shade, by the help of the one gas-burner which flared away over head.

"Drat the silk!" said Mrs. Duff at length. "One can't tell which is which, by candle-light. The green looks blue, and the blue looks green. Look at them two skeins, Polly: which *is* the green ? "

Miss Polly Dawson, a showy damsel with black hair and a cherry-coloured net at the back of it,—

one of the family that Roy was pleased to term the
ill-doing Dawsons, took the two skeins in her hand.

"Blest if I can tell!" was her answer. "It's
for doing up mother's green silk bonnet, so it won't
do to take blue. You be more used to it nor me,
Mrs. Duff."

"My eyes never was good for sorting silks by
this light," responded Mrs. Duff. "I'll tell you
what, Polly; you shall take 'em both. Your
mother must take the responsibility of fixing on
one herself; or let her keep 'em till the morning
and choose it then. She should have sent by
daylight. You can bring back the skein you don't
use to-morrow; but mind you keep it clean."

"Wrap 'em up," curtly returned Miss Polly
Dawson.

Mrs. Duff was proceeding to do so, when some
tall thin form, bearing a large bundle, entered the
shop in a fluster. It was Mrs. Peckaby. She sat
herself down on the only stool the shop contained,
and let the bundle slip to the floor.

"Give a body leave to rest a bit, Mother Duff!
I be turned a'most inside out."

"What's the matter?" asked Mrs. Duff, while
Polly Dawson surveyed her with a stare.

"There's a white cow in the pound. I can't tell
ye the turn it give me, coming sudden upon it. I
thought nothing less, at first glance, but it was the
white quadruple."

"What! hasn't that there white donkey come
yet?" demanded Polly Dawson; who, in conjunc-

tion with sundry others of her age and sex in the
village, was not sparing of her free remarks to
Mrs. Peckaby on the subject, thereby aggravating
that lady considerably.

"You hold your tongue, Polly Dawson, and
don't be brazen, if you can help it," rebuked Mrs.
Peckaby. "I was so took aback for the minute,
that I couldn't neither stir nor speak," she resumed
to Mrs. Duff. "But when I found it was nothing
but a old strayed wretch of a pounded cow, I a'most
dropped with the disappointment. So I thought I'd
come back here and take a rest. Where's Dan?"

"Dan's out," answered Mrs. Duff.

"Is he? I thought he might have took this
parcel down to Sykes's, and saved me the sight o'
that pound again and the deceiver in it. It's just
my luck!"

"Dan's gone up to Verner's Pride," continued
Mrs. Duff. "That fine French madmizel, as rules
there, come down for some trifles this evening,
and took him home with her to carry the parcel.
It's time he was back, though, and more nor time.
'Twasn't bigger, neither, nor a farthing bun, but
'twas too big for *her*. Isn't it a getting the season
for you to think of a new gownd, Mrs. Peckaby?"
resumed Mother Duff, returning to business. "I
have got some beautiful winter stuffs in."

"I hope the only new gownd as I shall want till
I gets to New Jerusalem, is the purple one I've
got prepared for it," replied Mrs. Peckaby. "I
don't think the journey's far off. I had a dream

last night as I saw a great crowd o' people dressed in white, a coming out to meet me. I look upon it as it's a token that I shall soon be there."

" I wouldn't go out to that there New Jerusalem if ten white donkeys come to fetch me!" cried Polly Dawson, tossing her head with scorn. "It *is* a nice place, by all that I have heard! Them saints—"

A most appalling interruption. Snorting, moaning, sobbing, his breath coming in gasps, his hair standing up on end, his eyes starting, and his face ghastly, there burst in upon them Master Dan Duff. That he was in the very height of terror, there could be no mistaking. To add to the confusion, he flung his arms out as he came in, and his hand caught one of the side panes of glass in the bow window and shattered it, the pieces falling amongst the displayed wares. Dan leaped in, caught hold of his mother with a spasmodic howl, and fell down on some bundles in a corner of the small shop.

Mrs. Duff was dragged down with him. She soon extricated herself, and stared at the boy in very astonishment. However inclined to play tricks, out of doors, Mr. Dan never ventured to play them, in. Polly Dawson stared. Susan Peckaby, forgetting New Jerusalem for once, sprang off her stool and stared. But that his terror was genuine, and Mrs. Duff saw that it was, Dan had certainly been treated then to that bugbear of his domestic life—a " basting."

"What has took you now?" sharply demanded Mrs. Duff, partly in curiosity, partly in wrath.

"I see'd a dead man," responded Dan, and he forthwith fell into convulsions.

They shook him, they pulled him, they pinched him. One laid hold of his head, another of his feet; but, make nothing of him, could they. The boy's face was white, his hands and arms were twitching, and froth was gathering on his lips. By this time the shop was full.

"Run across, one of you," cried the mother, turning her face to the crowd, "and see if you can find Mr. Jan Verner."

CHAPTER XV.

JAN VERNER was turning in at his own door—the surgery—at a swinging pace. Jan's natural pace was a deliberate one ; but Jan found so much to do, now he was alone in the business, that he had no resource but to move at the rate of a steam-engine. Otherwise he would never have got through his day's work. Jan had tried one assistant, who had proved to be more plague than profit, and Jan was better without him. Master Cheese, promoted now to tail-coats and turn-up collars, was coming on, and could attend to trifling cases. Master Cheese wished to be promoted also to "Mister" Cheese : but he remained obstinately excessively short, and people would still call him "Master." He appeared to grow in breadth instead of height, and underwent, in consequence, a perpetual inward mortification. Jan would tell him he should eat less and walk more ; but the advice was not taken.

Jan Verner was turning into the surgery at a swinging pace, and came in violent contact with Master Cheese, who was coming out at another sharp pace. Jan rubbed his chest, and Cheese his head.

"I say, Jan," said he, "can't you look where you're going?"

"Can't *you* look?" returned Jan. "Where are you off to?"

"There's something the matter at Duff's. About a dozen came here in a body, wanting you. Bob says Dan Duff was dying."

Jan turned his eyes on Bob, the surgery-boy. Bob answered the look:

"It's what they said, sir. They said as Dan Duff was a-dying and a-frothing at the mouth. It's about five minutes ago, sir."

"Did you go over?" asked Jan of Cheese. "I saw a crowd round Mrs. Duff's door."

"No I didn't. I am going now. I was in-doors, having my supper."

"Then you need not trouble yourself," returned Jan. "Stop where you are, and digest your supper."

He, Jan, was speeding off, when a fresh deputation arrived. Twenty anxious faces at the least, all in a commotion, their tongues going together. "Dan was frothing dreadful, and his legs was twitchin' like one in the epilepsies."

"What has caused it?" asked Jan. "I saw him well enough an hour or two ago."

"He see a dead man, sir; as it's said. We can't come to the bottom of it, 'cause of his not answering no questions. He be too bad, he be."

"He did see a dead man," put in Polly Dawson, who made one of the deputation, and was proud of being able to add her testimony to the asserted fact. "Leastways, he said he did. I was a-buying some silk, sir, in at Mother Duff's shop, and Susan Peckaby was in there too, she was, a-talking rubbish about her white donkey, when Dan flounders in upon us in a state not to be told, a-frightening of us dreadful, and a-smashing in the winder with his arm. And he said he'd seen a dead man."

Jan could not make sense of the tale. There was nobody lying dead in Deerham, that he knew of. He pushed the crowd round the door right and left to get space to enter. The shop was pretty full already, but numbers pushed in after Jan. Dan had been carried into the kitchen at the back of the shop, and was laid upon the floor, a pillow under his head. The kitchen was more crowded than the shop; there was not breathing space; and room could hardly be found for Jan.

The shop was Mrs. Duff's department. If she chose to pack it full of people to the ceiling, it was her affair: but Jan made the kitchen, where the boy lay, his.

"What's the matter with him, sir?" was the eager question to Jan, the moment he had cast his eyes on the invalid.

"I may be able to ascertain as soon as I have elbow room," replied Jan. "Suppose you give it me? Mrs. Duff may stop, but nobody else."

Jan's easy words carried authority in their tone, and the company turned tail and began to file out.

"Couldn't you do with me in, as well as his mother, sir?" asked Susan Peckaby. "I was here

when he came in, I was; and I knowed what it was
a'most afore he spoke. He have been frightened by
that thing in the pound. Only a few minute afore,
it had turned my inside a'most out."

"No, I can't," answered Jan. "I must have the
room clear. Perhaps I shall send away his mother."

"I should ha' liked to know for sure," meekly
observed Susan Peckaby, preparing to resign herself to her fate. "I hope you'll ask him, sir, when
he comes to, whether it were not that thing in the
pound as frightened him. I took it for some'at else,
more's the grief! but it looks, for all the world, like
a ghost in the moonlight."

"What is in the pound?" demanded Jan.

"It's a white cow," responded Susan Peckaby.
"And it strikes me as it's Farmer Blow's. He have
got a white cow, you know, sir, like he have got a
white pony, and they be always a giving me a turn,
one or t'other of 'em. I'd like old Blow to be
indicted for a pest, I would! a-keeping white
animals to upset folks. It's not a week ago that I
met that cow in the road at dusk,—strayed through
a gap in the hedge. Tiresome beast! a-causing my
heart to leap into my mouth!"

"If Dan have put himself into this state, and
done all this damage, through nothing but seeing of
a white cow, won't I baste him!" emphatically
rejoined Mrs. Duff.

Jan at length succeeded in getting the kitchen
clear. But for some time, in spite of all his skill
and attention—and he spared neither—he could

make no impression upon the unhappy Dan. His mother's bed was made ready for him—Dan himself sharing the accommodation of a dark closet in an ordinary way, in common with his brothers—and Jan carried him up to it. There he somewhat revived, sufficiently to answer a question or two rationally. It must be confessed that Jan felt some curiosity upon the subject: to suppose the boy had been thrown into that state, simply by seeing a white cow in the pound, was ridiculous.

"What frightened you?" asked Jan.

"I see'd a dead man," answered the boy. "Oh lor!"

"Well?" said Jan, with composure, "he didn't eat you. What is there in a dead man to be alarmed at? I have seen scores—handled 'em, too. What dead man was it?"

The boy pulled the bed-clothes over him, and moaned. Jan pulled them down again.

"Of course you can't tell! There's no dead man in Deerham. Was it in the churchyard?"

"No."

"Was it in the pound?" asked Jan, triumphantly, thinking he had got it right this time.

"No."

The answer was an unexpected one.

"Where was it, then?"

"Oh-o-o-o-oh!" moaned the boy, beginning to shake and twitch again.

"Now, Dan Duff, this won't do," said Jan. "Tell me quietly what you saw, and where you saw it."

"I see'd a dead man," reiterated Dan Duff. And it appeared to be all he was capable of saying.

"You saw a white cow on its hind legs," returned Jan. "That's what you saw. I am surprised at you, Dan Duff. I should have thought you more of a man."

Whether the reproof overcame Master Duff's nerves again, or the remembrance of the "dead man," certain it was, that he relapsed into a state which rendered it imprudent, in Jan's opinion, to continue for the present the questioning. One more only he put—for a sudden thought crossed him, which induced it.

"Was it in the copse at Verner's Pride?"

"'Twas at the Willow-pool: he was a-walking round it. Oh-o-o-o-o-oh!"

Jan's momentary fear was dispelled. A night or two back there had been a slight affray between Lionel's gamekeeper and some poachers: and the natural doubts arose whether anything fresh of the same nature had taken place. If so, Dan Duff might have come upon one of them, lying dead or wounded. The words—"walking round the pool"—did away with this. For the present, Jan departed.

But, if Dan's organs of disclosure are for the present in abeyance, there's no reason why we should not find out what we can for ourselves. You may be very sure that Deerham would not fail to do it.

The French madmizel—as Mrs. Duff styled her,

meaning, of course, Mademoiselle Benoite — had
called in at Mrs. Duff's shop and made a purchase.
It consisted—if you are curious to know—of pins
and needles, and a staylace. Not a parcel that would
have weighed her down, certainly, had she borne it
herself: but it pleased her to demand that Dan
should carry it for her. This she did, partly to
display her own consequence, chiefly that she might
have a companion home, for Mademoiselle Benoite
did not relish the walk alone by moonlight to
Verner's Pride. Of course young Dan was at the
beck and call of Mrs. Duff's customers, that being,
as Mademoiselle herself might have said, his *spécialité*. Whether a customer bought a parcel that
would have filled a van, or one that might have gone
inside a penny thimble, Master Dan was equally
expected to be in readiness to carry the purchase to
its destination at night, if called upon. Master
Dan's days being connected now with the brick-
fields, where his "spécialité" appeared to be, to
put layers of clay upon his clothes.

Accordingly, Dan started with Mademoiselle
Benoite. She had been making purchases at other
places, which she had brought away with her—
shoes, stationery, and various things, all of which
were handed over to the porter, Dan. They arrived
at Verner's Pride in safety, and Dan was ordered
to follow her in, and deposit his packages on the
table of the apartment that was called the steward's
room.

"One, two, three, four," counted Mademoiselle

Benoite, with French caution, lest he should have
dropped any by the way. "You go outside now,
Dan, and I bring you something from my pocket
for your trouble."

Dan returned outside accordingly, and stood
gazing at the laundry windows, which were lighted
up. Mademoiselle dived in her pocket, took something from thence, which she screwed carefully up
in a bit of newspaper, and handed it to Dan. Dan
had watched the process in a glow of satisfaction,
believing it could be nothing less than a silver
sixpence. How much more it might prove, Dan's
aspirations were afraid to anticipate.

"There!" said Mademoiselle, when she put it
into his hand. "Now you can go back to your
mother."

She shut the door in his face somewhat inhos-
pitably, and Dan eagerly opened his *cadeau*. It
contained—two lumps of fine white sugar.

"Mean old cat!" burst forth Dan. "If it
wasn't that mother 'ud baste me, I'd never bring
a parcel for her again, not if she bought up
the shop. Wouldn't I like to give all the French
a licking?"

Munching his sugar wrathfully, he passed across
the yard, and out at the gate. There he hesitated
which way home he should take, as he had hesitated
that far gone evening, when he had come up upon
the errand to poor Rachel Frost. More than four
years had elapsed since then, and Dan was now
fourteen: but he was a young and childish boy of

his age, which might be owing to the fact of his being so kept under by his mother.

"I have a good mind to trick her!" soliloquised he; alluding, it must be owned, to that revered mother. "She wouldn't let me go out to Bill Hook's to-night; though I telled her as it wasn't for no nonsense I wanted to see him, but about that there grey ferret. I will, too! I'll go back the field way, and cut down there. She'll be none the wiser."

Now this was really a brave resolve for Dan Duff. The proposed road would take him past the Willow-pool; and he, in common with other timorous spirits, had been given to eschew that place at night, since the end of Rachel. It must be supposed that the business, touching the grey ferret, was one of importance, for Dan to lose sight of his usual fears, and turn towards that pool.

Not once, from that time to this, had Dan Duff taken this road alone at night. From that cause probably, no sooner had he now turned into the lane, than he began to think of Rachel. He would have preferred to think of anything else in the world: but he found, as many others are obliged to find, that unpleasant thoughts cannot be driven away at will. It was not so much that the past night of misfortune was present to him, as that he feared to meet the ghost of Rachel.

He went on, glancing furtively on all sides, his face and his hair growing hotter and hotter. There, on his right, was the gate through which he had

entered the field to give chase to the supposed
cat; there, on the left, was the high hedge; before
him lay the length of lane traversed that evening
by the tall man, who had remained undiscovered
from that hour to this. Dan could see nothing
now; no tall man, no cat; even the latter might
have proved a welcome intruder. He glanced up
at the calm sky, at the bright moon riding over-
head. The night was perfectly still; a lovely night,
could Dan only have kept the ghosts out of his
mind.

Suddenly a horse, in the field on the other side
the hedge, set up a loud neigh, right in Dan's ear.
Coming thus unexpectedly, it startled Dan above
everything. He half resolved to go back, and
turned round and looked the way he had come.
But he thought of the grey ferret, and plucked up
some courage and went on again: intending, the
moment he came in sight of the Willow-pool, to
make a dash past it at his utmost speed.

The intention was not carried out. Clambering
over the gate which led to the enclosure, a more
ready way to Dan than opening it, he was brought
within view of the pool. There it was, down in the
dreary lower part, near the trees. The pool itself
was distinct enough, lying to the right, and Dan
involuntarily looked towards it. Not to have saved
his life, could Dan have helped looking.

Susan Peckaby had said to Jan, that her heart
leaped into her mouth at the sight of the white cow
in the pound. Poor Dan Duff might have said that

his heart·leaped right out of him, at sight now of
the Willow-pool. For there was some shadowy
figure moving round it.

Dan stood powerless. But for the gate behind
him he would have turned and run : to scramble
back over that, his limbs utterly refused. The
delay caused him, in spite of his fear, to discern
the very obvious fact, that the shadowy figure was
not that of a woman habited in white—as the
orthodox ghost of Rachel ought to have been—but
a man's, wearing dark clothes. There flashed into
Dan's remembrance the frequent nightly visits of
Robin Frost to the pond, bringing with it a ray
of relief.

Robin had been looked upon as little better than
a lunatic since the misfortune; but, to Dan Duff,
he appeared in that moment worth his weight in
gold. Robin's companionship was as good as anybody's to ward off the ghostly fears, and Dan set
off, full speed, towards him. To go right up to the
pond would take him a few yards out of his way to
Bill Hook's. What of that ? To exchange words
with a human tongue, Dan, in that moment of
superstitious fright, would have gone as many
miles.

He had run more than half the intervening distance, when he brought himself to a halt. It had
become evident to Dan's sight that it was not Robin
Frost. Whoever it might be, he was a head and
shoulders taller than Robin; and Dan moved up
more quietly, his eyes strained forward in the moon-

light. A suspicion came over him that it might be Mr. Verner: Dan could not, at the moment, remember anybody else so tall, unless it was Mr. Jan. The figure stood now with its back to him; apparently gazing into the pool. Dan advanced with slow steps; if it was Mr. Verner, he would not presume to intrude upon him: but when he came nearly close, he saw that it bore no resemblance to the figure of Mr. Verner. Slowly, glidingly, the figure turned round; turned its face right upon Dan, full in the rays of the bright moon; and the most awful yell you ever heard went forth upon the still night air.

It came from Dan Duff. What could have been its meaning? Did he think he saw the ghost, which he had been looking out for the last half-hour, poor Rachel's?—saw it beyond this figure which had turned upon him? Dan alone knew. That he had fallen into the most appalling terror, was certain. His eyes were starting, the drops of perspiration poured off him, and his hair rose up on end. The figure—just as if it had possessed neither sight nor hearing, neither sense nor sympathy for human sound—glided noiselessly away: and Dan went yelling on.

Towards home now. All thought of Bill Hook and the grey ferret was gone. Away he tore, the nearest way, which took him past the pound. He never saw the white cow: had the cow been a veritable ghost, Dan had not seen it then. The yells subsiding into moans, and the perspiration into fever heat, he gained his mother's, and broke the window, as you have heard, in passing in.

Such were the particulars; but as yet they were not known. The first person to elicit them was Roy the bailiff.

After Jan Verner had departed, saying he should be back by-and-by, and giving Mrs. Duff strict orders to keep the boy quiet, to allow nobody near him but herself, and, above all, no questioning, Mrs. Duff quitted him: "that he might get a bit o' sleep," she said. In point of fact, Mrs. Duff was burning to exercise her gossiping powers with those other gossipers below. To them she descended; and found Susan Peckaby holding forth upon the subject of the white cow.

"You be wrong, Susan Peckaby," said Mrs. Duff. "It warn't the white cow at all; Dan warn't a-nigh the pound. He told Mr. Jan so."

"Then what was it?" returned Susan Peckaby.

One of the present auditors was Roy the bailiff. He had only recently pushed in, and had stood listening in silence, taking note of the various comments and opinions. As silently, he moved behind the group, and was stealing up the stairs. Mrs. Duff placed herself before him.

"Where be you a-going, Mr. Roy? Mr. Jan said as not a soul was to go a-nigh him to disturb him with talk. A nice thing, it 'ud be, for it to settle on his brain!"

"I ain't a-going to disturb him," returned Roy. "I have seen something myself to-night that is not over-kind. I'd like to get a inkling if it's the same that has frighted him."

"Was it in the pound?" eagerly asked Mrs. Peckaby.

"The pound be smoked!" was the polite answer vouchsafed by Roy. "Thee'll go mad with th' white donkey one of these days."

"There can't be any outlet to it, but one," observed Mrs. Chuff, the blacksmith's wife, giving her opinion in a loud key. "He must ha' seen Rachel Frost's ghost."

"Have *you* been and seen that to-night, Mr. Roy?" cried Susan Peckaby.

"Maybe I have, and maybe I haven't," was Roy's satisfactory reply. "All I say is, I've seen something that I'd rather not have seen; something that 'ud have sent all you women into fits. 'Twarn't unlike Rachel, and 'twere clothed in white. I'll just go and take a look at Dan, Mother Duff. No fear o' my disturbing him."

Mother Duff, absorbed with her visitors, allowed him to go on without further impediment. The first thing Roy did, upon getting upstairs, was to shut the chamber door: the next, to arouse and question the suffering Dan. Roy succeeded in getting from him the particulars already related; and a little more: insomuch that Dan mentioned the name which the dead man had borne in life.

Roy sat and stared at him after the revelation, keeping silence. It may have been that he was digesting the wonder: it may have been that he was deliberating upon his answer.

"Look you here, Dan Duff," said he, by and by, holding the shaking boy by the shoulder. "You just breathe that name again to living mortal, and see if you don't get hung up by the neck for it. 'Twas nothing but Rachel's ghost. Them ghosts takes the form of anything that it pleases 'em to take; whether it's a dead man's, or whether it's a woman's, what do they care? There's no ghost but Rachel's 'ud be a-hovering over that pond. Where be your senses gone, not to know that?"

Poor Dan's senses appeared to be wandering somewhere yet: they certainly were not in him. He shook and moaned, and finally fell into the same sort of stupor as before. Roy could make nothing further of him, and he went down.

"Well," said he to the assemblage, "I've got it out of him. The minute he saw me, he stretched his arm out—'Mr. Roy,' says he, 'I'm sick to unburden myself to somebody:' and he up and told. He's fell off again now, like one senseless, and I question if he'd remember telling me."

"And what was it? And what was it?" questioned the chorus. "Rachel's ghost?"

"It was nothing less, you may be sure," replied Roy, his tone expressive of contempt that they should have thought it could be anything less. "The young idiot must take and go by the pond on this bright night, and in course he saw it. Right again his face, he says, it appeared; there wasn't no mistaking of it. It was a-walking round and round the pool."

Considerable shivering in the assembly. Polly Dawson, who was on its outskirts, shrieked, and pushed into its midst, as if it were a safer place. The women drew into a closer circle, and glanced round at an imaginary ghost behind their shoulders.

"Was it that as you saw yourself to-night, Mr. Roy?"

"Never mind me," was Roy's answer. "I ain't one to be startled to death at sight of a sperit, like boys and women is. I had my pill in what I saw, I can tell ye. And my advice to ye all is, keep within your own doors after nightfall."

Without further salutation, Roy departed. The women, with one accord, began to make for the staircase. To contemplate one who had just been in actual contact with the ghost — which some infidels had persistently asserted throughout was nothing but a myth—was a sight not to be missed. But they were driven back again. With a succession of yells, the like of which had never been heard, save at the Willow-pond that night, Dan appeared leaping down upon them, his legs naked and his short shirt flying behind him. To be left alone, a prey to ghosts or their remembrances, was more than the boy, with his consciousness upon him, could bear. The women yelled also, and fell back one upon another: not a few being under the impression that it was the ghost itself.

What was to be done with him? Before the

question was finally decided, Mrs. Bascroft, the landlady of the Plough and Harrow, who had made one of the company, went off to her bar, whence she hastened back again with an immense hot tumbler, three parts brandy, one part water, the whole of which was poured down the throat of Dan.

"There's nothing like it for restoring folks after a fright," remarked Mrs. Bascroft.

The result of the dose was, that Dan Duff sub· sided into a state of real stupor, so profound and prolonged that even Jan began to doubt whether he would awake from it.

CHAPTER XVI.

LIONEL VERNER sat over his morning letters, bending upon one of them a perplexed brow. A claim which he had settled the previous spring—at least, which he believed had been settled—was now forwarded to him again. That there was very little limit to his wife's extravagance, he had begun to know.

In spite of Sibylla's extensive purchases, made in Paris at the time of their marriage, she had contrived by the end of the following winter to run up a tolerable bill at her London milliner's. When they had gone to town in the early spring, this bill got presented to Lionel. Four hundred and odd pounds. He gave Sibylla a cheque for its amount, and some gentle loving words of admonition at the same time—not to spend him out of house and home.

A second account from the same milliner had arrived this morning—been delivered to him with other London letters. Why it should have been sent to him and not to his wife, he was unable to tell—unless it was meant as a genteel hint that payment would be acceptable. The whole amount was for eleven hundred pounds, but part of this purported to be "To bill delivered"—four hundred and odd pounds. The precise sum which Lionel believed to have been paid. Eleven hundred pounds! and all the other claims upon him! No wonder he sat with a bent brow. If things went on at this rate, Verner's Pride would come to the hammer.

He rose, the account in his hand, and proceeded to his wife's dressing-room. Among other habits, Sibylla was falling into that of indolence, scarcely ever rising to breakfast now. Or, if she rose, she did not come down. Mademoiselle Benoite came whisking out of a side room as he was about to enter.

"Madame's toilette is not made, sir," cried she, in a tart tone, as if she thought he had no right to enter.

"What of that?" returned Lionel. And he went in.

Just as she had got out of bed, save that she had a blue quilted silk dressing-gown thrown on, and her feet were thrust into blue quilted slippers, sat Sibylla, before a good fire. She leaned in an easy-chair, reading; a miniature breakfast service of Sèvres china, containing chocolate, on a low table at her side. Some people like to read a word or two of the Bible, as soon as conveniently may be, after getting up in the morning. Was that good book the study of Sibylla? Not at all. Her study was a French novel. By dint of patience, and the assistance of Mademoiselle Benoite in the hard

words and complicated sentences, Mrs. Verner contrived to arrive tolerably well at its sense.

"Good gracious!" she exclaimed, when Lionel
appeared, "are you not gone shooting with the
rest?"

"I did not go this morning," he answered, closing
the door, and approaching her.

"Have you taken breakfast?" she asked.

"Breakfast has been over a long while. Were I
you, Sibylla, when I had guests staying in the
house, I should try and rise to breakfast with
them."

"Oh you crafty Lionel! To save you the trouble
of presiding. Thank you," she continued, good-
humouredly, "I am more comfortable here. What
is this story about a ghost? The kitchen's in a
regular commotion, Benoite says."

"To what do you allude?" asked Lionel.

"Dan Duff is dying, or dead," returned Sibylla.
"Benoite was in Deerham last night, and brought
him home to carry her parcels. In going back
again, he saw, as he says, Rachel Frost's ghost, and
it terrified him out of his senses. Old Roy saw it,
too, and the news has travelled up here."

Sibylla laughed as she spoke. Lionel looked
vexed.

"They are very stupid," he said. "A pity but
they kept such stories to themselves. If they were
only as quiet as poor Rachel's ghost is, it might be
be better for some of them."

"Of course *you* would wish it kept quiet," said

Sibylla, in a tone full of significance. "I like to
hear of these frights—it is good fun."

He did not fathom in the remotest degree the
meaning of her tone. But he had not gone thither
to dispute about ghosts.

"Sibylla," he gravely said, putting the open
account into her hand, "I have received this bill
this morning."

"Sibylla ran her eyes over it with indifference:
first at the bill's head, to see whence it came, next
at its sum total.

"What an old cheat! Eleven hundred pounds!
I am sure I have not had the half."

Lionel pointed to the part ' bill delivered.' "Was
that not paid in the spring ? "

"How can I recollect? " returned Sibylla, speaking as carelessly as before.

"I think you may recollect if you try. I gave
you a cheque for the amount."

"Oh, yes, I do recollect now. It has not been
paid."

"But, my dear, I say I gave the cheque for it."

"I cashed the cheque myself. I wanted some
money just then. You can't think how fast money
goes in London, Lionel."

The avowal proved only what he suspected.
Nevertheless it hurt him greatly—grieved him to
his heart's core. Not so much the spending of the
money, as the keeping the fact from him. What a
lack of good feeling, of confidence, it proved.

He bent towards her, speaking gently, kindly.

Whatever might be her faults to him, her provoca-
tions, he could never behave otherwise to her than
as a thorough gentleman, a kind husband.

"It was not right to use that cheque, Sibylla.
It was made out in Madame Lebeau's name, and
should have been paid to her. But why did you not
tell me?"

Sibylla shrugged her shoulders in place of answer.
She had picked up many such little national habits
of Mademoiselle Benoite's. Very conspicuous just
then was the upright line on Lionel's brow.

"The amount altogether is, you perceive, eleven
hundred pounds," he continued.

"Yes," said Sibylla. "She's a cheat, that Madame
Lebeau. I shall make Benoite write her a French
letter, and tell her so."

"It must be paid. But it is a great deal of money.
I cannot continue to pay these large sums, Sibylla.
I have not the money to do it with."

"Not the money! When you know you are paying heaps for Lady Verner! Before you tell me not
to spend, you should cease supplying her."

Lionel's very brow flushed. "My mother has a
claim upon me only in a degree less than you have,"
he gravely said. "Part of the revenues of Verner's
Pride ought to have been hers years ago: and they
were not."

"If my husband had lived—if he had left me a
little child—Verner's Pride would have been his
and mine, and never yours at all."

"Hush, Sibylla! You don't know how these

allusions hurt me," he interrupted, in a tone of intense pain.

" They are true," said Sibylla.

"But not—forgive me, my dear, for saying it— not the less unseemly."

"Why do you grumble at me, then ? "

"I do not grumble," he answered, in a kind tone. " Your interests are mine, Sibylla, and mine are yours. I only tell you the fact—and a fact it is— that our income will not stand these heavy calls upon it. Were I to show you how much you have spent in dress since we were married,—what with Paris, London, and Heartburg, — the sum total would frighten you."

" You should not keep the sum total," resentfully spoke Sibylla. " Why do you add it up ? "

" I must keep my accounts correctly. My uncle taught me that."

" I am sure he did not teach you to grumble at me," she rejoined. " I look upon Verner's Pride as mine, more than yours : if it had not been for the death of my husband, you would never have had it."

Inexpressibly vexed—vexed beyond the power to answer, for he would not trust himself to answer— Lionel prepared to quit the room. He began to wish he had not had Verner's Pride, if this was to be its domestic peace. Sibylla petulantly threw the French book from her lap upon the table, and it fell down with its pages open.

Lionel's eyes caught its title, and a flush, not less deep than the preceding flush, darkened his brow.

He laid his open palm upon the page with an involuntary movement, as if he would guard it from the
eyes of his wife. That she should be reading that
notorious work!

" Where did you get this ? " he cried. " It is not
a fit book for you."

" There's nothing the matter with the book as far
as I have gone."

" Indeed you must not read it! Pray don't,
Sibylla! You will be sorry for it afterwards."

" How do you know it is not a fit book ? "

" Because I have read it."

" There! *You* have read it! And you would like
to deny the pleasure to me! Don't say you are never
selfish."

" Sibylla! What is fit for me to read, may be most
unfit for you. I read the book when I was a young
man : I would not read it now. Is it Benoite's ? "
he inquired, seeing the name in the first page.

" Yes it is."

Lionel closed the book. " Promise me, Sibylla,
that you will not attempt to read more of it. Give
it her back at once, and tell her to send it out of
the house, or to keep it under lock and key while it
remains within it."

Sibylla hesitated.

" Is it so very hard a promise ? " he tenderly
asked. " I would do a great deal more for you."

" Yes, Lionel, I will promise," she replied, a better
feeling coming over her. " I will give it her back
now. Benoite!"

She called loudly. Benoite heard, and came in.

"Mr. Verner says this is not a nice book. You may take it away."

Mademoiselle Benoite advanced with a red face, and took the book.

"Have you any more such books?" inquired Lionel, looking at her.

"No, sir, I not got one other," hardily replied she.

"Have the goodness to put this one away. Had your mistress been aware of the nature of the book, she had not suffered you to produce it."

Mademoiselle went away, her skirts jerking. Lionel bent down to his wife.

"You know that it *pains* me to find fault, Sibylla," he fondly whispered. "I have ever your welfare and happiness at heart. More anxiously, I think, than you have mine."

CHAPTER XVII

LIONEL VERNER was strolling out later in the day, and met the shooting-party coming home. After congratulating them on their good sport, he was turning home with them, when the gamekeeper intimated that he should be glad to speak a word to him in private. Upon which, Lionel let the gentlemen go on.

"What is it, Broom?" asked he.

"I'm much afeared, sir, if things are not altered, that there'll be murder committed some night," answered Broom, without circumlocution.

"I hope not," replied Lionel. "Are you and the poachers again at issue?"

"It's not about the poachers, hang 'em! It's about Robin Frost, sir. What on earth have come to him I can't conceive. This last few nights he have took to prowling out with a gun. He lays himself down in the copse, or a ditch, or the open field—no matter where—and there he stops, on the watch, with his gun always pointed."

"On the watch for what?" asked Lionel.

"He best knows himself, sir. He's going quite cracked, it's my belief; he have been half-way to it this long while. Sometimes he's trailing through the brushwood on all fours, the gun ever pointed; but mostly he's posted on the watch. He'll get shot for a poacher, or some of the poachers will shoot him, as sure as it's a gun that he carries."

"What can be his motive?" mused Lionel.

"I'm inclined to think, sir, though he is Robin Frost, that he's after the birds," boldly returned Broom.

"Then rely upon it that you think wrong, Broom," rebuked Lionel. "Robin Frost would no more go out poaching, than I should go out thieving."

"I saw him trailing along last night in the moon-light, sir. I saw his old father come up and talk to him, urging him to go home, as it seemed to me. But he couldn't get him; and the old man had to hobble back without Robin. Robin stopped in his cold berth on the ground."

"I did not think old Matthew was capable of going out at night."

"He did last night, sir; that's for certain. It was not far; only down away by the brick-kilns. There's a tale going abroad that Dan Duff was sent into mortal fright by seeing something that he took to be Rachel's ghost: my opinion is, that he must have met old Frost in his white smock-frock, and took him for a ghost. The moon did cast an un-common white shade last night. Though old Frost wasn't a-nigh the Willow-pool, nor Robin neither, and that's where they say Dan Duff got his fright. Formerly, Robin was always round that pool, but lately he has changed his beat. Anyhow, sir, perhaps you'd be so good as drop a warning to Robin of the risk he runs. He may mind you."

" I will," said Lionel.

The gamekeeper touched his hat, and walked away. Lionel considered that he might as well give Robin the warning then: and he turned towards the village. Before fairly entering it, he had met twenty talkative persons, who gave him twenty different versions of the previous night's doings, touching Dan Duff.

Mrs. Duff was at her door when Lionel went by. She generally was at her door, unless she was serving customers. He stopped to accost her.

" What's the truth of this affair, Mrs. Duff? " asked he. " I have heard many reports of it ? "

Mrs. Duff gave as succinct an account as it was in her nature to give. Some would have told it in a third of the time: but Lionel had patience; he was in no particular hurry.

" I have been one of them to laugh at the ghost, sir; a-saying that it never was Rachel's, and that it never walked," she added. " But I'll never do so again. Roy, he see it, as well as Dan."

" Oh! he saw it, too, did he," responded Lionel. with a good-natured smile of mockery. " Mrs. Duff, you ought to be too old to believe in ghosts," he more seriously resumed. " I am sure Roy is, whatever he may chose to say."

" If it was no ghost, sir, what could have put our Dan into that awful fright? Mr. Jan doesn't know as he'll overget it at all. He's a-lying without a bit of conscientiousness on my bed, his eyes shut, and his breath a-coming hard."

"Something frightened him, no doubt. The belief in poor Rachel's ghost has been so popular, that every night fright is attributed to that. Who was it went into a fainting fit in the road, fancying Rachel's ghost was walking down upon them; and it proved afterwards to have been only the miller's man with a sack of flour on his back?"

"Oh, that!" slightingly returned Mrs. Duff. "It was that stupid Mother Grind, before they went off with the Mormons. She'd drop at her shadder, sir, she would."

"So would some of the rest of you," said Lionel. "I am sorry to hear that Dan is so ill."

"Mr. Jan's in a fine way over him, sir. Mrs. Bascroft gave him just a taste of weak brandy and water, and Mr. Jan, when he come to know it, said we might just as well have give him pison; and he'd not answer for his life or his reason. A pretty thing it'll be for Deerham, if there's more lives to be put in danger, now the ghost have took to walk again! Mr. Bourne called in just now, sir, to learn the rights of it. He went up and see Dan: but nothing could he make of him. Would you be pleased to go up and take a look at him, sir?"

Lionel declined, and wished Mrs. Duff good day.

He could do the boy no good, and had no especial wish to look at him, although he had been promoted to the notoriety of seeing a ghost. A few steps further he encountered Jan.

"What is it that's the matter with the boy?" asked Lionel.

"He had a good fright; there's no doubt about that," replied Jan. "Saw a white cow on its hind legs, it's my belief. That wouldn't have been much: the boy would have been all right by now, but the women drenched him with brandy, and made him stupidly drunk. He'll be better this evening. I can't stop, Lionel: I am run off my legs to-day."

The commotion in the village increased as the evening approached. Jan knew that young Dan would be well—save for any little remembrance of the fright which might remain—when the fumes of the brandy had gone off; but he wisely kept his own counsel, and let the public think he was in danger. Otherwise, a second instalment of the brandy might have been administered behind Jan's back. To have a boy dying of fright from seeing a ghost was a treat in the marvellous line, which Deerham had never yet enjoyed. There had been no agitation like unto it, since the day of poor Rachel Frost.

Brave spirits, some of them! They volunteered to go out and meet the apparition. As twilight approached you could not have got into Mrs. Duff's shop, for there was the chief gathering. Arguments were being used to prove that, according to all logic, if a ghost appeared one night, it was safe to appear a second.

"Who'll speak up to go and watch for it?" asked Mrs. Duff. "I can't. I can't leave Dan. Sally

Green's a-sitting up by him now; for Mr. Jan says if he's left again, he shall hold me responsible. It don't stand to reason as I can leave Sally Green in charge of the shop, though I can leave her a bit with Dan. Not but what I'd go alone to the pond, and stop there; *I* haven't got no fear."

It singularly happened that those who were kept at home by domestic or other duties, had no fear; they, to hear them talk, would rather have enjoyed an encounter *solus* with the ghost, than not. Those who could plead no home engagement professed themselves willing to undertake the expedition in company; but freely avowed they would not go alone for the world.

"Come! who'll volunteer?" asked Mrs. Duff. "It 'ud be a great satisfaction to see the form it appears in, and have that set at rest. Dan, he'll never be able to tell, by the looks of him now."

"I'll go for one," said bold Mrs. Bascroft. "And them as joins me shall each have a good stiff tumbler of some'at hot afore starting, to prime 'em again the cold."

Whether it was the brave example set, or whether it was the promise accompanying it, certain it was, that there was no lack of volunteers now. A good round dozen started, filling up the Plough-and-Harrow bar, as Mrs. Bascroft dealt out her treat with no niggard hand.

"What's a-doing now?" asked Bascroft, a stupid-

looking man with red hair combed straight down
his forehead, and coloured shirt-sleeves, surveying
the inroad on his premises with surprise.

"Never you mind," sharply reproved his better
half. "These ladies is my visitors, and if I choose
to stand treat round, what's that to you? You takes
your share o' liquor, Bascroft."

Bascroft was not held in very great estimation by
the ladies generally, and they turned their backs
upon him.

"We are a-going out to see the ghost, if you
must know, Bascroft," said Susan Peckaby, who
made one of the volunteers.

Bascroft stared. "What a set of idiots you must
be!" grunted he. "Mr. Jan says as Dan Duff see
nothing but a white cow: he telled me so hisself.
Be you a-thinking to meet that there other white
animal on your road, Mrs. Peckaby?"

"Perhaps I am," tartly returned Mrs. Peckaby.

"One 'ud think so. *You* can't want to go out
to meet ghostesses; you be a-going out to your
saints at New Jerusalem. I'd whack that there
donkey for being so slow, when he did come, if
I was you."

Hastening away from Bascroft and his aggravating tongue, the expedition, having drained their
tumblers, filed out. Down by the pound—relieved
now of its caged inmate—went they, on towards
the willow pond. The tumblers had made them
brave. The night was light, as the preceding one
had been: the ground looked white, as if with frost,

and the air was cold. The pond in view, they halted, and took a furtive glance, beginning to feel somewhat chill. So far as these half glances allowed them to judge, there appeared to be nothing near to it, nothing upon its brink.

"It's of no good marching right up to it," said Mrs. Jones, the baker's wife. "The ghost mightn't come at all, if it saw all us there. Let's get inside the trees."

Mrs. Jones meant inside the grove of trees. The proposition was most acceptable, and they took up their position, the pond in view, peeping out, and conversing in a whisper. By and by they heard the church clock strike eight.

"I wish it 'ud make haste," exclaimed Susan Peckaby, with some impatience. "I don't never like to be away from home long together, for fear of that there blessed white animal arriving."

"He'd wait, wouldn't he?" sarcastically rejoined Polly Dawson. "He'd——"

A prolonged hush—sh—sh! from the rest restored silence. Something was rustling the trees at a distance. They huddled closer together, and caught hold one of another.

Nothing appeared. The alarm went off. And they waited, without result, until the clock struck nine. The artificial strength within them had cooled by that time, their ardour had cooled, and they were feeling chill and tired. Susan Peckaby was upon thorns, she said, and urged their departure.

" *You* can go if you like," was the answer.
" Nobody wants to keep you."

Susan Peckaby measured the distance between
the pond and the way she had to go, and came to the
determination to risk it.

" I'll make a rush for it, I think," said she.   " I
shan't see nothing.   For all I know, that quadruple
may be right afore our door now.   If he——"

Susan Peckaby stopped, her voice subsiding into
a shriek.   She, and those with her, became simul-
taneously aware that some white figure was bearing
down upon them.   The shrieks grew awful.

It proved to be Roy in his white fustian jacket.
Roy had never had the privilege of hearing a dozen
women shriek in concert before ; at least, like this.
His loud derisive laugh was excessively aggravating.
What with that, what with the fright his appearance
had really put them in, they all tore off, leaving
some hard words for him ; and never stopped to
take breath until they burst into the shop of Mrs.
Duff.

It was rather an ignominious way of returning,
and Mrs. Duff did not spare her comments.   If she
had went out to meet the ghost, sh'd ha' stopped
till the ghost came, *she* would !   Mrs. Jones rejoined
that them watched-for ghosts, as she had heered,
never did come—which she had said so afore she
went out !

Master Dan, considerably recovered, was down-
stairs then.   Rather pale and shaky, and accommo-
dated with a chair and pillow, in front of the kitchen

fire. The expedition pressed into the kitchen, and
five hundred questions were lavished upon the boy.

" What was it dressed in, Dan ?   Did you get a
good sight of her face, Dan ?   Did it look just as
Rachel used to look ?   Speak up, Dan."

" It warn't Rachel at all," replied Dan.

This unexpected assertion brought a pause of dis-
comfiture. " He's head ain't right yet," observed
Mrs. Duff, apologetically; " and that's why I've not
asked him nothing."

"Yes, it is right, mother," said Dan.   " I never
see Rachel last night.   I never said as I did."

Another pause : spent in contemplating Dan.   " I
knowed a case like this, once afore," observed old
Miss Till, who carried round the milk to Deerham.
" A boy got a fright, and they couldn't bring him to
at all.   Epsum salts did it at last.   Three pints of
'em they give, I think it was, and that brought his
mind round."

" It's a good remedy," acquiesced Mrs. Jones.
" There's nothing like plenty of Epsum salts for
boys.   I'd try 'em on him, Mother Duff."

" Dan, dear," said Susan Peckaby, insinuatingly
—for she had come in along with the rest, ignoring for the moment what might be waiting at
her door—" was it in the pound as you saw
Rachel's ghost ? "

" 'Twarn't Rachel's ghost as I did see," persisted
Dan.

" Tell us who it was, then ? " asked she, humouring him.

The boy answered. But he answered below his breath; as if he scarcely dared to speak the name aloud. His mother partially caught it.

"Whose?" she exclaimed, in a sharp voice, her tone changing. And Dan spoke a little louder.

"It was Mr. Frederick Massingbird's!"

CHAPTER XVIII.

OLD Matthew Frost sat in his room at the back of the kitchen. It was his bed-room and sitting-room combined. Since he had grown feeble, the bustle of the kitchen and of Robin's family disturbed him, and he sat much in his chamber, they frequently taking his dinner in to him.

A thoroughly comfortable arm-chair had Matthew. It had been the gift of Lionel Verner. At his elbow was a small round table, of very dark wood, rubbed to brightness. On that table Matthew's large Bible might generally be found open, and Matthew's spectacled eyes bending over it. But the Bible was closed to-day. He sat in deep thought. His hands clasped upon his stick; something after the manner of old Mr. Verner; and his eyes fixed through the open window at the September sun, as it played on the gooseberry and currant bushes in the cottage garden.

The door opened, and Robin's wife—her hands and arms white, for she was kneading dough—appeared, showing in Lionel: who had come on after his conversation with Mrs. Duff, as you read of in the last chapter; for it is necessary to go back

a few hours. One cannot tell two portions of a
history at one and the same time. The old man
rose, and stood leaning on his stick.

"Sit down, Matthew," said Lionel, in a kindly
tone. "Don't let me disturb you." He made him
go into his seat again, and took a chair opposite to
him.

"The time's gone, sir, for me to stand afore you.
That time must go for us all."

"Ay, that it must, Matthew, if we live. I came
in to speak to Robin. His wife says she does not
know where he is."

"He's here and there and everywhere," was
old Matthew's answer. "One never knows how
to take him, sir, or when to see him. My late
master's bounty to me, sir, is keeping us in
comfort, but I often ask Robin what he'll do
when I am gone. It gives me many an hour's
care, sir. Robin, he don't earn the half of a living
now."

"Be easy, Matthew," was Lionel's answer. "I
am not sure that the annuity, or part of it, will not
be continued to Robin. My uncle left it in my
charge to do as I should see fit. I have never
mentioned it, even to you: and I think it might
be as well for you not to speak of it to Robin. It
is to be hoped that he will get steady and hard-
working again: were he to hear that there was a
chance of his being kept without work, he might
never become so."

"The Lord bless my old master!" aspirated

Matthew, lifting his hands. "The Lord bless you, sir! There's not many gentlemen would do for us what him and you have."

Lionel bent his head forward, and lowered his voice to a whisper. "Matthew, what is this that I hear, of Robin's going about the grounds at night with a loaded gun?"

Matthew flung up his hands. Not with the reverence of the past minute, but with a gesture of despair. "Heaven knows what he does it for, sir! I'd keep him in: but it's beyond me."

"I know you would. You went yourself after him last night, Broom tells me."

Matthew's eyes fell. He hesitated much in his answer. "I—yes, sir,—I—I couldn't get him home. It's a pity."

"You got as far as the brick-kilns, I hear. I was surprised. I don't think you should be out at night, Matthew."

"No, sir, I am not a-going again."

The words this time were spoken readily enough. But, from some cause or other, the old man was evidently embarrassed. His eyes were not lifted, and his clear face had gone red. Lionel searched his imagination for a reason, and could only connect it with his son.

"Matthew," said he, "I am about to ask you a painful question. I hope you will answer it. Is Robin perfectly sane?"

"Ay, sir, as sane as I am. Unsettled he is, ever dwelling on poor Rachel, ever thinking of revenge:

but his senses be as much his as they ever were.
I wish his mind could be set at rest."

"At rest in what way?"

"As to who it was that did the harm to Rachel.
He has had it in his head for a long while, sir,
that it was Mr. John Massingbird: but he can't
be certain, and it's the uncertainty that keeps his
mind on the worrit."

"Do you know where he picked up the notion
that it was Mr. John Massingbird?" inquired
Lionel, remembering the conversation on the same
point that Robin had once held with him, on that
very garden bench, in the face of which he and
Matthew were now sitting.

Old Matthew shook his head. "I never could
learn, sir. Robin's a dutiful son to me, but he'd
never tell me that. I know that Mr. John Massingbird has been like a pill in his throat this many
a day. Oftentimes have I felt thankful that he was
dead, or Robin would surely have gone out to
where he was, and murdered him. Murder wouldn't
mend the ill, sir—as I have told him many a time."

"Indeed it would not," replied Lionel. "The
very fact of Mr. John Massingbird's being dead,
should have the effect of setting Robin's mind at
rest—if it was to him that his suspicions were
directed. For my part, I think Robin is wrong in
suspecting him."

"I think so too, sir. I don't know how it is, but
I can't bring my mind to suspect him more than
anybody else. I have thought over things in this

light, and I have thought 'em over in that light; and I'd rather incline to believe that she got acquainted with some stranger, poor dear! than that it was anybody known to us. Robin is in doubt : he has had some cause given him to suspect Mr. John Massingbird, but he is not sure, and it's that doubt, I say, that worrits him."

" At any rate, doubt or no doubt, there is no cause for him to go about at night with a gun. What does he do it for ? "

" I have asked him, sir, and he does not answer. He seems to me to be on the watch."

" On the watch for what ? " rejoined Lionel.

" I'm sure I don't know," said old Matthew. " If you'd say a word to him, sir, it might stop it. He got a foolish notion into his mind that poor Rachel's spirit might come again, and he'd used to be about the pond pretty near every moonlight night. That fancy passed off, and he has gone to his bed at night as the rest of us have, up to the last week or so, when he has taken to go out again, and to carry a gun."

" It was a foolish notion," remarked Lionel. " The dead do not come again, Matthew."

Matthew made no reply.

" I must try and come across Robin," said Lionel, rising. " I wish you would tell him to come up to me, Matthew."

" Sir, if you desire that he shall wait upon you at Verner's Pride, he will be sure to do so," said the old man, leaning on his stick as he stood.

"He has not got to the length of disobeying an order of yours. I'll tell him."

It happened that Lionel did "come across" Robin Frost. Not to any effect, however, for he could not get to speak to him. Lionel was striking across some fields towards Deerham Court, when he came in view of Roy and Robin Frost leaning over a gate, their heads together in close confab. It looked very much as though they were talking secrets. They looked up and saw him; but when he reached the place, both were gone. Roy was in sight, but the other had entirely disappeared. Lionel lifted his voice.

"Roy, I want you."

Roy could not feign deafness, although there was every appearance that he would like to do it. He turned and approached, putting his hand to his hat in a half surly manner.

"Where's Robin Frost?"

"Robin Frost, sir? He was here a minute or two agone. I met him accidental, and I stopped him to ask what he was about, that he hadn't been at work this three days. He went on his way then, down the gap. Did you want him, sir?"

Lionel Verner's perceptive faculties were tolerably developed. That Roy was endeavouring to blind him, he had no doubt. They had not met "accidental," and the topic of conversation had not been Robin's work—of that he felt sure. Roy and Robin Frost might meet and talk together all day long, it was nothing to him: why they should strive to deceive him was the only curious part about it. Both had striven to avoid meeting him; and Roy was talking to him now unwillingly. In a general way, Robin Frost was fond of meeting and receiving a word from Mr. Verner.

"I shall see him another time," carelessly remarked Lionel. " Not so fast, Roy,"—for the man was turning away—"I have not done with you. Will you be good enough to inform me what you were doing in front of my house last night ? "

" I wasn't doing anything, sir.   I wasn't there."

" Oh, yes, you were," said Lionel. " Recollect yourself. You were posted under the large yew tree on the lawn, watching my drawing-room windows."

Roy looked up at this, the most intense surprise in his countenance. " I never was on your lawn last night, sir; I wasn't near it. Leastways not nearer than the side field. I happened to be in that, and I got through a gap in the hedge, on to the high road."

" Roy, I believe that you *were* on the lawn last night, and watching the house," persisted Lionel, looking fixedly at his countenance. For the life of him he could not tell whether the man's surprise was genuine, his denial real. " What business had you there ? "

" I declare to goodness, if it was the last word I had to speak, that I was not on your lawn, sir,— that I did not watch the house. I did not go near the house. I crossed the side field, cornerwise, and

got out into the road ; and that's the nearest I was
to the house last night."

Roy spoke unusually impressive for him, and
Lionel began to believe that, so far, he was telling
truth. He did not make any immediate reply, and
Roy resumed.

"What cause have you got to accuse me, sir?
I shouldn't be likely to watch your house—why
should I ?"

"Some man was watching it," replied Lionel.
"As you were seen in the road shortly afterwards,
close to the side field, I came to the conclusion that
it was you."

"I can be upon my oath that it wasn't, sir,"
answered Roy.

"Very well," replied Lionel, "I accept your
denial. But allow me to give you a recommenda-
tion, Roy,—not to trouble yourself with my affairs
in any way. They do not concern you; they never
will concern you; therefore, don't meddle with
them."

He walked away as he spoke. Roy stood and
gazed after him, a strange expression on his
countenance. Had Lucy Tempest seen it, she
might have renewed her warning to Lionel. And
yet she would have been puzzled to tell the
meaning of the expression, for it did not look like
a threatening one.

Had Lionel Verner turned up Clay Lane, upon
leaving Matthew Frost's cottage, instead of down
it, to take a path across the fields at the back, he

would have encountered the Vicar of Deerham. That gentleman was paying parochial visits that day in Deerham, and in due course he came to Matthew Frost's. He and Matthew had long been upon confidential terms : the clergyman respected Matthew, and Matthew revered his pastor.

Mr. Bourne took the seat which Lionel had but recently vacated. He was so accustomed to the old man's habitual countenance that he could detect every change in it : and he saw that something was troubling him.

"I am troubled in more ways than one, sir," was the old man's answer. "Poor Robin, he's giving me trouble again : and last night, sir, I had a sort of fright. A shock, it may be said. I can't overget it."

"What was its nature ? " asked Mr. Bourne.

"I don't much like to speak of it, sir : and, beside yourself, there's not a living man that I'd open my lips to. It's an unpleasant thing to have upon the mind. Mr. Verner, he was here but a few minutes a-gone, and I felt before him like a guilty man that has something to conceal. When I have told it to you, sir, you'll be hard of belief."

"Is it connected with Robin ? "

"No, sir. But it was my going after Robin that led to it, as may be said. Robin, sir, has took these last few nights to go out with a gun. It has worrited me so, sir, fearing some mischief might ensue, that I couldn't sleep ; and last evening, I thought I'd hobble out and see if I couldn't get him home.

Chuff, he said, as he had seen him go toward the brickfield, and I managed to get down : and, sure enough, I came upon Robin. He was lying down at the edge of the field, watching, as it seemed to me. I couldn't get him home, sir. I tried hard, but 'twas of no use. He spoke respectful to me, as he always does : 'Father, I have got my work to do, and I must do it. You go back home, and go to sleep in quiet.' It was all I could get from him, sir, and at last I turned to go back——"

"What was Robin doing?" interrupted Mr. Bourne.

"Sir, I suppose it's just some fancy or other that he has got into his head, as he used to get after the poor child died. Mr. Verner has just asked me whether he is sane, but there's nothing of that sort wrong about him. You mind the clump of trees that stands out, sir, between here and the brickfield, by the path that would lead to Verner's Pride?" added old Matthew in an altered tone.

"Yes," said Mr. Bourne.

"I had just got past it, sir, when I saw a figure crossing that bare corner from the other trees. A man's shape, it looked like. Tall and shadowy it was, wearing what looked like a long garment, or a woman's riding-habit, trailing nearly on the ground. The very moment my eyes fell upon it, I felt that it was something strange, and when the figure passed me, turning its face right upon me,—I *saw* the face, sir."

Old Matthew's manner was so peculiar, his pause

so impressive, that Mr. Bourne could only gaze at
him, and wait in wonder for what was coming.

"Sir, it was the face of one who has been dead
these two years past—Mr. Frederick Massingbird."

If the rector had gazed at old Matthew before, he
could only stare now. That the calm, sensible old
man should fall into so extraordinary a delusion,
was incomprehensible. He might have believed it
of Deerham in general, but not of Matthew Frost.

"Matthew, you must have been deceived," was
his quiet answer.

"No, sir. There never was another face like Mr.
Frederick Massingbird's. Other features may have
been made like his—it's not for me to say they have
not—but whose else would have the black mark
upon it? The moonlight was full upon it, and
I could see even the little lines shooting out from
the cheek, so bright was the night. The face
was turned right upon me as it passed, and I am
as clear about its being his as I am that it was
me looking at it."

"But you know it is a thing absolutely impossible," urged Mr. Bourne. "I think you must
have dreamt this, Matthew."

Old Matthew shook his head. "I wouldn't have
told you a dream, sir. It turned me all in a maze.
I never felt the fatigue of a step all the way home
after it. When I got in, I couldn't eat my supper;
I couldn't go to bed. I sat up thinking, and the
wife, she came in and asked what ailed me that
I didn't go to rest. I had got no sleep in my eyes,

Q 2

I told her, which was true : for, when I did get to
bed, it was hours afore I could close 'em."

" But, Matthew, I tell you that it is impossible.
You must have been mistaken."

" Sir, until last night, had anybody told me such
a thing, I should have said it was impossible. You
know, sir, I have never been given to such fancies.
There's no doubt, sir ; there's *no doubt* that it was
the spirit of Mr. Frederick Massingbird."

Matthew's clear intelligent eye was fixed firmly
on Mr. Bourne's—his face, as usual, bending a
little forward. Mr. Bourne had never believed in
" spirits: " clergymen, as a rule, do not. A half
smile crossed his lips.

" Were you frightened ? " he asked.

" I was not frightened, sir, in the sense that you,
perhaps, put the question. I was surprised ;
startled. As I might have been surprised and
startled at seeing anybody I least expected to see
—somebody that I had thought was miles away.
Since poor Rachel's death, sir, I have lived, so to
say, in communion with spirits : what with Robin's
talking of his hope to see *hers*, and my constantly
thinking of her ; knowing also that it can't be long,
in the course of nature, before I am one myself, I
have grown to be, as it were, familiar with the dead
in my mind. Thus, sir, in that sense, no fear came
upon me last night. I don't think, sir, I should
feel fear at meeting or being alone with a spirit, any
more than I should at meeting a man. But I was
startled and disturbed."

"Matthew," cried Mr. Bourne, in some perplexity, "I had always believed you superior to these foolish things. Ghosts might do well enough for the old days, but the world has grown older and wiser. At any rate, the greater portion of it has."

"If you mean, sir, that I was superior to the belief in ghosts, you are right. I never had a grain of faith in such superstition in my life; and I have tried all means to convince my son what folly it was of him to hover round about the willow pond, with any thought that Rachel might 'come again.' No, sir, I have never been given to it."

"And yet you deliberately assure me, Matthew, that you saw a ghost last night!"

"Sir, that it was Mr. Frederick Massingbird, dead or alive, that I saw, I must hold to. We know that he is dead, sir: his wife buried him in that far land; so what am I to believe? The face looked ghastly white: not like a person's living."

Mr. Bourne mused. That Frederick Massingbird was dead and buried, there could not be the slightest doubt. He hardly knew what to make of old Matthew. The latter resumed.

"Had I been flurried or terrified by it, sir, so as to lose my presence of mind, or if I was one of those timid folks that see signs in dreams, or take every white post to be a ghost, that they come to on a dark night, you might laugh at and disbelieve me. But I tell it to you, sir, as you say, deliberately: just as it happened. I can't have much longer time to live, sir; but I'd stake it all on the truth that it

was the spirit of Mr. Frederick Massingbird. When
you have once known a man, there are a hundred
points by which you may recognise him, beyond
possibility of being mistaken.   They have got a
story in the place, sir, to-day—as you may have
heard—that my poor child's ghost appeared to Dan
Duff last night, and that the boy has been senseless
ever since.   It has struck me, sir, that perhaps he
also saw what I did."

Mr. Bourne paused.   "Did you say anything of
this to Mr. Verner ? "

"Not I, sir.   As I tell you, I felt like a guilty
man in his presence, one with something to hide.
He married Mr. Fred's widow, pretty creature, and
it don't seem a nice thing to tell him.   If it had
been the other gentleman's spirit, Mr. John's, I
should have told him at once."

Mr. Bourne rose.   To argue with old Matthew
in his present frame of mind, appeared to be about
as useless a waste of time as to argue with Susan
Peckaby on the subject of the white donkey.   He
told him he would see him again in a day or two,
and took his departure.

But he did not dismiss the subject from his
thoughts.   No, he could not do that.   He was
puzzled.   Such a tale from one like old Matthew—
calm, pious, sensible, and verging on the grave,
made more impression on Mr. Bourne than all
Deerham could have made.   Had Deerham come
to him with the story, he would have flung it to the
winds.

He began to think that some person, from evil
design or love of mischief, must be personating
Frederick Massingbird. It was a natural conclusion. And Matthew's surmise, that the same thing
might have alarmed Dan Duff, was perfectly probable. Mr. Bourne determined to ascertain the
latter fact, as soon as Dan should be in a state of
sufficient convalescence, bodily and mentally, to
give an account. He had already paid one visit to
Mrs. Duff's—as that lady informed Lionel.

Two or three more visits he paid there during the
day, but not until night did he find Dan revived.
In point of fact, the clergyman penetrated to the
kitchen just after that startling communication had
been made by Dan. The women were standing in
consternation when the vicar entered : one of them
strongly recommending that the copper furnace
should be heated, and Dan plunged into it to
" bring him round."

" How is he now ? " began Mr. Bourne. " Oh !
I see : he is sensible."

" Well, sir, I don't know," said Mrs. Duff. " I'm
afraid as his head's a-going right off. He persists
in saying now that it wasn't the ghost of Rachel at
all,—but somebody else's."

" If he was put into a good hot furnace, sir, and
kep' at a even heat up to biling pint for half an
hour—that is, as near biling as his skin could bear
it—I know it'ud do wonders," spoke up Mrs. Chuff.
" It's a excellent remedy, where there's a furnace
convenient, and water not short."

" Suppose you allow me to be alone with him for a few minutes," suggested Mr. Bourne. " We will try and find out what will cure him, won't we, Dan ?"

The women filed out one by one. Mr. Bourne sat down by the boy, and took his hand. In a soothing manner he talked to him, and drew from him by gentle degrees the whole tale, so far as Dan's memory and belief went. The boy shook in every limb as he told it. He could not boast immunity from ghostly fears as did old Matthew Frost.

" But, my boy, you should know that there are no such things as ghosts," urged Mr. Bourne. " When once the dead have left this world, they do not come back to it again."

" I see'd it, sir," was Dan's only argument—an all-sufficient one with him. " It was stood over the pool, it was, and it turned round right upon me as I went up. I see the porkypine on his cheek, sir, as plain as anything."

The same account as old Matthew's!

" How was the person dressed ?" asked Mr. Bourne. " Did you notice ?"

" It had got on some'at long—a coat or a skirt, or some'at. It was as thin as thin, sir."

" Dan, shall I tell you what it was—as I believe ? It was somebody dressed up to frighten you and other timid persons."

Dan shook his head. " No, sir, 'twasn't. 'Twas the ghost of Mr. Frederick Massingbird."

CHAPTER XIX

STRANGE rumours began to be rife in Deerham. The extraordinary news told by Dan Duff would have been ascribed to some peculiar hallucination of that gentleman's brain, and there's no knowing but that the furnace might have been tried as a cure, had not other testimony arisen to corroborate it. Four or five different people, in the course of as many days—or rather nights—saw, or professed to have seen, the apparition of Frederick Massingbird.

One of them was Master Cheese. He was one night coming home from paying a professional visit —in slight, straightforward cases Jan could trust him —when he saw by the roadside what appeared to be a man standing up under the hedge, as if he had taken his station there to look at the passers-by.

"He's up to no good," quoth Master Cheese to himself. "I'll go and dislodge the fellow."

Accordingly Master Cheese turned off the path where he was walking, and crossed the waste bit— only a yard or two in breadth—that ran by the side of the road. Master Cheese, it must be confessed, did not want for bravery; he had a great deal rather face danger of any kind than hard work; and the rumour about Fred Massingbird's ghost had been rare nuts for him to crack. Up he went, having no thought in his head at that moment of ghosts, but rather of poachers.

"I say, you fellow—" he was beginning, and there he stopped dead.

He stopped dead, both in step and tongue. The figure, never moving, never giving the faintest indication that it was alive, stood there like a statue. Master Cheese looked in its face, and saw the face of the late Frederick Massingbird.

It is *not* pleasant to come across a dead man at moonlight—a man whose body has been safely reposing in the ground ever so long ago. Master Cheese did not howl as Dan Duff had done. He set off down the road: he was too fat to propel himself over or through the hedge, though that was the nearest way: he took to his heels down the road, and arrived in an incredibly short space of time at home, bursting into the surgery and astonishing Jan and the surgery boy.

"I say, Jan, though, haven't I had a fright?"

Jan, at the moment, was searching in the prescription-book. He raised his eyes, and looked over the counter. Master Cheese's face had turned white, and drops of wet were pouring off it—in spite of his bravery.

"What have you been at?" asked Jan.

"I saw the thing they are talking about, Jan. It *is* Fred Massingbird's."

Jan grinned. That Master Cheese's fright was

genuine there could be no mistaking, and it amused Jan excessively.

"What had you been taking?" asked he, in his incredulity.

"I had taken nothing," retorted Master Cheese, who did not like the ridicule. "I had not had the opportunity of taking anything—unless it was your medicine. Catch me tapping that! Look here, Jan. I was coming by Crow Corner, when I saw a something standing back in the hedge. I thought it was some poaching fellow hiding there, and went up to dislodge him. Didn't I wish myself up in the skies? It was the face of Fred Massingbird."

"The face of your fancy," slightingly returned Jan.

"I swear it was, then! There! There's no mistaking *him*. The hedgehog on his cheek looked larger and blacker than ever."

Master Cheese did not fail to talk of this abroad: the surgery boy, Bob, who had listened with open ears, did not fail to talk of it, and it spread throughout Deerham; additional testimony to that, already accumulated. In a few days' time, the commotion was at its height; nearly the only persons who remained in ignorance of the reported facts being the master and mistress of Verner's Pride, and those connected with them, relatives on either side.

That some great internal storm of superstition was shaking Deerham, Lionel knew. In his happy ignorance, he attributed it to the rumour which had first been circulated, touching Rachel's ghost. He

was an ear-witness to an angry colloquy at home.
Some indispensable trifle for his wife's toilette was
required suddenly from Deerham one evening, and
Mademoiselle Benoite ordered that it should be
sent for. But not one of the maids would go. The
French woman insisted, and there ensued a stormy
war. The girls, one and all, declared they'd rather
give up their service, than go abroad after nightfall.

When the fears and the superstitions came palpably in Lionel's way, he made fun of it—as Jan
might have done. Once or twice he felt half provoked; and asked the people, in a tone between
earnest and jest, whether they were not ashamed of
themselves. Little reply made they: not one of
them but seemed to shrink from mentioning to
Lionel Verner the name that the ghost had borne
in life.

On nearly the last evening that it would be light
during this moon, Mr. Bourne started from home
to pay a visit to Mrs. Hook, the labourer's wife.
The woman had been ailing for some time: partly
from natural illness, partly from chagrin—for her
daughter Alice was the talk of the village—and she
had now become seriously ill. On this day Mr.
Bourne had accidentally met Jan: and, in conversing upon parish matters, he had inquired after
Mrs. Hook.

"Very much worse," was Jan's answer. "Unless
a change takes place, she'll not last many days."

The clergyman was shocked: he had not deemed

her to be in danger. " I will go and see her to-day," said he. " You can tell her that I am coming."

He was a conscientious man; liking to do his duty: and especially kind to those that were in sickness or trouble. Neither did he willingly break a specific promise. He made no doubt that Jan delivered the message: and therefore he went; though it was late at night when he started, other duties having detained him throughout the day.

His most direct way from the vicarage to Hook's cottage, took him past the willow pond. *He* had no fear of ghosts, and therefore he chose it, in preference to going down Clay Lane, which was further round. The willow pool looked lonely enough as he passed it, its waters gleaming in the moonlight, its willows bending. A little farther on, the clergyman's ears became alive to the sound of sobs, as from a person in distress. There was Alice Hook, seated on a bench underneath some elm-trees, sobbing enough to break her heart.

However the girl might have got herself under the censure of the neighbourhood, it is a clergyman's office to console, rather than to condemn. And he could not help liking pretty Alice : she had been one of the most tractable pupils in his Sunday-school. He addressed her as soothingly, as considerately, as though she were one of the first ladies in his parish : harshness would not mend the matter now. Her heart opened to the kindness.

" I've broke mother's heart, and killed her !"

cried she, with a wild burst of sobs. "But for me, she might have got well."

"She may get well still, Alice," replied the vicar. "I am going on to see her now. What are you doing here?"

"I am on my way, sir, to get the fresh physic for her. Mr. Jan, he said this morning as somebody was to go for it: but the rest have been out all day. As I came along, I got thinking of the time, sir, when I could go about by daylight with my head up, like the best of 'em; and it overcame me."

She rose up, dried her eyes with her shawl, and Mr. Bourne proceeded onwards. He had not gone far, when something came rushing past him from the opposite direction. It seemed more like a thing than a man, with its swift pace—and he recognised the face of Frederick Massingbird.

Mr. Bourne's pulses stood still, and then gave a bound onwards. Clergyman though he was, he could not, for his life, have helped the queer feeling which came over him. He had sharply rebuked the superstition in his parishioners; had been inclined to ridicule Matthew Frost; had cherished a firm and unalterable belief that some foolish wight was playing pranks with the public; but all these suppositions and convictions faded in this moment: and the clergyman felt that that which had rustled past was the veritable dead-and-gone Frederick Massingbird, in the spirit or in the flesh.

He shook the feeling off—or strove to shake it. That it was Frederick Massingbird in the flesh he did not give a second supposition to: and that it could be Frederick Massingbird in the spirit, was opposed to every past belief of the clergyman's life. But he had never seen such a likeness: and though the similarity in the features might be accidental, what of the black star?

He strove to shake the feeling off; to say to himself that some one, bearing a similar face, must be in the village; and he went on to his destination. Mrs. Hook was better: but she was lying in the place unattended, all of them out somewhere or other. The clergyman talked to her and read to her: and then waited impatiently for the return of Alice. He did not care to leave the woman alone.

"Where are they all?" he asked, not having inquired before.

They were gone to the wake at Broxley, a small place some two miles distant. Of course! Had Mr. Bourne remembered the wake, he need not have put the question.

An arrival at last. It was Jan. Jan, attentive to poor patients as he was to rich ones, had come striding over, the last thing. They asked him if he had seen anything of Alice in his walk. But Jan had come across from Deerham Court, and that would not be the girl's road. Another minute, and the husband came in. The two gentlemen left together.

"She is considerably better, to-night," remarked Jan. "She'll get about now, if she does not fret too much over Alice."

"It is strange where Alice can have got to," remarked Mr. Bourne. Her prolonged absence, coupled with the low spirits the girl appeared to be in, rather weighed upon his mind. "I met her as I was coming here an hour ago," he continued. "She ought to have been home long before this."

"Perhaps she has encountered the ghost," said Jan, in a joke.

"I saw it to-night, Jan."

"Saw what?" asked Jan, looking at Mr. Bourne.

"The—the party that appears to be personating Frederick Massingbird."

"Nonsense!" uttered Jan.

"I did. And I never saw such a likeness in my life."

"Even to the porcupine," ridiculed Jan.

"Even to the porcupine," gravely replied Mr. Bourne. "Jan, I am not joking. Moreover, I do not consider it a subject for a joke. If any one is playing the trick, it is an infamous thing, most disrespectful to your brother and his wife. And if not——"

"If not—what?" asked Jan.

"In truth, I stopped because I can't continue. Frederick Massingbird's spirit it cannot be—unless all our previous belief in the non-appearance of spirits is to be upset—and it cannot be Frederick Massingbird in life. He died in Australia, and was buried there. I am puzzled, Jan."

Jan was not. Jan only laughed. He believed there must be something in the moonlight that deceived the people, and that Mr. Bourne had caught the infection from the rest.

"Should it prove to be a trick that any one is playing," resumed the clergyman, "I shall——"

"Halloa!" cried Jan. "What's this? Another ghost?"

They had nearly stumbled over something lying on the ground. A woman, dressed in some light material. Jan stooped.

"It's Alice Hook!" he cried.

The spot was that at which Mr. Bourne had seen her sitting. The empty bottle for medicine in her hand told him that she had not gone upon her errand. She was insensible and cold.

"She has fainted," remarked Jan. "Lend a hand, will you, sir?"

Between them they got her on the bench, and the stirring revived her. She sighed once or twice, and opened her eyes.

"Alice, girl, what is it? How were you taken ill?" asked the vicar.

She looked up at him; she looked at Jan. Then she turned her eyes in an opposite direction, glanced fearfully round, as if searching for some sight that she dreaded; shuddered, and relapsed into insensibility.

"We must get her home," observed Jan.

"There are no means of getting her home in her present state, unless she is carried," said Mr. Bourne.

"That's easy enough," returned Jan. And he

caught her up in his long arms, apparently having to exert little strength in the action. " Put her petticoats right, will you ?" cried he, in his uncere- monious fashion.

The clergyman put her things as straight as he could, as they hung over Jan's arm. " You'll never be able to carry her, Jan," said he.

" Not carry her !" returned Jan. " I could carry you, if put to it."

And away he went, bearing his burden as tenderly and easily as though it had been a little child. Mr. Bourne could hardly keep pace with him.

" You go on, and have the door open," said Jan, as they neared the cottage. " We must get her in without the mother hearing, up-stairs."

They had the kitchen to themselves. Hook, the father, a little the worse for what he had taken, had gone to bed, leaving the door open for his children. They got her in quietly, found a light, and placed her in a chair. Jan took off her bonnet and shawl; he was handy as a woman ; and looked about for something to give her. He could find nothing except water. By-and-by she got better.

Her first movement, when she fully recovered her senses, was to clutch hold of Jan on the one side, of Mr. Bourne on the other.

" Is it gone ?" she gasped, in a voice of the most intense terror.

" Is what gone, child ?" asked Mr. Bourne.

" The ghost," she answered. " It came right up,

sir, just after you left me. I'd rather die than see it again."

She was shaking from head to foot. There was no mistaking that her terror was intense. To attempt to meet it with confuting arguments would have been simply folly, and both gentlemen knew that it would. Mr. Bourne concluded that the same sight, which had so astonished him, had been seen by the girl.

"I sat down again after you went, sir," she re-sumed, her teeth chattering. "I knew there was no mighty hurry for my being back, as you had gone on to mother, and I sat on ever so long, and it came right up again me, brushing my knees with its things as it passed. At the first moment I thought it might be you coming back to say some-thing to me, sir, and I looked up. It turned its face upon me, and I never remembered nothing after that."

"Whose face?" questioned Jan.

"The ghost's, sir. Mr. Fred Massingbird's."

"Bah!" said Jan. "Faces look alike in the moonlight."

"'Twas his face," answered the girl, from between her shaking lips. "I saw its every feature, sir."

"Porcupine and all?" retorted Jan, ironically.

"Porkypine and all, sir. I'm not sure that I should have knowed it at first, but for the porky-pine."

What were they to do with the girl? Leave her there, and go? Jan, who was more skilled in

ailments than Mr. Bourne, thought it possible that
the fright had seriously injured her.

"You must go to bed at once," said he. "I'll just
say a word to your father."

Jan was acquainted with the private arrangements
of the Hooks' household. He knew that there was
but one sleeping apartment for the whole family—
the room above, where the sick mother was lying.
Father, mother, sons, and daughters all slept there
together. The "house" consisted of the kitchen
below and the room above it. There were many such
on the Verner estate.

Jan, carrying the candle to guide him, went softly
up the creaky staircase. The wife was sleeping.
Hook was sleeping, too, and snoring heavily. Jan
had something to do to awake him: shaking seemed
useless.

"Look here," said he, in a whisper, when the
man was aroused, "Alice has had a fright, and I
think she may perhaps be ill through it. If so,
mind you come for me without loss of time. Do
you understand, Hook?"

Hook signified that he did.

"Very well," replied Jan. "Should——"

"What's that! what's that?"

The alarmed cry came from the mother. She
had suddenly awoke.

"It's nothing," said Jan. "I only had a word to
say to Hook. You go to sleep again, and sleep
quietly."

Somehow Jan's presence carried reassurance with

it to most people. Mrs. Hook was contented. "Is Ally not come in yet?" asked she.

"Come in, and down - stairs," replied Jan. "Good night. Now," said he to Alice, when he returned to the kitchen, "you go on to bed and get to sleep: and don't get dreaming of ghosts and goblins."

They were turning out at the door, the clergyman and Jan, when the girl flew to them in a fresh attack of terror.

"I daren't be left alone," she gasped. "Oh, stop a minute! Pray stop, till I be gone up-stairs."

"Here," said Jan, making light of it. "I'll marshal you up."

He held the candle, and the girl flew up the stairs as fast as young Cheese had flown from the ghost. Her breath was panting, her bosom throbbing. Jan blew out the candle, and he and Mr. Bourne departed, merely shutting the door. Labourers' cottages have no fear of midnight robbers.

"What do you think now?" asked Mr. Bourne, as they moved along.

Jan looked at him. "*You* are not thinking, surely, that it is Fred Massingbird's ghost!"

"No. But I should advise Mr. Verner to place a watch, and have the thing cleared up—who it is, and what it is."

"Why Mr. Verner?"

"Because it is on his land that the disturbance is occurring. This girl has been seriously frightened."

"You may have cause to know that, before many hours are over," answered Jan.

"Why! you don't fear that she will be seriously ill?"

، "Time will show," was all the answer given by Jan. "As to the ghost, I'll either believe in him, or disbelieve him, when I come across him. If he were a respectable ghost, he'd confine himself to the churchyard, and not walk in unorthodox places, to frighten folks."

They looked somewhat curiously at the seat near which Alice had fallen; at the willow pond, farther on. There was no trace of a ghost about then—at least, that they could see—and they continued their way. In emerging upon the high road, whom should they meet but old Mr. Bitterworth and Lionel, arm in arm. They had been to an evening meeting of the magistrates at Deerham, and were walking home together.

To see the vicar and surgeon of a country village in company by night, imparts the idea that some one of its inhabitants may be in extremity. It did so now to Mr. Bitterworth:

"Where do you come from?" he asked.

"From Hook's," answered Jan. "The mother's better to-night: but I have had another patient there. The girl Alice has seen the ghost, or fancied that she saw it, and was terrified, literally, out of her senses."

"How is she going on?" asked Mr. Bitterworth.

"Physically, do you mean, sir?"

"No, I meant morally, Jan. If all accounts are true, the girl has been losing herself."

"Law!" said Jan. "Deerham has known that this many a month past. I'd try and stop it, if I were Lionel."

"Stop what?" asked Lionel.

"I'd build 'em better dwellings," composedly went on Jan. "They might be brought up to decency then."

"It's true that decency can't put its head into such dwellings as that of the Hooks'," observed the vicar. "People have accused me of showing leniency to Alice Hook, since the scandal has been known; but I cannot show harshness to her when I think of the home the girl was reared in."

The words pricked Lionel. None could think worse of the homes than he did. He spoke in a cross tone: we are all apt to do so, when vexed with ourselves. "What possesses Deerham to show itself so absurd just now? Ghosts! They only affect fear, it is my belief."

"Alice Hook did not affect it, for one," said Jan. "She may have been frightened to some purpose. We found her lying on the ground, insensible. They are stupid, though, all the lot of them."

"Stupid is not the name for it," remarked Lionel. "A little superstition, following on Rachel's peculiar death, may have been excusable, considering the ignorance of the people here, and the tendency to superstition inherent in human nature. But why it should have been revived now, I cannot imagine."

Mr. Bitterworth and Jan had walked on. The vicar touched Lionel on the arm, not immediately to follow them.

"Mr. Verner, I do not hold good with the policy which seems to prevail, of keeping this matter from you," he said, in a confidential tone. "I cannot see the expediency of it in any way. It is not Rachel Frost's ghost that is said to be terrifying people."

"Whose then?" asked Lionel.

"Frederick Massingbird's."

Lionel paused, as if his ears deceived him.

"*Whose?*" he repeated.

"Frederick Massingbird's."

"How perfectly absurd!" he presently exclaimed.

"True," said Mr. Bourne. "So absurd that, were it not for a circumstance which has happened to-night, I scarcely think I should have brought myself to repeat it. My conviction is, that some person bearing an extraordinary resemblance to Frederick Massingbird is walking about to terrify the neighbourhood."

"I should think there's not another face living, that bears a resemblance to Fred Massingbird's," observed Lionel. "How have you heard this?"

"The first to tell me of it was old Matthew Frost. He saw him plainly, believing it to be Frederick Massingbird's spirit — although he had never believed in spirits before. Dan Duff holds to it that *he* saw it; and now Alice Hook: besides others. I turned a deaf ear to all, Mr. Verner; but to-night

I met one so like Frederick Massingbird that, were Massingbird not dead, I could have sworn it was himself. It was wondrously like him, even to the mark on the cheek."

"I never heard such a tale!" uttered Lionel.

"That is precisely what I said—until to-night. I assure you the resemblance is so great, that if we have all female Deerham in fits, I shall not wonder. It strikes me—it is the only solution I can come to —that some one is personating Frederick Massingbird for the purpose of a mischievous joke—though how they get up the resemblance is another thing. Let me advise you to see into it, Mr. Verner."

Mr. Bitterworth and Jan were turning round in front, waiting; and the vicar hastened on, leaving Lionel glued to the spot where he stood.

CHAPTER XX

PEAL! peal! peal! came the sound of the night-bell at Jan's window as he lay in bed. For Jan had caused the night-bell to be hung there since he was factotum. "Where's the good of waking-up the house?" remarked Jan : and he made the alteration.

Jan got up with the first sound, and put his head out at the window. Upon which, Hook—for he was the applicant—advanced. Jan's window being, as you may remember, nearly on a level with the ground, presented favourable auspices for holding a face to face colloquy with night visitors.

"She's mortal bad, sir," was Hook's salutation.

"Who is?" asked Jan. "Alice, or the missis?"

"Not the missis, sir. The other. But I shouldn't ha' liked to trouble you, if you hadn't ordered me."

"I won't be two minutes," said Jan.

It seemed to Hook that Jan was only one, so speedily did he come out. A belief was popular in Deerham that Mr. Jan slept with his clothes on : no sooner would a night summons be delivered to Jan, than Jan was out with the summoner, ready for the start. Before he had closed the surgery door, through which he had to pass, there came another peal, and a woman ran up to him. Jan recognised her for the cook of a wealthy lady in the Belvedere Road, a Mrs. Ellis.

"Law, sir! what a provident mercy that you are up and ready!" exclaimed she. "My mistress is attacked again."

"Well, you know what to do," returned Jan. "You don't want me."

"But she do want you, sir. I have got orders not to go back without you."

"I suppose she has been eating cucumber again," remarked Jan.

"Only a bit of it, sir. About the half of a small one, she took for her supper. And now the spasms is on her dreadful."

"Of course they are," replied Jan. "She knows how cucumber serves her. Well, I can't come. I'll send Mr. Cheese, if you like. But he can do no more good than you can. Give her the drops and get the hot flannels; that's all."

"You are going out, sir!" cried the woman, in a tone that sounded as if she would like to be impertinent. "*You* are come for him, I suppose?" turning a sharp tongue upon Hook.

"Yes, I be," humbly replied Hook. "Poor Ally—"

The woman set up a scream. "You'd attend *her*, that miserable castaway, afore you'd attend my mistress!" burst out she to Jan. "Who's Ally Hook, by the side of folks of standing?"

"If she wants attendance, she must have it," was the composed return of Jan. "She has got a body and a soul to be saved, as other folks have. She is in danger; your mistress is not."

"Danger! What has that got to do with it?" angrily answered the woman. "You'll never get paid there, sir."

"I don't expect it," returned Jan. "If you'd like Cheese, that's his window," pointing to one in the house. "Throw a handful of gravel up, and tell him I said he was to attend."

Jan walked off with Hook. He heard a crash of gravel behind him; so, concluded the cook was flinging at Mr. Cheese's window in a temper. As she certainly was: giving Mr. Jan some hard words in the process. Just as Lady Verner had never been able to inculcate suavity on Jan, so Dr. West had found it a hopeless task to endeavour to make Jan understand that, in medical care, the rich should be considered before the poor. Take, for example, that *bête noire* of Deerham just now, Alice Hook, and put her by the side of a born duchess: Jan would have gone to the one who had most need of him, without reference to which of the two it might be. Evidently there was little hope for Jan.

Jan, with his long legs, outstripped the stooping and hard-worked labouring man. In at the door and up the stairs he went, into the sleeping room.

Did you ever pay a visit to a room of this social grade? If not, you will deem the introduction of this one highly coloured. Had Jan been a head and shoulders shorter he might have been able to stand up in the lean-to attic, without touching the lath and plaster of the roof. On a low bedstead, on a flock mattress, lay the mother and two children, about eight and ten. How they made room for Hook also, was a puzzle. Opposite to it, on a straw mattress, slept three sons, grown up, or nearly so; between these beds was another straw mattress where lay Alice and her sister, a year younger: no curtains, no screens, no anything. All were asleep, with the exception of the mother and Alice: the former could not rise from her bed; Alice appeared too ill to rise from hers. Jan stooped his head and entered.

A few minutes, and he set himself to arouse the sleepers. They might make themselves comfortable in the kitchen, he told them, for the rest of the night: he wanted room in the place to turn himself round, and they must go out of it. And so he bundled them out. Jan was not given to stand upon ceremony. But it is not a pleasant room to linger in, so we will leave Jan to it.

It was pleasanter at Lady Verner's. Enough of air, and light, and accommodation there. But even in that desirable residence it was not all *couleur de rose.* Vexations intrude into the most luxurious home, whatever may be the superfluity of room, the admirable style of the architecture: and they were just now agitating Deerham Court.

On the morning which rose on the above night—

as lovely a morning as ever September gave us —Lady Verner and Lucy Tempest received each a letter from India. Both were from Colonel Tempest. The contents of Lady Verner's annoyed her, and the contents of Lucy's annoyed *her*.

It appeared that some considerable time back, nearly, if not quite, twelve months, Lucy had privately written to Colonel Tempest, urgently requesting to be allowed to go out to join him. She gave no reason or motive for the request, but urged it strongly. That letter, in consequence of the moving about of Colonel Tempest, had only just reached him: and now had arrived the answer to it. He told Lucy that he should very shortly be returning to Europe: therefore it was useless for her to think of going out.

So far, so good. However Lucy might have been vexed or disappointed at the reply—and she was both; still more at the delay which had taken place—there the matter would have ended. But Colonel Tempest, having no idea that Lady Verner was a stranger to this request; inferring, on the contrary, that she was a party to it, and must therefore be growing tired of her charge, had also written to her an elaborate apology for leaving Lucy so long upon her hands, and for being unable to comply with her wish to be relieved of her. This enlightened Lady Verner as to what Lucy had done.

She was very angry. She was worse than angry; she was mortified. And she questioned Lucy a great deal more closely than that young lady liked, as to what her motive could have been, and why she was tired of Deerham Court.

Lucy, all self-conscious of the motive by which she had been really actuated, stood before her like a culprit. " I am not tired of Deerham Court, Lady Verner. But I wished to be with papa."

" Which is equivalent to saying that you wish to be away from me," retorted my lady. " I ask you why ? "

" Indeed, Lady Verner, I am pleased to be with you; I like to be with you. It was not to be away from you that I wrote. It is a long while since I saw papa: so long, that I seem to have forgotten what he is like."

" Can you assure me, in all open truth, that the wish to be with Colonel Tempest was your sole reason for writing, unbiassed by any private feeling touching Deerham ? " returned Lady Verner, searching her face keenly. " I charge you answer me, Lucy."

Lucy could not answer that it was her sole reason, unless she told an untruth. Her eyes fell under the gaze bent upon her.

" I see," said Lady Verner. " You need not equivocate more. Is it to me that you have taken a dislike ? or to any part of my arrangements ? "

" Believe me, dear Lady Verner, that it is neither to you nor to your home," she answered, the tears rising to her eyes. " Believe me, I am as happy here as I ever was : on that score I have no wish to change."

It was an unlucky admission of Lucy's, "on that score." Of course, Lady Verner immediately pressed to know on what other score the wish might be founded. Lucy pleaded the desire to be with her father, which Lady Verner did not believe ; and she pleaded nothing else. It was not satisfactory to my lady, and she kept Lucy the whole of the morning, harping upon the sore point.

Lionel entered, and interrupted the discussion. Lady Verner put him in possession of the facts. That for some cause which Lucy refused to explain, she wanted to leave Deerham Court; had been writing, twelve months back, to Colonel Tempest, to be allowed to join him in India; and the negative answer had arrived but that morning. Lady Verner would like the motive for her request explained : but Lucy was obstinate, and would not explain it.

Lionel turned his eyes on Lucy. If she had stood self-conscious before Lady Verner, she stood doubly self-conscious now. Her eyelashes were drooping, her cheeks were crimson.

" She says she has no fault to find with me, no fault to find with the arrangements of my house," pursued Lady Verner. " Then I want to know what else it is that should drive her away from Deerham. Look at her, Lionel! That is how she stands : unable to give me an answer."

Lady Verner might equally well have said, Look

at Lionel. *He* stood self-conscious also. Too well he knew the motive—absence from him—which had actuated Lucy. From him, the married man; the man who had played her false; away, anywhere, from witnessing the daily happiness of him and his wife. He read it all, and Lucy saw that he did.

" It were no such strange wish, surely, to be where my dear papa is!" she exclaimed, the crimson of her cheeks turning to scarlet.

" No," murmured Lionel, " no such strange wish. I wish *I* could go to India, and free the neighbourhood of my presence !"

A curious wish ! Lady Verner did not understand it. Lionel gave her no opportunity to inquire its meaning, for he turned to quit the room and the house. She rose and laid her hand upon his arm to detain him.

" I have an engagement," pleaded Lionel.

" A moment yet. Lionel, what *is* this nonsense that is disturbing the equanimity of Deerham ? About a ghost !"

" Ah, what indeed?" returned Lionel, in a careless tone, as if he would make light of it. " You know what Deerham is, mother. Some think Dan Duff saw his own shadow; some, a white cow in the pound. Either is sufficient marvel for Deerham."

" So vulgar a notion !" reiterated Lady Verner, resuming her seat, and taking her essence bottle in her delicately gloved hand. " I wonder you don't stop it, Lionel."

"I!" cried Lionel, opening his eyes in considerable surprise. "How am I to stop it?"

"You are the lord of Deerham. It is vulgar, I say, to have such a report afloat on your estate."

Lionel smiled. "I don't know how you are to put away vulgarity from stargazers and villagers. Or ghosts, either—if they once get ghosts in their heads."

He finally left the Court, and turned towards home. His mother's words about the ghost had brought the subject to his mind. If, indeed, it had required bringing: but the whispered communication of the vicar the previous night had scarcely been out of his thoughts since. It troubled him. In spite of himself, of his good sense and reason, there was an undercurrent of uneasiness at work within him. Why should there be? Lionel could not have explained had he been required to do it. That Frederick Massingbird was dead and buried, there could be no shade of doubt: and ghosts had no place in the creed of Lionel Verner. All true: but the consciousness of uneasiness was there, and he could not ignore it.

In the last few days, the old feeling touching Lucy had been revived with unpleasant force. Since that night which she had spent at his house, when they saw, or fancied they saw, a man hiding himself under the tree, he had thought of her more than was agreeable; more than was right, he would have said, but that he saw not how to avoid it. The little episode of this morning at his mother's house had served to open his eyes most completely: to show him how intense was his love for Lucy Tempest. It must be confessed that his wife did little towards striving to retain his love.

He went along, thinking of these things: he would have put them from him; but he could not. The more he tried, the more unpleasantly vivid they became. " Tush!" said Lionel. " I must be getting nervous! I'll ask Jan to give me a draught."

He was passing Dr. West's as he spoke, and he turned into the surgery. Sitting on the bung of a large stone jar was Master Cheese, his attitude a disconsolate one, his expression of countenance rebellious.

" Is Mr. Jan at home?" asked Lionel.

" No, he's not at home, sir," replied Master Cheese, as if the fact were some personal grievance of his own. " Here's all the patients, all the making up of the physic left in my charge, and I'd like to know how I am to do it? I can't go out to fifty folks at a time?"

" And so you expedite the matter by not going to one! Where is Mr. Jan?"

" He was fetched out in the night to that beautiful Ally Hook," grumbled Master Cheese. " It's a shame, sir, folks are saying, for him to give his time to *her*. I had to leave my warm bed and march out to that fanciful Mother Ellis, through it, who's always getting the spasms. And I had about forty poor here this morning, and couldn't

s 2

get a bit of comfortable breakfast for 'em. Miss
Debb, she never kept my bacon warm, or anything; and somebody had eaten the meat out of
the veal pie when I got back. Jan *will* have
those horrid poor here twice a week, and if I
speak against it, he tells me to hold my tongue."

" But is Mr. Jan not back yet from Hook's ? "

" No, sir, he's not," was the resentful response.
" He has never come back at all since he went,
and that was at four o'clock this morning. If he
had gone to cut off all the arms in the house, he
couldn't have been longer! And I wish him joy
of it! He'll get no breakfast. They have got
nothing for themselves but bread and water."

Lionel left his draught an open question, and
departed. `As he turned into the principal street
again, he saw Master Dan Duff at the door of
his mother's shop. A hasty impulse prompted
Lionel to question the boy of what he saw that
unlucky night; or believed he saw. He crossed
over; but Master Dan retreated inside the shop.
Lionel followed him.

" Well, Dan! Have you overcome the fright
of the cow yet ? "

" Twarn't a cow, please, sir," replied Dan,
timidly. " 'Twere a ghost."

" Whose ghost ? " returned Lionel.

Dan hesitated. He stood first on one leg then
on the other.

" Please, sir, 'twarn't Rachel's," said he, presently.

" Whose then ? " repeated Lionel.

" Please, sir, mother said I warn't to tell you. Roy, he said, if I told it to anybody, I should be took and hunged."

" But I say that you are to tell me," said Lionel. And his pleasant tone, combined, perhaps, with the fact that he was Mr. Verner, effected more with Dan Duff than his mother's sharp tone or Roy's threatening one.

" Please, sir," glancing round to make sure that his mother was not within hearing, " 'twere Mr. Fred Massingbird's. They can't talk me out on't, sir. I see'd the porkypine as plain as I see'd him. He were—"

Dan brought his information to a summary stand-still. Bustling down the stairs was that revered mother. She came in, curtseying fifty times to Lionel. " What could she have the honour of serving him with ? " He was leaning over the counter, and she concluded he had come to patronise the shop.

Lionel laughed. "I am a profitless customer, I believe, Mrs. Duff. I was only talking to Dan."

Dan sidled off to the street-door. Once there, he took to his heels, out of harm's way. Mr. Verner might get telling his mother more particulars, and it was as well to be at a safe distance.

Lionel, however, had no intention to betray trust. He stood chatting a few minutes with Mrs. Duff. He and Mrs. Duff had been great friends when he was an Eton boy: many a time had he ransacked her shop over for flies and gut and other fishing tackle, a supply of which Mrs. Duff professed to keep. She listened to him with a somewhat pre-occupied manner : in point of fact, she was debating a question with herself.

" Sir," said she, rubbing her hands nervously one over the other, " I should like to make bold to ask a favour of you. But I don't know how it might be took. I'm fearful it might be took as a cause of offence."

" Not by me. What is it ? "

" It's a delicate thing, sir, to have to ask about," resumed she. " And I shouldn't venture, sir, to speak to *you*, but that I'm so put to it, and that I've got it in my head it's through the fault of the servants."

She spoke with evident reluctance. Lionel, he scarcely knew why, leaped to the conclusion that she was about to say something regarding the subject then agitating Deerham—the ghost of Frederick Massingbird. Unconsciously to him-self, the pleasant manner changed to one of constraint.

" Say what you have to say, Mrs. Duff."

" Well, sir—but I'm sure I beg a hundred thou-sand pardings for mentioning of it—it's about the bill," she answered, lowering her voice. " If I could be paid, sir, it 'ud be the greatest help to me. I don't know hardly how to keep on."

No revelation touching the ghost could have given

Lionel the surprise imparted by these ambiguous words. But his constraint was gone.

"I do not understand you, Mrs. Duff. What bill?"

"The bill what's owing to me, sir, from Verner's Pride. It's a large sum for me, sir,—thirty-two pound odd. I have to keep up my payments for my goods, sir, whether or not, or I should be a bankrupt to-morrow. Things is hard upon me just now, sir: though I don't want everybody to know it. There's that big son o' mine, Dick, out o' work. If I could have the bill, or only part of it, it 'ud be like a God-send."

"Who owes you the bill?" asked Lionel.

"It's your good lady, sir, Mrs. Verner."

"*Who?*" echoed Lionel, his accent quite a sharp one.

"Mrs. Verner, sir."

Lionel stood gazing at the woman. He could not take in the information: he believed there must be some mistake.

"It were for things supplied between the time Mrs. Verner came home after your marriage, sir, and when she went to London in the spring. The French Madmizel, sir, came down and ordered some on 'em; and Mrs. Verner herself, sir, ordered others."

Lionel looked around the shop. He did not disbelieve the woman's words, but he was in a maze of astonishment. Perhaps a doubt of the Frenchwoman crossed his mind.

"There's nothing here that Mrs. Verner would wear!" he exclaimed.

"There's many odds and ends of things here, sir, as is useful to a lady's tilette—and you'd be surprised, sir, to find how such things mounts up when they be had continual. But the chief part o' the bill, sir, is for two silk gownds as was had of our traveller. Mrs. Verner, sir, she happened to be here when he called in one day last winter, and she saw his patterns, and she chose two dresses, and said she'd buy 'em of me if I ordered 'em. Which in course I did, sir, and paid for 'em, and sent 'em home. I saw her wear 'em both, sir, after they was made up, and very nice they looked."

Lionel had heard quite enough. "Where is the bill?" he inquired.

"It have been sent in, sir, long ago. When I found Mrs. Verner didn't pay it afore she went away, I made bold to write and ask her. Miss West she give me the address in London, and said she wished she could pay me herself. I didn't get a answer, sir, and I made bold to write again, and I never got one then. Twice I have been up to Verner's Pride, sir, since you come home this time, but I can't get to see Mrs. Verner. That French Madmizel's one o' the best I ever see at putting folks off. Sir, it goes again the grain to trouble you; and if I could have got to see Mrs. Verner, I never would have said a word. Perhaps if you'd be so good as to tell her, sir, how hard I'm put to it, she'd send me a little."

"I am sure she will," said Lionel. "You shall have your money to-day, Mrs. Duff."

He turned out of the shop, a scarlet spot of emotion on his cheek. Thirty-two pounds owing to poor Mrs. Duff! Was it *thoughtlessness* on Sibylla's part? He strove to beat down the conviction that it was a less excusable error.

But the Verner pride had been wounded to its very core.

CHAPTER XXI.

GATHERED before a target on the lawn, in their archery costume gleaming with green and gold, was a fair group, shooting their arrows in the air. Far more went into the air than struck the target. They were the visitors of Verner's Pride: and Sibylla, the hostess, was the gayest, the merriest, the fairest among them.

Lionel came on to the terrace, descended the steps, and crossed the lawn to join them: as courtly, as apparently gay, as if that bill of Mrs. Duff's was not making havoc of his heartstrings. They all ran to surround him: it was not often they had so attractive a host to surround: and attractive men are, and always will be, welcome to women. A few minutes, a quarter of an hour given to them, an unruffled smoothness on his brow, a smile upon his lips, and then he contrived to draw his wife aside.

"Oh, Lionel, I forgot to tell you," she exclaimed. "Poynton has been here. He knows of the most charming pair of grey ponies, he says. And they can be ours if secured at once."

"I don't want grey ponies," replied Lionel.

"But I do," cried Sibylla. "You say I am too timid to drive. It is all nonsense; I should soon get over the timidity. I *will* learn to drive, Lionel. Mrs. Jocelyn, come here," she called out.

Mrs. Jocelyn, a young and pretty woman, almost as pretty as Sibylla, answered to the summons.

"Tell Mr. Verner what Poynton said about the ponies."

"Oh, you must not miss the opportunity," cried Mrs. Jocelyn to Lionel. "They are perfectly beautiful, the man said. Very dear, of course; but you know nobody looks at money when buying horses for a lady. Mrs. Verner must have them. You might secure them to-day."

"I have no room in my stables for more horses," said Lionel, smiling at Mrs. Jocelyn's eagerness.

"Yes you have, Lionel," interposed his wife. "Or, if not, room must be made. I have ordered the ponies to be brought."

"I shall send them back," said Lionel, laughing.

"Don't you wish your wife to take to driving, Mr. Verner? Don't you like to see a lady drive? Some do not."

"I think there is no necessity for a lady to drive, while she has a husband at her side to drive for her," was the reply of Lionel.

"Well—if I had such a husband as you to drive for me, I don't know but I might subscribe to that doctrine," candidly avowed Mrs. Jocelyn. "*I* would not miss these ponies, were I Mrs. Verner. You can drive them, you know. They are calling me. It is my turn, I suppose."

She ran back to the shooting. Sibylla was following her, but Lionel caught her hand and drew her into a covered walk. Placing her hand within his arm, he began to pace it.

"I must go back, too, Lionel."

"Presently. Sibylla, I have been terribly vexed this morning."

"Oh, now Lionel, don't you begin about 'vexing,'" interrupted Sibylla, in the foolish, light, affected manner, which had grown worse of late, more intolerable to Lionel. "I have ordered the ponies. Poynton will send them in; and if there's really not room in the stables, you must see about it, and give orders that room must be made."

"I cannot buy the ponies," he firmly said. "My dear, I have given in to your every wish, to your most trifling whim; but, as I told you a few days ago, these ever-recurring needless expenses I cannot stand. Sibylla"—and his voice grew hoarse—"do you know that I am becoming embarrassed?"

"I don't care if you are," pouted Sibylla. "I must have the ponies."

His heart ached. Was this the loving wife—the intelligent companion for whom he had once yearned?—the friend who should be as his own soul? He had married the Sibylla of his imagination; and he woke to find Sibylla—what she was. The disappointment was heavy upon him always;

but there were moments when he could have cried out aloud in its sharp bitterness.

"Sibylla, you know the state in which some of my tenants live ; the miserable dwellings they are forced to inhabit. I must change this state of things. I believe it to be a duty for which I am accountable to God. How am I to set about it if you ruin me ?"

Sibylla put her fingers to her ears. "I can't stand to listen when you preach, Lionel. It is as bad as a sermon."

It was ever thus. He could not attempt to reason with her. Anything like sensible conversation she could not or would not hold. Lionel, considerate to her as he ever was, felt provoked.

"Do you know that this unfortunate affair of Alice Hook's is laid remotely to me ?" he said, with a sternness, which he could not help, in his tone. "People are saying that if I gave them decent dwellings, decent conduct would ensue. It is so. God knows that I feel its truth more keenly than my reproachers."

"The dwellings are good enough for the poor."

"Sibylla? You cannot think it. The laws of God and man alike demand a change. Child," he continued in a softer tone, as he took her hand in his, "let us bring the case home to ourselves. Suppose that you and I had to sleep in a room a few feet square, no chimney, no air, and that others tenanted it with us ? Girls and boys growing up : nay, grown up, some of them ; men and women as

we are, Sibylla. The beds huddled together, no
space between them ; sickness, fever— "

"I am only shutting my ears," interrupted
Sibylla. "You pretend to be so careful of me—you
would not even let me go to that masked ball in
Paris—and yet you put these horrid pictures into
my mind! I think you ought to be ashamed of it,
Lionel. People sleeping in the same room with
us ! "

"If the picture be revolting, what must be the
reality ? " was his rejoinder. "*They* have to
endure it."

"They are used to it," retorted Sibylla. "They
are brought up to nothing better."

"Just so. And therefore their perceptions of
right and wrong are deadened. The wonder is, not
that Alice Hook has lost herself, but that— "

"I don't want to hear about Alice Hook," interrupted Sibylla. "She is not very good to talk
about."

"I have been openly told, Sibylla, that the
reproach should lie at my door."

"I believe it is not the first reproach of the
kind that has been cast on you," answered Sibylla,
with cutting sarcasm.

He did not know what she meant, or in what
sense to take the remark; but his mind was too
pre-occupied to linger on it. "With these things
staring me in the face, how can I find money for
superfluous vanities ? The time has come when I
am compelled to make a stand against it. I will, I

must, have decent dwellings on my estate, and I shall set about the work without a day's loss of time. For that reason, if for no other, I cannot buy the ponies."

" I have bought them," coolly interrupted Sibylla.

" Then, my dear, you must forgive me if countermand the purchase. I am resolute, Sibylla," he continued, in a firm tone. " For the first time since our marriage, I must deny your wish. I cannot let you bring me to beggary, because it would also involve you. Another year or two of this extravagance, and I should be on the verge of it."

Sibylla flung his arms from her. " Do you want to keep me as a beggar ? I will have the ponies ! "

He shook his head. " The subject is settled, Sibylla. If you cannot think for yourself, I must think for you. But it was not to speak of the ponies that I brought you here. What is it that you owe to Mrs. Duff ? "

Sibylla's colour heightened. " It is no business of yours, Lionel, what I owe her. There may be some trifle or other down in her book. It will be time enough for you to concern yourself with my little petty debts when you are asked to pay them."

" Then that time is the present one, with regard to Mrs. Duff. She applied to me for the money this morning. At least, she asked if I would speak to you—which is the same thing. She says you owe her thirty-two pounds. Sibylla, I had far rather been stabbed than have heard it."

"A fearful sum, truly, to be doled out of your coffers!" cried Sibylla, sarcastically. "You'll never recover it, I should think!"

"Not that, not that," was the reply of Lionel, his tone one of pain. "Sibylla! have you *no* sense of the fitness of things? Is it seemly for the mistress of Verner's Pride to keep a poor woman, as Mrs. Duff is, out of her money; a humble shop-keeper who has to pay her way as she goes on?"

"I wish Fred had lived! He would never have taken me to task as you do."

"I wish he had!" was the retort in Lionel's heart: but he bit his lips to silence : exchanging the words, after a few minutes' pause, for others.

"You would have found Frederick Massingbird a less indulgent husband to you than I have been," he firmly said. "But these remarks are profitless, and will add to the comfort of neither you nor me. Sibylla, I shall send, in your name, to pay this bill of Mrs. Duff's. Will you give it me?"

"I daresay Bénoite can find it, if you choose to ask her."

"And, my dear, let me beg of you not to contract these paltry debts. There have been others, as you know. I do not like that Mrs. Verner's name should be thus bandied in the village. What you buy in the village, pay for at once."

"How can I pay while you stint me?"

"Stint you!" repeated Lionel, in amazement. "*Stint* you!"

"It's nothing but stinting—going on at me as you

do!" she sullenly answered. "You would like to deprive me of the horses I have set my mind upon! You know you would!"

"The horses you cannot have, Sibylla," he answered, his tone a decisive one. "I have already said it."

It aroused her anger. "If you don't let me have the horses, and all other things I want, I'll go where I can have them."

What did she mean? Lionel's cheek turned white with the taunt the words might be supposed to imply. He held her two hands in his, pressing them nervously.

"You shall not force me to quarrel with you, Sibylla," he continued, with emotion. "I have almost registered a vow that no offensive word or conduct on your part shall make me forget myself for a moment; or render me other than an ever considerate, tender husband. It may be that our marriage was a mistake for both of us; but we shall do well to make the best of it. It is the only course remaining."

He spoke in a strangely earnest tone: one of deep agitation. Sibylla was aroused. She had believed that Lionel blindly loved her. Otherwise she might have been more careful to retain his love: there's no knowing.

"How do you mean that our marriage was a mistake for both of us?" she hastily cried.

"You do your best to remind me continually that it must be so," was his reply.

" Psha !" returned Sibylla.   And Lionel, without
another word, quitted her and walked away.   In
these moments, above all others, would the image
of Lucy Tempest rise up before his sight.   Beat it
down as he would, it was ever present to him.   A
mistake in his marriage !   Ay ; none save Lionel
knew how fatal a one.

He passed on direct to the terrace, avoiding the
lawn, traversed it, and went out at the large gates.
Thence he made his way to Poynton's, the veterinary
surgeon, who also dealt in horses.   At least, dealt
in them so far as that he would buy and sell when
employed to do so.

The man was in his yard, watching a horse go
through his paces.   He came forward to meet Lionel.

" Mrs. Verner has been talking to you about
some ponies, she tells me," began Lionel.   " What
are they ?"

" A very handsome pair, sir.   Just the thing
for a lady to drive.   They are to be sold for a
hundred and fifty pounds.   It's under their value."

" Spirited ?"

" Yes.   They have their mettle about them.
Good horses always have, you know, sir.   Mrs.
Verner has given me the commission."

" Which I am come to rescind," replied Lionel,
calling up a light smile to his face.   " I cannot have
my wife's neck risked by her attempting to drive
spirited ponies, Poynton.   She knows nothing of
driving, is constitutionally timid, and—in short, I
do not wish the order executed."

" Very well, sir," was the man's reply. " There's no harm done. I was at Verner's Pride with that horse that's ill, and Mrs. Verner spoke to me about some ponies. It was only to-day I heard these were in the market, and I mentioned them to her. But, for all I know, they may be already sold."

Lionel turned to walk out of the yard. " After Mrs. Verner shall have learnt to drive, then we shall see : perhaps we may buy a pair," he remarked. " My opinion is that she will not learn : after a trial or two she will give it up."

" All right, sir."

*

CHAPTER XXII.

JAN was coming up the road from Deerham with long strides, as Lionel turned out of Poynton's yard. Lionel advanced leisurely to meet him.

" One would think you were walking for a wager, Jan !"

" Ay," said Jan. " This is my first round to-day. Bitterworths have sent for me in desperate haste. Folks always get ill at the wrong time."

" Why don't you ride ?" asked Lionel, turning with Jan, and stepping out at the same pace.

" There was no time to get the horse ready. I can walk it nearly as fast. I have had no breakfast yet."

" No breakfast !" echoed Lionel.

" I dived into the kitchen and caught up a piece of bread out of the basket. Half my patients must do without me to-day. I have only just got away from Hook's."

" How is the girl ?"

" In great danger," replied Jan.

" She is ill, then ?"

" So ill that I don't think she'll last the day out. The child's dead. I must cut across the fields back

there again, after I have seen what's amiss at,
Bitterworth's."

The words touching Alice Hook caused quite a
shock to Lionel. " It will be a sad thing, Jan, if
she should die ! "

" I don't think I can save her. This comes of
the ghost. I wonder how many more folks will get
frightened to death."

Lionel paused. " Was it really that alone that
frightened the girl, and caused her illness ? How
very absurd the thing sounds ! And yet serious."

" I can't make it out," remarked Jan. " Here's
Bourne now, says he saw it. There's only one
solution of the riddle that I can come to."

" What's that ? " asked Lionel.

" Well," said Jan, " it's not a pleasant one."

" You can tell it me, Jan, pleasant or unpleasant."

" Not pleasant for you, I mean, Lionel. I'll tell
you if you like."

Lionel looked at him.

" Speak ! "

" I think it must be Fred Massingbird himself."

The answer appeared to take Lionel by surprise.
Possibly he had not admitted the doubt.

" Fred Massingbird himself ! I don't understand
you, Jan."

" Fred himself, in life," repeated Jan. " I fancy
it will turn out that he did not die in Australia.
He may have been very ill perhaps, and they
fancied him dead : and now he is well, and has
come over."

Every vestige of colour forsook Lionel's face.

"Jan!" he uttered, partly in terror, partly in anger. "Jan!" he repeated from between his bloodless lips. "Have you thought of the position in which your hint would place my wife?—the reflection it would cast upon her? How dare you?"

"You told me to speak," was Jan's composed answer. "I said you'd not like it. Speaking of it, or keeping silence, won't make it any the better, Lionel."

"What could possess you to think of such a thing?"

"There's nothing else that I can think of. Look here! *Is* there such a thing as a ghost? Is that probable?"

"Nonsense! No," said Lionel.

"Then what can it be, unless it's Fred himself? Lionel, were I you, I'd look the matter full in the face. It is Fred Massingbird, or it is not. If not, the sooner the mystery is cleared up the better, and the fellow brought to book and punished. It's not to be submitted to that he is to stride about for his own pastime, terrifying people to their injury. Is Alice Hook's life nothing? Were Dan Duff's senses nothing? — and, upon my word, I once thought there was good-by to them."

Lionel did not answer. Jan continued.

"If it is Fred himself, the fact can't be long concealed. He'll be sure to make himself known. Why he should not do it at once, I can't imagine. Unless—"

" Unless what ? " asked Lionel.

" Well, you are so touchy on all points relating to Sibylla, that one hesitates to speak," continued Jan. " I was going to say, unless he fears the shock to Sibylla; and would let her be prepared for it by degrees."

" Jan," gasped Lionel, " it would kill her."

" No it wouldn't," dissented Jan. " She's not one to be killed by emotion of any sort. Or much stirred by it, as I believe, if you care for my opinion. It would not be pleasant for you or for her, but she'd not die of it."

Lionel wiped the moisture from his face. From the moment Jan had first spoken, a conviction seemed to arise within him that the suggestion would turn out to be only too true a one—that the ghost, in point of fact, was Frederick Massingbird in life."

" This is awful ! " he murmured. " I would sacrifice my own life to save Sibylla from pain."

" Where'd be the good of that ? " asked practical Jan. " If it is Fred Massingbird in the flesh, she's his wife and not yours : your sacrificing yourself— as you call it, Lionel—would not make her any the less or the more so. I am abroad a good deal at night, especially now, when there's so much sickness about, and I shall perhaps come across the fellow. Won't I pin him if I get the chance."

" Jan," said Lionel, catching hold of his brother's arm to detain him as he was speeding away, for they had reached the gate of Verner's Pride, " be cautious that not a breath of this suspicion escapes you. For my poor wife's sake."

"No fear," answered Jan. "If it gets about, it won't be from me, mind. I am going to believe in the ghost henceforth, you understand. Except to you and Bourne."

"If it gets about," mechanically answered Lionel, repeating the words which made most impression upon his mind. "You think it will get about?"

"Think! It's safe to," answered Jan. "Had old Frost and Dan Duff and Cheese not been great gulls, they'd have taken it for Fred himself; not his ghost. Bourne suspects. From a hint he dropped to me just now at Hook's, I find he takes the same view of the case that I do."

"Since when have you suspected this, Jan?"

"Not for many hours. Don't keep me, Lionel. Bitterworth may be dying, for aught I know, and so may Alice Hook."

Jan went on like a steam-engine. Lionel remained, standing at his entrance-gate, more like a prostrate being than a living man.

Thought after thought crowded upon him. If it was really Frederick Massingbird in life, how was it that he had not made his appearance before? Where had he been all this while? Considerably more than two years had elapsed since the supposed death. To the best of Lionel's recollection, Sibylla had said Captain Canonby *buried* her husband: but it was a point into which Lionel had never minutely inquired. Allow that Jan's sugges-

tion was correct—that he did not die—where had
he been since? What had prevented him from
joining or seeking his wife? What prevented him
doing it now? From what motive could he be in
concealment in the neighbourhood, stealthily prowling about at night? Why did he not appear
openly? Oh, it could not, — it could not be
Frederick Massingbird!

Which way should he bend his steps? Indoors,
or away? Not indoors! He could scarcely *bear*
to see his wife, with this dreadful uncertainty upon
him.   Restless, anxious, perplexed, miserable,
Lionel Verner turned towards Deerham.

There are some natures upon whom a secret,
awful as this, tells with appalling force, rendering
it next to impossible to keep silence. The imparting it to some friend, the speaking of it, appears to
be a matter of dire necessity. It was so in this
instance to Lionel Verner.

He was on his way to the vicarage. Jan had
mentioned that Mr. Bourne shared the knowledge
—if knowledge it could be called : and he was one
in whom might be placed entire trust.

He walked onwards, like one in a fever dream,
nodding mechanically in answer to salutations;
answering he knew not what, if words were spoken
to him. The vicarage joined the churchyard, and
the vicar was standing in the latter as Lionel came
up, watching two men who were digging a grave.
He crossed over the mounds to shake hands with
Lionel.

Lionel drew him into the vicarage garden, amidst the trees. It was shady there; the outer world shut out from eye and ear.

"I cannot beat about the bush; I cannot dissemble," began Lionel, in deep agitation. "Tell me your true opinion of this business, for the love of heaven! I have come down to ask it of you."

The vicar paused. "My dear friend, I feel almost afraid to give it to you."

"I have been speaking with Jan. He thinks it may be Frederick Massingbird — not dead, but alive."

"I fear it is," answered the clergyman. "Within the last half-hour I have fully believed that it is."

Lionel leaned his back against a tree, his arms folded. Tolerably calm outwardly: but he could not get the healthy blood back to his face. "Why within the last half-hour more than before?" he asked. "Has anything fresh happened?"

"Yes," said Mr. Bourne. "I went down to Hook's: the girl's not expected to live the day through—but that you may have heard from Jan. In coming away, your gamekeeper met me. He stopped, and began asking my advice in a mysterious manner—whether, if a secret affecting his master had come to his knowledge, he ought, or ought not, to impart it to his master. I felt sure what the man was driving at—that it could be no other thing than this ghost affair—and gave him a hint to speak out to me in confidence. Which he did."

" Well ? " rejoined Lionel.

" He said," continued Mr. Bourne, lowering his voice, " that he passed a man last night who, he was perfectly certain, was Frederick Massingbird. Not Frederick Massingbird's ghost, as foolish people were fancying, Broom added, but Massingbird himself. He was in doubt whether or not it was his duty to acquaint Mr. Verner : and so he asked me. I bade him not acquaint you," continued the vicar, " but to bury the suspicion within his own breast, breathing a word to none."

Evidence upon evidence ! Every moment brought less loop-hole of escape for Lionel to lean upon. " How can it be ? " he gasped.   " If he is not dead, where can he have been all this while ? "

" I conclude it will turn out to be one of those every-day occurrences that have little marvel at all in them. My thoughts were busy upon it, while standing over the grave yonder. I suppose he must have been to the Diggings. Possibly laid up there from illness, and letters may have miscarried."

" You feel little doubt upon the fact itself—that it is Frederick Massingbird ? "

" I feel none. It is certainly he. Won't you come in and sit down ? "

" No, no," said Lionel. And, drawing his hand from the vicar's, he went forth again, he, and his heavy weight. Frederick Massingbird alive !

CHAPTER XXIII.

THE fine September morning had turned to a rainy afternoon. A heavy mist hung upon the trees, the hedges, the ground; something akin to the mist which had fallen upon Lionel Verner's spirit. The day had grown more like a November one: the clouds were leaden-coloured, the rain fell; even the little birds sought the shelter of their nests.

One, there was, who walked in it, his head uncovered, his brow bared. Not a bird, but a man. He was in the height of his fever dream. It is not an inapt name for his state of mind. His veins coursed as with fever; his thoughts took all the vague uncertainty of a dream. Little heeded he that the weather had become chilly, or that the waters fell upon him!

What must be his course? What ought it to be? The more he dwelt on the revelation of that day, the deeper grew his conviction that Frederick Massingbird was alive, breathing the very air that he breathed. What ought to be his course? If this were so, his wife was—not his wife.

It was obvious that his present, immediate course

ought to be to solve the doubt: to set it at rest.
But how? It could only be done by unearthing
Frederick Massingbird; or he who bore so strange
a resemblance to him. And where was he to be
looked for? To track the hiding-place of a "ghost"
is not an easy matter; and Lionel had no clue
where to find the track of this one. If staying in
the village, he must be concealed in some house;
lying *perdu* by day. It was very strange that it
should be so; that he should not openly show
himself.

There was another way by which perhaps the
doubt might be solved—as it suddenly occurred to
Lionel. And that was through Captain Cannonby.
If this gentleman really was with Frederick Massingbird when he died, and saw him buried, it
was evident that it could not be Frederick come
back to life. In that case, who or what it might
be, Lionel did not stay to speculate: his business
lay in ascertaining by the most direct means in his
power, whether it was, or was not, Frederick Massingbird. How was it possible to do this: how
could it be possible to set the question at rest?

By a very simple process, it may be answered—
the waiting for time and chance. Ay, but do you
know what that waiting involves, in a case like
this? Think of the state of mind that Lionel
Verner must live under, during the suspense!

He made no doubt that the man who had been
under the tree on the lawn a few nights before,
watching his window, whom they had set down as

being Roy, was Frederick Massingbird. And yet, it was scarcely believable. Where now was Lionel to look for him? He could not, for Sibylla's sake, make inquiries in the village in secret or openly: he could not go to the inhabitants and ask—have you seen Frederick Massingbird? or say to each individual, I must send a police officer to search your house, for I suspect Frederick Massingbird is somewhere concealed, and I want to find him. For *her* sake he could not so much as breathe the name, in connection with his being alive.

Given that it was Frederick Massingbird, what could possibly prevent his making himself known? As he dwelt upon this problem, trying to solve it, the idea taken up by Lucy Tempest—that the man under the tree was watching for an opportunity to harm him—came into his mind. *That*, surely, could not be the solution! If he had taken Frederick Massingbird's wife to be his wife, he had done it in all innocence. Lionel spurned the notion as a preposterous one: nevertheless, a remembrance crossed him of the old days when the popular belief at Verner's Pride had been, that the younger of the Massingbirds was of a remarkably secretive and also of a revengeful nature. But, all that, he barely glanced at: the terrible fear touching Sibylla absorbed him.

He was leaning against a tree in the covered walk near Verner's Pride, the walk which led to the willow-pond, his head bared, his brow bent with the most unmistakeable signs of care, when something

not unlike a small white balloon came flying down
the path. A lady, with her silk dress turned over
her shoulders, leaving only the white lining ex-
posed to view. She was face to face with Lionel
before she saw him.

" Lucy ! " he exclaimed, in extreme surprise.

Lucy Tempest laughed, and let her dress drop
into a more dignified position. "I and Decima
went to call on Mrs. Bitterworth," she explained,
"and Decima is staying there. It began to rain
as I came out, so I turned into the back walk and
put my dress up to save it. Am I not economical,
Mr. Verner ? "

She spoke quickly. Lionel thought it was done
with a view to hide her agitation. "You cannot go
home through this rain, Lucy. Let me take you
indoors : we are close to Verner's Pride."

" No, thank you," said Lucy, hastily, "I must go
back to Lady Verner. She will not be pleased at
Decima's staying out, therefore I must return.
Poor Mrs. Bitterworth has had an attack of—what
did they call it?—spasmodical croup, I think. She
is better now, and begged Decima to stay with her
the rest of the day: Mr. Bitterworth and the rest
of them are out. Jan says it is highly dangerous
for the time it lasts."

" She has had something of the same sort before,
I remember," observed Lionel. "I wish you would
come in, Lucy. If you must go home, I will send
you in the carriage : but I think you might stay and
dine with us."

A soft colour mantled in Lucy's cheeks. She
had never made herself a familiar acquaintance at
Lionel Verner's. He had observed it, if no one
else had. Sibylla had once said to her that she
hoped they should be great friends, that Verner's
Pride would see a great deal of her. Lucy had
never responded to the wish. A formal visit with
Decima or Lady Verner when she could not help
herself; but alone, in a social manner, she had
never put her foot over the threshold of Verner's
Pride.

"You are very kind. I must go home at once.
The rain will not hurt me."

Lionel, self-conscious, did not urge it further.
"Will you remain here, then, under the trees, while
I go home and get an umbrella?"

"Oh dear no, I don't want an umbrella; thank
you all the same. I have my parasol, you see."

She took her dress up again as she spoke; not
high, as it was previously, but turning it a little.
"Lady Verner scolds me so if I spoil my things,"
she said, in a tone of laughing apology. "She buys
me very good ones, and orders me to take care of
them. Good-by, Mr. Verner."

Lionel took the hand in his which she held
out. But he turned with her, and then loosed it
again.

"You are not coming with me, Mr. Verner?"

"I shall see you home."

"But—I had rather you did not. I prefer—not
to trouble you."

"Pardon me, Lucy. I cannot suffer you to go alone."

It was a calm reply, quietly spoken. There were no fine phrases of its being "no trouble," that the "trouble was a pleasure," as others might indulge in. Fine phrases from them! from the one to the other! Neither could have spoken them.

Lucy said no more, and they walked on side by side in silence, both unpleasantly self-conscious. Lionel's face had resumed its strange expression of care. Lucy had observed it when she came up to him; she observed it still.

"You look as though you had some great trouble upon you, Mr. Verner," she said, after awhile.

"Then I look what is the truth. I have one, Lucy."

"A heavy one?" asked Lucy, struck with his tone.

"A grievously heavy one. One that does not often fall to the lot of man."

"May I know it?" she timidly said.

"No, Lucy. If I could speak it, it would only give you pain; but it is of a private nature. Possibly it may be averted; it is at present a suspected dread, not a confirmed one. Should it become confirmed, you will learn it in common with all the world."

She looked up at him, puzzled; sympathy in her mantling blush, in her soft dark earnest eyes. He could not avoid contrasting that truthful face with another's frivolous one : and I can't help it

if you blame him. He did his best to shake off
the feeling, and looked down at her with a careless
smile.

"Don't let it give you concern, Lucy. My
troubles must rest upon my own head."

"Have you seen any more of that man who was
watching? Roy."

"No. But I don't believe now that it was Roy.
He strongly denies it, and I have had my suspicions
diverted to another quarter."

"To one who may be equally wishing to do you
harm ? "

"I cannot say. If it be the party I—I suspect,
he may deem that I have done him harm."

"You ! " echoed Lucy. "And have you ? "

"Yes. Unwittingly. It seems to be my fate, I
think, to work harm upon—upon those whom I
would especially shield from it."

Did he allude to her ? Lucy thought so, and
the flush on her cheeks deepened. At that moment
the rain began to pour down heavily. They were
then passing the thicket of trees where those ad-
venturous ghost-hunters had taken up their watch
a few nights previously, in view of the willow-pond.
Lucy stepped underneath their branches.

"Now," said Lionel, "should you have done well
to accept my offer of Verner's Pride as a shelter, or
not ? "

"It may only be a passing storm," observed Lucy.
"The rain then was nothing."

Lionel took her parasol and shook the wet off

it. He began to wonder how Lucy would get home. No carriage could be got to that spot, and the rain, coming down now, was not, in his opinion, a passing storm.

"Will you promise to remain here, Lucy, while I get an umbrella ? " he presently asked.

"Why ! where could you get an umbrella from ? "

"From Hook's, if they possess such a thing. If not, I can get one from Broom's."

" But you would get so wet, going for it ! "

Lionel laughed as he went off.

" I don't wear a silk dress ; to be scolded for it, if it gets spoiled."

Not ten steps had he taken, however, when who should come striding through an opening in the trees, but Jan. Jan was on his way from Hook's cottage, a huge brown cotton umbrella over his head, more useful than elegant.

" What, is that you, Miss Lucy ! Well, I should as soon have thought of seeing Mrs. Peckaby's white donkey ! "

" I am weather-bound, Jan," said Lucy. " Mr. Verner was about to get me an umbrella."

" To see if I could get one," corrected Lionel. " I question if the Hooks possess such a commodity."

" Not they," cried Jan. " The girl's rather better," added he unceremoniously. " She may get through it now ; at least there's a shade of a chance. You can have my umbrella, Miss Lucy."

"Won't you let me go with you, Jan?" she asked.

"Oh, I can't stop to take you to Deerham Court," was Jan's answer, given with his accustomed plainness. "Here, Lionel!"

He handed over the umbrella, and was walking off.

"Jan, Jan, you will get wet," said Lucy.

It amused Jan. "A wetting more or less is nothing to me," he called out, striding on.

"Will you stay under shelter a few minutes yet, and see whether it abates?" asked Lionel.

Lucy looked up at the skies, stretching her head beyond the trees to do so.

"Do you think it will abate?" she rejoined.

"Honestly to confess it, I think it will get worse," said Lionel. "Lucy, you have thin shoes on! I did not see that, until now."

"Don't you tell Lady Verner," replied Lucy, with the pretty dependent manner which she had brought from school with her, and which she probably would never lose. "She would scold me for walking out in them."

Lionel smiled, and held the great umbrella—large enough for a carriage—close to the trees, that it might shelter her as she came forth.

"Take my arm, Lucy."

She hesitated for a single moment—a hesitation so temporary that any other than Lionel could not have observed it, and then took his arm. And again they walked on in silence. In passing down

Clay Lane—the way Lionel took—Mrs. Peckaby was standing at her door.

"On the look out for the white donkey, Mrs. Peckaby?" asked Lionel.

The husband, inside, heard the words and flew into a tantrum.

"She's never on the look out for nothing else, sir : asking pardon for saying it to you."

Mrs. Peckaby clasped her hands together.

"It 'll come!" she murmured. "Sometimes, sir, when my patience is well nigh exhausted, I has a vision of the New Jerusalem in the night, and is revived. It 'll come, sir, the quadruple 'll come!"

"I wonder," laughed Lucy, as they walked on, "whether she will go on to the end of her life expecting it?"

"If her husband will allow her," answered Lionel. "But by what I have heard since I came home, his patience is—as she says by her own with reference to the white ' quadruple'—well nigh exhausted."

"He told Decima, the other day, that he was sick of the theme and of her folly, and he wished the New Jerusalem had her and the white donkey together. Here we are!" added Lucy, as they came in front of Deerham Court. "Lionel, please, let me go in the back way—Jan's way. And then Lady Verner will not see me. She will say I ought not to have come through the rain."

"She 'll see the shoes and the silk dress, and

she 'll say you should have stopped at Verner's Pride, as a well-trained young lady ought," returned Lionel.

He took her safely to the back door, opened it, and sent her in.

" Thank you very much," said she, holding out her hand to him. "I have given you a disagreeable walk, and now I must give you one back again."

" Change your shoes at once, and don't talk foolish things," was Lionel's answer.

CHAPTER XXIV.

THE THUNDER-STORM.

A WET walk back Lionel certainly had : but, wet or dry, it was all the same in his present distressed frame of mind. Arrived at Verner's Pride, he found his wife dressed for dinner, and the centre of a host of guests gay as she was. No opportunity, then, to question her about Frederick Massingbird's death, and how far Captain Cannonby was cognisant of the particulars.

He had to change his own things. It was barely done by dinner-time ; and he sat down to table, the host of many guests. His brow was smooth, his speech was courtly ; how could any of them suspect that a terrible dread was gnawing at his heart ? Sibylla, in a rustling silk dress and a coronet of diamonds, sat opposite to him, in all her dazzling beauty. Had she suspected what might be in store for her, those smiles would not have chased each other so incessantly on her lips.

Sibylla went up to bed early. She was full of caprices as a wayward child. Of a remarkably chilly nature—as is the case, sometimes, where the constitution is delicate—she would have a fire in her dressing-room night and morning all the year round, even in the heat of summer. It pleased her this evening to desert her guests suddenly: she had the headache, she said.

The weather on this day appeared to be as capricious as Sibylla, as strangely curious as the great fear which had fallen upon Lionel. The fine morning had changed to the, rainy, misty, chilly afternoon ; the afternoon to a clear, bright evening; and that evening had now become overcast with portentous clouds.

Without much warning the storm burst forth: peals of thunder reverberated through the air, flashes of forked lightning played in the sky. Lionel hastened up-stairs: he remembered how these storms terrified his wife.

She had knelt down to bury her head amidst the soft cushions of a chair when Lionel entered her dressing-room. " Sibylla !" he said.

Up she started at the sound of his voice, and flew to him. There lay her protection; and in spite of her ill-temper and her love of aggravation, she felt and recognised it. Lionel held her in his sheltering arms, bending her head down upon his breast, and drawing his coat over it, so that she might see no ray of light: as he had been wont to do in former storms. As a timid child was she at these times : humble, loving, gentle: she felt as if she were on the threshold of the next world, that the next moment might be her last. Others have been known to experience the same dread in a thunder-storm :

and, to be thus brought, as it were, face to face with death, takes the spirit out of people.

He stood, patiently holding her. Every time the thunder burst above their heads, he could feel her heart beat against his. One of her arms was round him; the other he held; all wet it was with fear. He did not speak: he only clasped her closer every now and then, that she might be reminded of her shelter.

Twenty minutes or so, and the violence of the storm abated. The lightning grew less frequent, the thunder distant and more distant. At length the sound wholly ceased, and the lightning subsided into that harmless sheet lightning which is so beautiful to look at in the far-off horizon.

" It is over," he whispered.

She lifted her head from its resting place. Her blue eye was bright with excitement, her delicate cheek was crimson, her golden hair fell in a dishevelled mass around. Her gala robes had been removed, with the diamond coronet, and the storm had surprised her writing a note in her dressing-gown. In spite of the sudden terror which overtook her, she did not forget to put the letter—so far as had been written of it—safely away. It was not expedient that her husband's eyes should fall upon it: Sibylla had many answers to write now to importunate creditors.

" Are you sure, Lionel ?"

" Quite sure. Come and see how clear it is. You are not alarmed at the sheet lightning."

He put his arm round her, and led her to the
window. As he said, the sky was clear again.
Nearly all traces of the storm had passed away :
there had been no rain with it; and, but for the
remembrance of its sound in their ears, they might
have believed that it had not taken place. The
broad lands of Verner's Pride lay spreading out before them; the lawns and the terrace underneath : the
sheet-lightning illumined the heavens incessantly,
rendering objects nearly as clear as in the day.

Lionel held her to his side, his arm round her.
She trembled still; trembled excessively; her
bosom heaved and fell beneath his hand.

"When I die, it will be in a thunder-storm," she
whispered.

"You foolish girl!" he said, his tone half a
joking one, wholly tender. "What can have given
you this excessive fear of thunder, Sibylla?" ·

"I was always frightened at a thunder-storm.
Deborah says mamma was. But I was not so *very*
frightened until a storm I witnessed in Australia.
It killed a man!" she added, shivering and nestling nearer to Lionel.

"Ah!"

"It was only a few days before Frederick left
me, when he and Captain Cannonby went away
together," she continued. "We had hired a carriage, and had gone out of the town ever so far.
There was something to be seen there; I forget
what now; races perhaps. I know a good many
people went; and an awful thunder-storm came on.

Some ran under the trees for shelter ; some would not : and the lightning killed a man. Oh, Lionel, I shall never forget it ! I saw him carried past ; I saw his face ! Since then I have felt ready to die myself with the fear."

She turned her face, and hid it upon his bosom. Lionel did not attempt to soothe the *fear ;* he knew that for such fear time alone is the only cure. He whispered words of soothing to *her ;* he stroked fondly her golden hair. In these moments, when she was gentle, yielding, clinging to him for protection, three parts of his old love for her would come back again. The lamp, which had been turned on to its full blaze of light, was behind them, so that they might have been visible enough to anybody standing in the nearer portion of the grounds.

" Captain Cannonby went away with Frederick Massingbird," observed Lionel, approaching by degrees to the questions he wished to ask. " Did they start together ? "

" Yes. Don't talk about it, Lionel."

" My dear wife, I must talk about it," he gravely answered. " You have always put me off in this manner, so that I know little or nothing of the circumstances. I have a reason for wishing to become cognisant of those past particulars. Surely," he added, a shade of deeper feeling in his tone, " at this distance of time it cannot be so very painful to your feelings to speak of Frederick Massingbird. *I* am by your side."

" What is the reason that you wish to know ? "

·" A little matter that regarded him and Cannonby. Was Cannonby with him when he died ? "

Sibylla, subdued still, yielded to the wish, as she would probably have yielded at no other time.

" Of course he was with him. They were but a day's journey from Melbourne. I forget the name of the place : a sort of small village or settlement, I believe, where the people halted that were going to, or returning from the diggings. Frederick was taken worse as they got there, and in a few hours he died."

" Cannonby remaining with him ? "

" Yes. I am sure I have told you this before, Lionel. I told it to you on the night of my return." -

He was aware she had. He could not say : " But I wish to press you upon the points ; to ascertain beyond doubt that Frederick Massingbird did really die ; that he is not living." " Did Cannonby stay until he was buried ? " he asked aloud.

" Yes."

" You are sure of this ? "

Sibylla looked at him curiously. She could not think why he was recalling this ; why want to know it ?

" I am sure of it only so far as that Captain Cannonby told me so," replied Sibylla.

The reservation struck upon him with a chill : it seemed to be a confirmation of his worst fears. Sibylla continued, for he did not speak :

"Of course he stayed with him until he was buried. When Captain Cannonby came back to me at Melbourne, he said he had waited to lay him in the ground. Why should he have said it, if he did not?"

"True," murmured Lionel.

"He said the burial-service had been read over him. I remember that, well. I reproached Captain Cannonby with not having come back to me immediately, or sent for me that I might at least have seen him dead, if not alive. He excused himself by saying that he did not think I should like to see him: and he had waited to bury him before returning."

Lionel fell into a reverie. If this, that Captain Cannonby had stated, was correct, there was no doubt that Frederick Massingbird was safely dead and buried. But he could not be sure that it was correct: Captain Cannonby may not have relished waiting to see a dead man buried: although he had affirmed so much to Sibylla. A thousand pounds would Lionel have given out of his pocket at that moment, for one minute's interview with Captain Cannonby.

"Lionel!"

The call came from Sibylla with sudden intensity, half startling him. She had got one of her fingers pointed to the lawn.

"Who's that—peeping forth from underneath the yew-tree?"

The same place, the same tree which had been

pointed to by Lucy Tempest! An impulse, for which Lionel could not have accounted, caused him to turn round and put out the lamp.

"Who can it be?" wondered Sibylla. "He appears to be watching us. How foolish of any of them to go out! *I* should not feel safe under a tree, although that lightning is only sheet-lightning."

Every perceptive faculty that Lionel Verner possessed was strained upon the spot. He could make out a tall man; a man whose figure bore—unless his eyes and his imagination combined to deceive him—a strong resemblance to Frederick Massingbird's. Had it come to it? Were he and his rival face to face; was she, by his own side now, about to be bandied between them?—belonging, save by the priority of the first marriage ceremony, no more to one than to the other? A stifled cry, suppressed instantly, escaped his lips; his pulses stood still, and then throbbed on with painful violence.

"Can you discern him, Lionel?" she asked. "He is going away—going back amidst the trees. Perhaps because he can't see us any longer, now you have put the light out. Who is it? Why should he have stood there, watching us?"

Lionel snatched her to him with an impulsive gesture. He would have sacrificed his life willingly, to save Sibylla from the terrible misfortune that appeared to be falling upon her.

CHAPTER XXV.

A CASUAL MEETING ON THE RIVER.

A MERRY breakfast-table. Sibylla, for a wonder, up, and present at it. The rain of the preceding day, the storm of the night had entirely passed away, and as fine a morning as could be wished was smiling on the earth.

"Which of you went out before the storm was over, and ventured under the great yew-tree?"

It was Mrs. Verner who spoke. She looked at the different gentlemen present, and they looked at her. They did not know what she meant.

"You *were* under it, one of you," persisted Sibylla.

All, save one, protested that they had neither been out nor under the tree. That one—it happened to be Mr. Gordon, of whom casual mention has been made—confessed to having been on the lawn, so far as crossing it went; but he did not go near the tree.

"I went out with my cigar," he observed, " and had strolled some distance from the house when the storm came on. I stood in the middle of a field and watched it. It was grandly beautiful."

"I wonder you were not brought home dead!" ejaculated Sibylla.

Mr. Gordon laughed. "If you once witnessed the thunder-storms that we get in the tropics, Mrs. Verner, you would not associate these with danger."

"I have seen dreadful thunder-storms, apart from what we get here, as well as you, Mr. Gordon," returned Sibylla. "Perhaps you will deny that anybody's ever killed by them in this country. But why did you halt underneath the yew-tree?"

"I did not," he repeated. "I crossed the lawn, straight on to the upper end of the terrace. I did not go near the tree."

"Some one did, if you did not. They were staring right up at my dressing-room window. I was standing at it with Mr. Verner."

Mr. Gordon shook his head. "Not guilty, so far as I am concerned, Mrs. Verner. I met some man, when I was coming home, plunging into the thicket of trees as I emerged from them. It was he, possibly."

"What man?" questioned Sibylla.

"I did not know him. He was a stranger. A tall, dark man with stooping shoulders, and something black upon his cheek."

"Something black upon his cheek;" repeated Sibylla, thinking the words bore an odd sound.

"A large black mark it looked like. His cheek was white—sallow would be the better term—and he wore no whiskers, so it was a conspicuous looking brand. In the moment he passed me, the lightning rendered the atmosphere as light as—"

"Sibylla!" almost shouted Lionel, "we are waiting for more tea in this quarter. Never mind Gordon."

They looked at him with surprise. He was lean-ing towards his wife; his face crimson, his tones agitated. Sibylla stared at him, and said, if he called out like that, she would not get up another morning. Lionel replied, talking fast; and just then the letters were brought in. Altogether, the subject of the man with the mark upon his cheek dropped out of the discussion.

Breakfast over, Lionel put his arm within Mr. Gordon's and drew him outside upon the terrace. Not to question him upon the man he had seen: Lionel would have been glad that that encounter should pass out of Mr. Gordon's remembrance, as affording less chance of Sibylla's hearing of it again ; but to get information on another topic. He had been rapidly making up his mind during the latter half of breakfast, and had come to a decision.

" Gordon, can you inform me where Captain Can-nonby is to be found ? "

" Can you inform me where the comet that visited us last year may be met with this ? " returned Mr. Gordon. " I'd nearly as soon undertake to find out the locality of the one as of the other. Cannonby did go to Paris ; but where he may be now, is quite another affair."

" Was he going there for any length of stay ? "

" I fancy not. Most likely he is back in Lon-don by this time. Had he told me he was coming back, I should have paid no attention to it. He never knows his own mind two hours together."

"I particularly wish to see him," observed Lionel. "Can you give me any address where he may be found in London?—if he has returned?"

"Yes. His brother's in Westminster. I can give you the exact number and address by referring to my note-book. When Cannonby's in London, he makes it his head-quarters. If he is away, his brother may know where he is."

"His brother may be out of town also. Few men are in it at this season."

"If they can get out. But Dr. Cannonby can't. He is a physician, and must stop at his post, season or no season."

"I am going up to town to-day," remarked Lionel, "and——"

"You are! For long?"

"Back to-morrow, I hope: perhaps to-night. If you will give me the address, I'll copy it down."

Lionel wrote it down: but Mr. Gordon told him there was no necessity: any little ragged boy in the street could direct him to Dr. Cannonby's. Then he went to make his proposed journey known to Sibylla. She was standing near one of the terrace pillars, looking up at the sky, her eyes shaded with her hand. Lionel drew her inside an unoccupied room.

"Sibylla, a little matter of business is calling me to London," he said. "If I can catch the half-past ten train, I may be home again to-night, late."

"How sudden!" cried Sibylla. "Why didn't
you tell me? What weather shall we have to-day,
do you think?"

"Fine. But it is of little consequence to me
whether it be fine or wet."

"Oh!" I was not thinking of you," was the careless reply. "I want it to be fine for our archery."

"Good-bye," he said, stooping to kiss her. "Take
care of yourself."

"Lionel, mind, I shall have the ponies," was her
answer, given in a pouting, pretty, affected manner.

Lionel smiled, shook his head, took another kiss,
and left her. Oh, if he could but shield her from
the tribulation that too surely seemed to be omi-
nously looming!

The lightest and fleetest carriage he possessed
had been made ready, and was waiting for him at
the stables. He got in there, and drove off with
his groom, saying farewell to none, and taking
nothing with him but an overcoat. As he drove
past Mrs. Duff's shop, the remembrance of the bill
came over him. He had forwarded the money to
her the previous night in his wife's name.

He caught the train; was too soon for it; it was
five minutes behind time. If those who saw him
depart could but have divined the errand he was
bent on, what a commotion would have spread over
Deerham! If the handsome lady, seated opposite
to him, the only other passenger in that compart-
ment, could but have read the cause which rendered
him so self-absorbed, so insensible to her attrac-

tions, she would have gazed at him with far more interest.

"Who is that gentleman?" she privately asked of the guard when she got the opportunity.

"Mr. Verner, of Verner's Pride."

He sat back on his seat, heeding nothing. Had all the pretty women of the kingdom been ranged before him, in a row, they had been nothing to Mr. Verner then. Had Lucy Tempest been there, he had been equally regardless of her. If Frederick Massingbird were indeed in life, Verner's Pride was no longer his: but it was not of that he thought: it was of the calamity that would involve his wife. A calamity which, to the refined, sensitive mind of Lionel Verner, was almost worse than death itself.

What would the journey bring forth for him? Should he succeed in seeing Captain Cannonby? He awaited the fiat with feverish heat; and wished the fast express engine would travel faster.

The terminus gained at last, a Hansom took him to Dr. Cannonby's. It was half-past two o'clock. He leaped out of the cab and rang, entering the hall when the door was opened.

"Can I see Dr. Cannonby?"

"The doctor's just gone out, sir. He will be home at five."

It was a sort of checkmate, and Lionel stood looking at the servant—as if the man could tele-graph some impossible aërial message to his master to bring him back then.

"Is Captain Cannonby staying here?" was his next question.

"No, sir. He was staying here, but he went away this morning."

"He is home from Paris then?"

"He came back two or three days ago, sir," replied the servant.

"Do you know where he is gone?"

"I don't, sir. I fancy it's somewhere in the country."

"Dr. Cannonby would know?"

"I dare say he would, sir. I should think so."

Lionel turned to the door. Where was the use of his lingering? He looked back to ask a question.

"You are sure that Captain Cannonby has gone out of town?"

"Oh yes, sir."

He descended the steps, and the man closed the door upon him. Where should he go? What should he do with himself for the next two and a half mortal hours? Go to his club? Or to any of the old spots of his London life? Not he: some familiar faces might be in town; and he was in no mood for familiar faces then.

Sauntering hither, sauntering thither, he came to Westminster Bridge. One of the steamers was approaching the pier to take in passengers, on its way down the river. For want of some other mode in which to employ his time, Lionel went down to the embarking place, and stepped on board.

Does *any* thing in this world happen by chance?

What secret unknown impulse could have sent
Lionel Verner on board that steamer ?   Had Dr.
Cannonby been at home he would not have gone
near it : had he turned to the right hand instead of
to the left, on leaving Dr. Cannonby's house, the
boat would never have seen him.

It was not crowded, as those steamers sometimes
are crowded, suggesting visions of the bottom of
the river.   The day was fine ; warm for September,
but not too hot; the gliding down the stream
delightful.   With a heart at ease, Lionel would
have found it so : as it was, he could scarcely have
told whether he was going down the stream or up,
whether it was wet or dry.   He could see but one
thing—the image of Frederick Massingbird.

As the boat drew up to the Temple pier, the only
person, waiting to embark, was a woman ; a little
body in a faded brown silk dress.   Whether, seeing
his additional freight was to be so trifling, the
manager of the steamer did not take the usual care
to bring it alongside, certain it is, that in some way
the woman fell, in stepping on board; her knees on
the boat, her feet hanging down to the water.
Lionel, who was sitting near, sprang forward and
pulled her out of danger.

"I declare I never ought to come aboard these
nasty steamers ! " she exclaimed, as he placed her
in a seat.   " I'm greatly obliged to you, sir : I might
have gone in, else; there's no saying.   The last
time I was aboard one I was in danger of being
killed.   I fell through the port-hole, sir."

"Indeed!" responded Lionel, who could not be so discourteous as not to answer. "Perhaps your sight is not good?"

"Well, yes it is, sir, as good as most folks, at middle age. I get timid aboard 'em, and it makes me confused and awkward, and I suppose I don't mind where I put my feet. This was in Liverpool, sir, a week or two ago. It was a passenger-ship just in from Australia, and the bustle and confusion aboard was dreadful—they say it's mostly so with them vessels that are coming home. I had gone down to meet my husband, sir; he has been away four years—and it's a pity he ever went, for all the good he has done. But he's back safe himself, so I must not grumble."

"That's something," said Lionel.

"True, sir. It would have been a strange thing if I had lost my life just as he had come home. And I should, but for a gentleman on board. He seized hold of me by the middle, and somehow con-trived to drag me up again. A strong man he must have been! I shall always remember him with gratitude, I'm sure : as I shall you, sir. His name, my husband told me afterwards, was Massingbird."

All Lionel's inertness was gone at the sound of the name. "Massingbird?" he repeated.

"Yes, sir. He had come home in the ship from the same port as my husband—Melbourne. Quite a gentleman, my husband said he was, with grand relations in England. He had not been out there over long—hardly as long as my husband, I fancy

—and my husband don't think he has made much, any more than himself has."

Lionel had regained all his outward impassiveness. He stood by the talkative woman, his arms folded. "What sort of a looking man was this Mr. Massingbird?" he asked. "I knew a gentleman once of that name, who went to Australia."

The woman glanced up at him, measuring his height. "I should say he was as tall as you, sir, or close upon it, but he was broader made, and had got a stoop in the shoulders. He was dark; had dark eyes and hair, and a pale face. Not the clear paleness of your face, sir, but one of them sallow faces that get darker and yellower with travelling; never red."

Every word was as fresh testimony to the suspicion that it was Frederick Massingbird. "Had he a black mark upon his cheek?" inquired Lionel.

"Likely he might have had, sir, but I couldn't see his cheeks. He wore a sort of fur cap with the ears tied down. My husband saw a good bit of him on the voyage, though he was only a middle-deck passenger, and the gentleman was a cabin. His friends have had a surprise before this," she continued, after a pause. "He told my husband that they all supposed him dead; had thought he had been dead these two years past and more; and he had never sent home to contradict it."

Then it *was* Frederick Massingbird! Lionel Verner quitted the woman's side, and leaned over the rail of the steamer, apparently watching the water. He could not, by any dint of reasoning or supposition, make out the mystery. How Frederick Massingbird could be alive; or, being alive, why he had not come home before to claim Sibylla—why he had not claimed her before she left Australia—why he did not claim her now he was come. A man without a wife might go roving where he would and as long as he would, letting his friends think him dead if it pleased him ; but a man with a wife could not in his sane senses, be supposed to act so. It was a strange thing, his meeting with this woman— a singular coincidence : one that he would hardly have believed, if related to him, as happening to another.

It was striking five when he again knocked at Dr. Cannonby's. He wished to see Captain Cannonby still ; it would be the crowning confirmation: but he had no doubt whatever that that gentleman's report would be : " I saw Frederick Massingbird die—as I believed, and I quitted him immediately. I conclude that I must have been in error in supposing he was dead."

Dr. Cannonby had returned, the servant said. He desired Lionel to walk in, and threw open the door of the room. Seven or eight people were sitting in it, waiting. The servant had evidently mistaken him for a patient, and placed him there to wait his turn with the rest. He took his card from his pocket, wrote on it a few words, and desired the servant to carry it to his master.

The man came back with an apology. " I beg your pardon, sir. Will you step this way ? "

The physician was bowing a lady out as he
entered the room—a room lined with books, and
containing casts of heads. He came forward to
shake hands, a cordial-mannered man. He knew
Lionel by reputation, but had never seen him.

"My visit was not to you, but to your brother,"
explained Lionel. "I was in hopes to have found
him here."

"Then he and you have been playing at cross-
purposes to-day," remarked the doctor, with a smile.
"Lawrence started this morning for Verner's Pride."

"Indeed!" exclaimed Lionel. "Cross-purposes
indeed!" he muttered to himself.

"He heard some news in Paris which concerned
you, I believe, and hastened home to pay you a
visit."

"Which concerned me!" repeated Lionel.

"Or rather Mrs. Massingbird—Mrs. Verner, I
should say."·

A sickly smile crossed Lionel's lips. Mrs. Massingbird! Was it already known? "Why," he
asked, "did you call her Mrs. Massingbird?"

"I beg your pardon for my inadvertence, Mr.
Verner," was the reply of Dr. Cannonby. "Lawrence knew her as Mrs. Massingbird, and on his
return from Australia he frequently spoke of her
to me as Mrs. Massingbird, so that I got into the
habit of thinking of her as such. It was not until
he went to Paris that he heard she had exchanged
the name for that of Verner."

A thought crossed Lionel that *this* was the news

which had taken Captain Cannonby down to him.
He might know of the existence of Frederick
Massingbird, and had gone to break the news to
him, Lionel; to tell him that his wife was not his
wife.

"You do not know precisely what his business
was with me ? " he inquired, quite wistfully.

"No, I don't. I don't know that it was much
beyond the pleasure of seeing you and Mrs. Verner."

Lionel rose. "If I—"

"But you will stay and dine with me, Mr.
Verner ? "

"Thank you, I am going back at once. I wished
to be home this evening if possible, and there's
nothing to hinder it now."

"A letter or two has come for Lawrence since
the morning," observed the doctor as he shook
hands. "Will you take charge of them for him ? "

"With pleasure."

Dr. Cannonby turned to a letter rack over the
mantelpiece, selected three letters from it, and
handed them to Lionel.

Back again all the weary way. His strong suspicions were no longer suspicions now, but confirmed certainties. The night grew dark: it was
not darker than the cloud which had fallen upon his
spirit.

Thought was busy with his brain. How could it
be otherwise? Should he get home to find the
news public property? Had Captain Cannonby
made it known to Sibylla? Most fervently did he

hope not. Better that he, Lionel, should be by her
side to help her to bear it when the dreadful news
came out. Next came another thought. Suppose
Frederick Massingbird should have discovered himself? should have gone to Verner's Pride to take
possession?—*his* home now; his wife. Lionel
might get back to find that he had no longer a place
there.

Lionel found his carriage waiting at the station.
He had ordered it to be so. Wigham was with it.
A very coward now, he scarcely dared ask questions.

"Has Captain Cannonby arrived at the house to-
day, do you know, Wigham?"

"Who, sir?"

"A strange gentleman from London. Captain
Cannonby."

"I can't rightly say, sir. I have been about in
the stables all day. I saw a strange gentleman cross
the yard just at dinner-time, one I'd never seen
afore. May be it was him."

A feeling came over Lionel that he could not see
Captain Cannonby before them all. Better send
for him to a private room, and get the communication over. What his after course would be was
another matter. Yes: better in all ways.

"Drive round to the yard, Wigham," he said, as
the coachman was about to turn on to the terrace.
And Wigham obeyed.

He stepped out. He went in at the back door,
almost as if he were slinking into the house
stealthily, traversed the passages, and gained the

lighted hall. At the very moment that he put his feet on its tesselated floor, a sudden commotion was heard up the stairs. A door was flung open, and Sibylla, with cheeks inflamed and breath panting, flew down, her convulsive cries echoing through the house. She saw Lionel, and threw herself into his arms.

"Oh Lionel, what is this wicked story?" she sobbed. "It is not true! It cannot be true that I am not your wife, that——"

"Hush, my darling!" he whispered, placing his hand across her mouth. "We are not alone!"

They certainly were not! Out of the drawing-rooms, out of the dining-room, had poured the guests; out of the kitchen came peeping the servants. Deborah West stood on the stairs like a statue, her hands clasped; and Mademoiselle Benoite frantically inquired what anybody had been doing to her mistress. All stared in amazement. She, in that terrible state of agitation; Lionel supporting her with his white and haughty face.

"It is nothing," he said, waving them off. "Mrs. Verner is not well. Come with me, Sibylla."

Waving them off still, he drew her into the study, closed the door, and bolted it. She clung to him like one in the extremity of terror, her throat heaving convulsively.

"Oh Lionel! is it true that he is come back? That he did not die? What will become of me? Tell me that they have been deceiving me; that it is not true!"

He could not tell her so. He wound his arms tenderly round her and held her face to his breast, and laid his own down upon it. " Strive for calmness," he murmured, his heart aching for her. " I will protect you so long as I shall have the power."

CHAPTER XXVI.

Miss Deborah West did not believe in ghosts.
Miss Deb, setting aside a few personal weaknesses
and vanities, was a strong-minded female, and no
more believed in ghosts than she did in Master
Cheese's delicate constitution, which required to be
supplied with an unlimited quantity of tarts and
other dainties to keep up his strength between
meals. The commotion respecting Frederick Massingbird, that his ghost had arrived from Australia,
and "walked," reached the ears of Miss Deb. It
reached them in this way.

Miss Deb and her sister, compelled to economy
by the scanty allowance afforded by Dr. West, had
no more helpmates in the household department
than were absolutely necessary, and the surgery boy,
Bob, found himself sometimes pressed into aiding
in the domestic service. One evening Miss Deb
entered the surgery, and caught Master Cheese
revelling in a hat-full of walnuts by gaslight. This
was the evening of the storm, previously mentioned.

"Where's Bob?" asked she. "I want a message
taken to Mrs. Broom's about those pickled mushrooms that she is doing for me."

"Bob's out," responded Master Cheese. "Have a walnut, Miss Deb?"

"I don't mind. Are they ripe?" answered Miss Deb.

Master Cheese, the greediest chap alive, picked out the smallest he could find, politely cracked it with his teeth, and handed it to her.

"You'll not get Bob over to Broom's at this hour," cried he. "Jan can't get him to Mother Hook's with her medicine after dark. Unless it's made up so that he can take it by daylight, they have to send for it."

"What's that for?" asked Miss Deb.

Master Cheese cracked on at his walnuts. "You have not heard the tale that's going about, I suppose, Miss Deb?" he presently said.

"I have not heard any tale," she answered.

"And I don't know that I must tell it you," continued Master Cheese, filling his mouth with five or six quarters at once, unpeeled. "Jan ordered me to hold my tongue in-doors."

"It would be more respectful, Master Cheese, if you said Mr. Jan," rebuked Miss Deborah. "I have told you so often."

"Who cares?" returned Master Cheese. "Jan doesn't. The fact is, Miss Deb, that there's a ghost about at night just now."

"Have they got up that folly again? Rachel Frost rests a great deal quieter in her grave than some of you do in your beds."

"Ah, but it's not Rachel's this time," significantly responded Master Cheese. "It's somebody else's."

"Whose is it, then?" asked Miss Deb, struck with his manner.

"I'll tell you if you won't tell Jan. "It's—don't start, Miss Deb—it's Fred Massingbird's."

Miss Deb did not start. She looked keenly at Master Cheese, believing he might be playing a joke upon her. But there were no signs of joking in his countenance. It looked, on the contrary, singularly serious, not to say awe-struck, as he leaned forward to bring it nearer Miss Deborah's.

"It is a fact that Fred Massingbird's ghost is walking," he continued. "Lots have seen it. I have seen it. You'd have heard of it, as every body else has, if you had not been Mrs. Verner's sister. It's an unpleasantly queer thing for her, you know, Miss Deb."

"What utter absurdity!" cried Deborah.

"Wait till you see it, before you say it's absurdity," replied Master Cheese. "If it's not Fred Massingbird's ghost, it is somebody's that's the exact image of him."

Miss Deborah sat down on a stone jar, and got Master Cheese to tell her the whole story. That he should put in a few exaggerations, and so increase the marvel, was only natural. But Deborah West heard sufficient to send her mind into a state of uneasy perplexity.

"You say Mr. Jan knows of this?" she asked.

"There's nobody about that doesn't know of it

except you and the folks at Verner's Pride," responded Master Cheese. " I say, don't you go and tell Jan that you made me betray it to you, Miss Deb ! You'll get me into a row if you do."

But this was the very thing that Miss Deb resolved to do. Not to get Master Cheese into a "row," but that she saw no other way of allaying her uncertainty. Ghosts were utterly excluded from Deborah West's creed; and why so many people should be suddenly testifying that Frederick Massingbird's was to be seen, she could not understand. That there must be something in it more than the common absurdity of such tales, the state of Alice Hook appeared to testify.

" Can Bob be spared to go over to Broom's in the morning ? " she asked after a long pause of silence, given apparently to the contemplation of Master Cheese's intense enjoyment of his walnuts; in reality, to deep thought.

" Well, I don't know," answered the young gentleman, who never was ready to accord the services of Bob in-doors, lest it might involve any little extra amount of exertion for himself. " There's a sight of medicine to be taken out just now. Jan's got a great deal to do, and I am nearly worked off my legs."

" It looks like it," retorted Miss Deborah. " Your legs will never be much the worse for the amount of work you do. Where's Mr. Jan ? "

" He went out to go to Hook's," replied Master Cheese, a desperately hard walnut proving nearly too much for his teeth. "He'll take a round, I dare say, before he comes in."

Deborah returned in-doors. Though not much inclined to reticence in general, she observed it now, saying nothing to Amilly. The storm came on, and they sat and watched it. Supper time approached, and Master Cheese was punctual. He found some pickled herrings on the table, of which he was uncommonly fond, and ate them as long as Miss West would supply his plate. The meal was over when Jan came in.

"Don't trouble to have anything brought back for me," said he. "I'll eat a bit of bread and cheese." He was not like his assistant: his growing days were over.

Master Cheese went straight up to bed. He liked to do so as soon as supper was over, lest any summons came, and he should have to go out. Easy Jan, no matter how tired he might be, would attend himself, sooner than wake up Master Cheese —a ceremony more easy to attempt than to accomplish. Fortifying himself with about a pound of sweet cake, which he kept in his box, as a dessert to the herrings, and to refresh his dreams, Master Cheese put himself into bed.

Jan meanwhile finished his bread and cheese, and rose. "I wonder whether I shall get a whole night of it to-night?" said he, stretching himself. "I didn't have much bed last night."

"Have you to go out again, Mr. Jan?"

"No. I shall look to the books a bit, and then

turn in. Good night, Miss Deborah ; good night, Miss Amilly."

" Good night," they answered.

Amilly drew to the fire. The chilly rain of the afternoon had caused them to have one lighted. She put her feet on the fender, feeling the warmth comfortable. Deborah sent the supper-tray away, and then left the room. Stealing out of the side door quietly, she tripped across the narrow path of wet gravel, and entered the surgery. Jan had got an account-book open on the counter, and was leaning over it, a pen in his hand.

" Don't be frightened, Mr. Jan ; it's only me," said Deborah, who did not at all times confine herself to the rules of severe grammar. " I'll shut the door, if you please, for I want to say a word to yourself alone."

" Is it more physic that you want ? " asked Jan. " Has the pain in the side come again ? "

" It is not about pains or physic," she answered, drawing nearer to the counter. " Mr. Jan,"—dropping her voice to a confidential whisper,—" would you be so good as to tell me the truth of this story that is going about ? "

Jan paused. " What story ? " he rejoined.

" This ghost story. They are saying, I understand, that—that—they are saying something about Frederick Massingbird."

" Did Cheese supply you with the information ? " cried Jan, imperturbable as ever.

" He did. But I must beg you not to scold him

for it—as he thought you might do. It was I who drew the story from him. He said you cautioned him not to speak of it to me or Amilly. I quite appreciate your motives, Mr. Jan, and feel that it was very considerate of you. But now that I have heard it, I want to know particulars from somebody more reliable than Master Cheese."

"I told Lionel I'd say nothing to any soul in the parish," said Jan, open and single-minded as though he had been made of glass. "But he'd not mind my making you an exception—as you have heard it. You are Sibylla's sister."

"*You* don't believe in its being a ghost?"

Jan grinned. "I!" cried he. "No, I don't."

"Then what do you suppose it is, that's frightening people? And why should they be frightened?"

Jan sat himself down on the counter, and whirled his legs over to the other side, clearing the galli-pots; so that he faced Miss Deborah. Not to waste time, he took the mortar before him. And there he was at his ease; his legs hanging, and his hands pounding.

"What should you think it is?" inquired he.

"How can I think, Mr. Jan? Until an hour or two ago, I had not heard of the rumour. I suppose it is somebody who walks about at night to frighten people. But it is curious that he should look like Frederick Massingbird. Can you understand it?"

"I am afraid I can," replied Jan, pounding away.

"Will you tell me, please, what you think."

"Can't you guess at it, Miss Deb?"

Miss Deb looked at him, beginning to think his manner as mysterious as Master Cheese's had been.

"I can't guess at it at all," she presently said. "Please to tell me."

"Then don't you go and drop down in a fit when you hear it," was the rejoinder of Jan. "I suppose it is Fred himself."

The words took her utterly by surprise. Not at first did she understand their meaning. She stared at Jan, her eyes and her mouth gradually opening.

"Fred himself?" she mechanically uttered.

"I suppose so. Fred himself. Not his ghost."

"Do you mean that he has come to life again?" she rapidly rejoined.

"Well, you can call it so if you like," said Jan. "I expect that, in point of fact, he has never been dead. The report of his death must have been erroneous: one of those unaccountable mistakes that do sometimes happen to astonish the world."

Deborah West took in the full sense of the words, and sunk down on the big stone jar. She turned all over of a burning heat: she felt her hands beginning to twitch with emotion.

"You mean that he is alive?—that he has never been dead?" she gasped.

Jan nodded.

"Oh, Mr. Jan! Then, what is—what is Sibylla?"

"Ah," said Jan, "that's just it. She's the wife of both of 'em—as you may say."

For any petty surprise or evil, Miss Deborah would have gone off in a succession of screams, of pseudo-faints. *This* evil was all too real, too terrible. She sat with her trembling hands clasped to pain, looking hopelessly at Jan.

He told her all he knew; all that was said by others.

" Dan Duff's nothing," remarked he; "and Cheese is nothing; and others, who profess to have seen it, are nothing: and old Frost's not much. But I'd back Bourne's calmness and sound sense against the world, and I'd back Broom's."

" And they have both seen it ? "

" Both," replied Jan. " Both are sure that it is Frederick Massingbird."

" What will Mr. Verner do ? " she asked, looking round with a shudder, and not speaking above her breath.

" Oh, that's his affair," said Jan. " It's hard to guess what he may do : he is one that won't be dictated to. If it were some people's case, they'd say to Sibylla, ' Now you have got two husbands, choose which you'll have, and keep to him.' "

" Good heavens, Mr. Jan ! " exclaimed Miss Deb, shocked at the loose sentiments the words appeared to indicate. " And suppose she should choose the second ? Have you thought of the sin ? The second *can't* be her husband : it would be as bad as those Mormons."

" Looking at it in a practical point of view, I can't see much difference, which of the two she chooses," returned Jan. " If Fred was her hus-

band once, Lionel's her husband now : practically I
say, you know, Miss Deb."

Miss Deb thought the question was going rather
into metaphysics, a branch of science which she did
not understand, and so was content to leave the
controversy.

"Any way, it is dreadful for her," she said, with
another shiver. "Oh, Mr. Jan, do you think it
can really be true ?"

"*I* think that there's not a doubt of it," he
answered, stopping in his pounding. "But you
need not think so, Miss Deb."

"How am I to help thinking so ?" she simply
asked.

"You needn't think either way until it is proved.
As I suppose it must be, shortly. Let it rest till
then."

"No, Mr. Jan, I differ from you. It is a question
that ought to be sought out and probed; not left to
rest. Does Sibylla know it ?"

"Not she. Who'd tell her ? Lionel won't, I
know. It was for her sake that he bound me to
silence."

"She ought to be told, Mr. Jan. She ought to
leave her husband—I mean Mr. Lionel—this very
hour, and shut herself up until the doubt is
settled."

"Where should she shut herself?" inquired
Jan, opening his eyes. "In a convent ? Law,
Miss Deb ! If somebody came and told me I had
got two wives, should you say I ought to make a

start for the nearest monastery? How would my patients get on?"

Rather metaphysical again. Miss Deb drew Jan back to plain details—to the histories of the various ghostly encounters. Jan talked and pounded: she sat on her hard seat and listened: her brain more perplexed than it could have been with any meta-physics, known to science. Eleven o'clock disturbed them, and Miss Deborah started as if she had been shot.

"How could I keep you until this time!" she exclaimed. "And you, scarcely in bed for some nights!"

"Never mind, Miss Deb," answered good-natured Jan. "It's all in the day's work."

He opened the door for her, and then bolted himself in for the night. For the night, that is, if Deerham would allow it to him. Hook's daughter was slowly progressing towards recovery, and Jan would not need to go to her.

Amilly was nodding over the fire, or, rather, where the fire had been, for it had gone out. She inquired with wonder what her sister had been doing, and where she had been. Deborah replied that she had been busy: and they went up-stairs to bed.

But not to sleep—for one of them. Deborah West lay awake through the live-long night, tossing from side to side in her perplexity and thought. Somewhat strict in her notions, she deemed it a matter of stern necessity, of positive duty, that Sibylla should retire, at any rate for a time, from the scenes of busy life. To enable her to do this, the news must be broken to her. But how?

Ay, how? Deborah West rose in the morning with the difficulty unsolved. She supposed she must do it herself. She believed it was as much a duty laid upon her, the imparting these tidings to Sibylla, as the separating herself from all social ties, the instant it was so imparted, would be the duty of Sibylla herself. Deborah West went about her occupations that morning, one imperative sentence ever in her thoughts: " It must be done! it must be done! "

She carried it about with her, ever saying it, through the whole day. She shrank, both for Sibylla's sake and her own, from the task she was imposing upon herself; and, as we all do when we have an unpleasant office to perform, she put it off to the last. Early in the morning she had said, I will go to Verner's Pride after breakfast and tell her; breakfast over, she said, I will have my dinner first and go then.

But the afternoon passed on, and she did not go. Every little trivial domestic duty was made an excuse for delaying it. Miss Amilly, finding her sister unusually bad company, went out to drink tea with some friends. The time came for ordering in tea at home, and still Deborah had not gone.

She made the tea and presided at the table. But she could eat nothing—to the inward gratification of Master Cheese. There happened to be shrimps : a dish which that gentleman preferred, if anything, to pickled herrings, and by Miss Deborah's want of appetite he was able to secure her share and his own, including the heads and tails. He would uncommonly have liked to secure Jan's share also ; but Miss Deborah filled a plate andput them aside, against Jan came in. Jan's pressure of work caused him of late to be irregular at his meals.

Scarcely was the tea over, and Master Cheese gone, when Mr. Bourne called. Deborah, the one thought uppermost in her mind, closed the door, and spoke out what she had heard. The terrible fear, her own distress, Jan's belief that it was Fred himself, Jan's representation that Mr. Bourne also believed it. Mr. Bourne, leaning forward until his pale face and his iron-grey hair nearly touched hers, whispered in answer that he did not think there was a doubt of it.

Then Deborah did nerve herself to the task. On the departure of the vicar she started for Verner's Pride and asked to see Sibylla. The servants would have shown her to the drawing-room, but she preferred to go up to Sibylla's chamber. The company were yet in the dining-room.

How long Sibylla kept her waiting there, she scarcely knew. Sibylla was not in the habit of putting herself to inconvenience for her sisters. The message was taken to her—that Miss West waited in her chamber—as she entered the drawing-room. And there Sibylla let her wait. One or two more messages to the same effect were subsequently delivered : they produced no impression, and Deborah began to think she should not get to see her that night.

But Sibylla came up at length, and Deborah entered upon her task. Whether she accomplished it clumsily, or whether Sibylla's ill-disciplined mind was wholly in fault, certain it is that there ensued a loud and unpleasant scene. The scene to which you were a witness. Scarcely giving herself time to take in more than the bare fact hinted at by Deborah—that her first husband was believed to be alive—not waiting to inquire a single particular, she burst out of the room and went shrieking down the stairs, flying into the arms of Lionel, who at that moment had entered.

CHAPTER XXVII.

LIONEL VERNER could not speak comfort to his wife. Or, at the best, comfort of a most negative nature. He held her to him in the study, the door locked against intruders. They were somewhat at cross-purposes. Lionel supposed that the information had been imparted to her by Captain Cannonby; he never doubted but that she had been told Frederick Massingbird had returned and was on the scene; that he might come in any moment —even that very present one as they spoke—to put in his claim to her. Sibylla, on the contrary, did not think (what little she was capable of thinking) that Lionel had had previous information of the matter.

"What am I to do?" she cried, her emotion becoming hysterical. "Oh, Lionel! don't you give me up!"

"I would have got here earlier had there been means," he soothingly said, wisely evading all answer to the last suggestion. "I feared he would be telling you in my absence: better that you should have heard of it from me."

She lifted her face to look at him. "Then you know it!"

"I have known it this day or two. My journey to-day—"

She broke out into a most violent fit of emotion, shrieking, trembling, clinging to Lionel, calling out at the top of her voice that she would not leave him. All his efforts were directed to stilling the noise. He implored her to be tranquil; to remember there were listeners around: he pointed out that, until the blow actually fell, there was no necessity for those listeners to be made cognisant of it. All that he *could* do for her protection and comfort, he would do, he earnestly said. And Sibylla subsided into a softer mood and cried quietly.

"I'd rather die," she sobbed, "than have this disgrace brought upon me."

Lionel put her into the large arm-chair, which remained in the study still: the old arm-chair of Mr. Verner. He stood by her and held her hands, his pale face, grave, sad, loving, bent towards her with the most earnest sympathy. She lifted her eyes to it, whispering:

"Will they say you are not my husband?"

"Hush, Sibylla! There are moments, even yet, when I deceive myself into a fancy that it may be somehow averted. *I cannot* understand how he can be alive. Has Cannonby told you whence the error arose?"

She did not answer. She began to shake again; she tossed back her golden hair. Some blue ribbons had been wreathed in it for dinner: she pulled them out and threw them on the ground, her hair partially falling with their departure.

"I wish I could have some wine?"

He moved to the door to get it for her. "Don't you let *her* in, Lionel," she called out as he unlocked it.

"Who?"

"That Deborah. I hate her now," was the ungenerous remark.

Lionel opened the door, called to Tynn, and desired him to bring wine. "What time did Captain Cannonby get here?" he whispered, as he took it from the butler.

"Who, sir?" asked Tynn.

"Captain Cannonby."

Tynn paused, like one who does not understand. "There's no gentleman here of that name, sir. A Mr. Rushworth called to-day, and my mistress asked him to stay dinner. He is in the drawing-room now. There is no other stranger."

"Has Captain Cannonby not been here at all?" reiterated Lionel. "He left London this morning to come."

Tynn shook his head to express a negative. "He has not arrived, sir."

Lionel went in again, his feelings undergoing a sort of revulsion, for there now peeped out a glimmer of hope. So long as the nearly certain conviction on Lionel's mind was not confirmed by positive testimony—as he expected Captain Cannonby's would be—he could not entirely lose sight of all hope. That he most fervently prayed the blow might not fall, might even now be averted, you will readily believe. Sibylla had not been to him the wife he had fondly hoped for; she provoked him every hour in the day; she appeared to do what she could, wilfully to estrange his affection. He was conscious of all this; he was all too conscious that his inmost love was another's, not hers: but he lost sight of himself in anxiety for her: it was for her sake he prayed and hoped. Whether she was his wife by law, or not; whether she was loved or hated, Lionel's course of duty lay plain before him now: to shield her, so far as he might be allowed, in all care and tenderness. He would have shed his last drop of blood to promote her comfort; he would have sacrificed every feeling of his heart for her sake.

The wine in his hand, he turned into the room again. A change had taken place in her aspect. She had left the chair, and was standing against the wall opposite the door, her tears dried, her eyes unnaturally bright, her cheeks burning.

"Lionel," she uttered, a catching of the breath betraying her emotion, "if *he* is alive, whose is Verner's Pride?"

"His," replied Lionel, in a low tone.

She shrieked out, very much after the manner of a petulant child. "I won't leave it!—I won't leave Verner's Pride! You could not be so cruel as to wish me. Who says he is alive? Lionel, I ask you who it is that says he is alive?"

"Hush, my dear! This excitement will do you a world of harm, and it cannot mend the matter, however it may be. I want to know who told you of this, Sibylla. I supposed it to be Cannonby: but Tynn says Cannonby has not been here."

The question appeared to divert her thoughts into another channel. "Cannonby! What should bring him here? Did you expect him to come?"

"Drink your wine, and then I will tell you," he said, holding the glass towards her.

She pushed the wine from her capriciously. "I don't want wine now. I am hot. I should like some water."

"I will get it for you directly. Tell me, first of all, how you came to know of this?"

"Deborah told me. She sent for me out of the drawing-room where I was so happy, to tell me this horrid tale. Lionel"—sinking her voice again to a whisper—"is—he—here?"

"I cannot tell you—— "

"But you must tell me," she passionately interrupted. "I will know. I have a right to know it, Lionel."

"When I say I cannot tell you, Sibylla, I mean that I cannot tell you with any certainty. I will tell you all I do know. Some one is in the neighbourhood who bears a great resemblance to him. He is seen sometimes at night: and—and—I have other testimony that he has returned from Australia."

"What will be done if he comes here?"

Lionel was silent.

" Shall you fight him ? "

" Fight him ! " echoed Lionel. " No."

"You will give up Verner's Pride without a struggle ! You will give up me ! Then, are you a coward, Lionel Verner ? "

" You know that I would give up neither willingly, Sibylla."

Grievously pained was his tone as he replied to her. She was meeting this as she did most other things—without sense or reason; not as a thinking, rational being. Her manner was loud, her emotion violent : but, deep and true, her grief was *not*. Depth of feeling, truth of nature, were qualities that never yet had place in Sibylla Verner. Not once, throughout all their married life, had Lionel been so painfully impressed with the fact as he was now.

" Am I to die for the want of that water ? " she resumed. " If you don't get it for me I shall ring for the servants to bring it."

He opened the door again without a word. He knew quite well that she had thrown in that little shaft about ringing for the servants, because it would not be pleasant to him that the servants should intrude upon them then. Outside the door, about to knock at it, was Deborah West.

" I must go home," she whispered. " Mr. Verner, how sadly she is meeting this ! "

The very thought that was in Lionel's heart. But, not to another would he cast a shade of reflection on his wife.

"It is a terrible thing for any one to meet," he answered. "I could have wished, Miss West, that you had not imparted it to her. Better that I should have done it, when it must have been done."

"I did it from a good motive," was the reply of Deborah, who was looking sadly down-hearted, and had evidently been crying. "She ought to leave you until some certainty shall be arrived at."

"Nonsense! No!" said Lionel. "I beg you— I *beg* you, Miss West, not to say anything more that can distress or disturb her. If the—the— explosion comes, of course it must come; and we must all meet it as we best may, and see then what is best to be done."

"But it is not right that she should remain with you in this uncertainty," urged Deborah, who could be obstinate when she thought she had cause. "The world will not deem it to be right. You should remember this."

"I do not act to please the world. I am responsible to God and my conscience."

"Responsible to —— Good gracious, Mr. Verner!" returned Deborah, every line in her face expressing astonishment. "You call keeping her with you acting as a responsible man ought! If Sibylla's husband is living, you must put her away from your side."

"When the time shall come. Until then, my duty—as I judge it—is to keep her by my side; to shelter her from harm and annoyance, petty as well as great."

"You deem *that* your duty!"

"I do," he firmly answered. "My duty to her and to God."

Deborah shook her head and her hands. "It ought not to be let go on," she said, moving nearer to the study-door. "I shall urge the leaving you upon her."

Lionel calmly laid his hand upon the lock. "Pardon me, Miss West. I cannot allow my wife to be subjected to it."

"But if she is not your wife?"

A streak of red came into his pale face. "It has yet to be proved that she is not. Until that time shall come, Miss West, she *is* my wife, and I shall protect her as such."

"You will not let me see her?" asked Deborah, for his hand was not lifted from the handle.

"No. Not if your object be the motives you avow. Sleep a night upon it, Miss West, and see if you do not change your mode of thinking and come over to mine. Return here in the morning with words of love and comfort for her, and none will welcome you more sincerely than I."

"Answer me one thing, Mr. Verner. Do you believe in your heart that Frederick Massingbird is alive and has returned?"

"Unfortunately I have no resource but to believe it," he replied.

"Then, to your way of thinking, I can never come," returned Deborah in some agitation. "It is just sin, Mr. Verner, in the sight of Heaven."

"I think not," he quietly answered. "I am content to let Heaven judge me, and the motives that actuate me : a judgment more merciful than man's."

Deborah West, in her conscientious, but severe rectitude, turned to the hall door and departed, her hands uplifted still. Lionel ordered Tynn to attend Miss West home. He then procured some water for his wife and carried it in, as he had previously carried in the wine.

A fruitless service. Sibylla rejected it. She wanted neither water nor anything else, were all the thanks Lionel received, querulously spoken. He laid the glass upon the table : and, sitting down by her side in all patience, he set himself to the work of soothing her, gently and lovingly as though she had been what she was showing herself—a wayward child.

CHAPTER XXVIII.

MISS WEST and Tynn proceeded on their way. The side path was dirty, and she chose the middle of the road, Tynn walking a step behind her. Deborah was of an affable nature, Tynn a long attached and valued servant, and she chatted with him familiarly. Deborah, in her simple good heart, could not have been brought to understand why she should not chat with him. Because he was a servant and she a lady, she thought there was only the more reason why she should, that the man might not be unpleasantly reminded of the social distinction between them.

She pressed down, so far as she could, the heavy affliction that was weighing upon her mind. She spoke of the weather, the harvest, of Mrs. Bitterworth's recent dangerous attack, of other trifling topics patent at the moment to Deerham. Tynn chatted in his turn, never losing his respect of words and manner ; a servant worth anything never does. Thus they progressed towards the village, utterly unconscious that a pair of eager eyes were following and an evil tongue was casting anathemas towards them.

The owner of the eyes and tongue was wanting to hold a few words of private colloquy with Tynn. Could Tynn have seen right round the corner of the pillar of the outer gate when he went out, he would have detected the man waiting there in ambush. It was Giles Roy. Roy was aware that Tynn sometimes attended departing visitors to the outer gate. Roy had come up, hoping that he might so attend them on this night. Tynn did appear, with Miss West, and Roy began to hug himself that fortune had so far favoured him : but when he saw that Tynn departed with the lady, instead of only standing politely to watch her off, Roy growled out vengeance against the unconscious offenders.

" He's a-going to see her home belike," snarled Roy, in soliloquy, following them with angry eyes and slow footsteps. " I must wait till he comes back—and be shot to both of 'em ! "

Tynn left Miss West at her own door, declining the invitation to go in and take a bit of supper with the maids, or a glass of beer. He was trudging back again, his arms behind his back and wishing himself at home, for Tynn, fat and of short breath, did not like much walking, when, in a lonely part of the road, he came upon a man sitting astride upon a gate.

" Halloa ! is that you, Mr. Tynn ? Who'd ha' thought of seeing you out to-night ? "

For it was Mr. Roy's wish, from private motives of his own, that Tynn should not know he had been looked for, but should believe the encounter to be

accidental. Tynn turned off the road, and leaned
his elbow upon the gate, rather glad of the opportunity to stand a minute and get his breath. It was
somewhat up-hill to Verner's Pride, the whole of
the way from Deerham.

"Are you sitting here for pleasure?" asked he of
Roy.

"I'm sitting here for grief," returned Roy; and
Tynn was not sharp enough to detect the hollow
falseness of his tone. "I had to go up the road
to-night on a matter of business, and, walking back
by Verner's Pride, it so overcome me that I was
glad to bring myself to a anchor."

"How should walking by Verner's Pride overcome
you?" demanded Tynn.

"Well," said Roy, "it was the thoughts of poor
Mr. and Mrs. Verner did it. He didn't behave to
me over liberal in turning me from the place I'd
held so long under his uncle, but I've overgot that
smart; it's past and gone. My heart bleeds for him
now, and that's the truth."

For Roy's heart to "bleed" for any fellow-creature
was a marvel that even Tynn, unsuspicious as he
was, could not take in. Mrs. Tynn repeatedly
assured him that he had been born into the world
with one sole quality—credulity. Certainly Tynn
was unusually inclined to put faith in fair outsides.
Not that Roy could boast much of the latter
advantage.

"What's the matter with Mr. Verner?" he asked
of Roy.

Roy groaned dismally. " It's a thing that is come
to my knowledge," said he—" a awful misfortin that
is a-going to drop upon him. I'd not say a word to
another soul but you, Mr. Tynn ; but you be his
friend if anybody be, and I feel that I must either
speak or bust."

Tynn peered at Roy's face. As much as he could
see of it, for the night was not a very clear one.

" It seems quite a providence that I happened to
meet you," went on Roy, as if any meeting with the
butler had been as far from his thoughts as an
encounter with somebody at the North Pole.
" Things does turn out lucky sometimes."

" I must be getting home," interposed Tynn.
" If you have anything to say to me, Roy, you had
better say it. I may be wanted."

Roy—who was standing now, his elbow leaning
on the gate—brought his face nearer to Tynn's.
Tynn was also leaning on the gate.

" Have you heered of this ghost that's said to be
walking about Deerham ? " he asked, lowering his
voice to a whisper. " Have you heered whose they
say it is ? "

Now, Tynn had heard. All the retainers, male
and female, at Verner's Pride had heard. And
Tynn, though not much inclined to give credence
to ghosts in a general way, had felt somewhat
uneasy at the tale. More on his mistress's account
than on any other score : for Tynn had the sense
to know that such a report could not be pleasing to
Mrs. Verner, should it reach her ears.

"I can't think why they do say it," replied Tynn, answering the man's concluding question. "For my own part, I don't believe there's anything in it. I don't believe in ghosts."

"Neither didn't a good many more, till now that they have got orakelar demonstration of it," returned Roy. "Dan Duff see it, and a'most lost his senses; that girl of Hook's see it, and you know, I suppose, what it did for *her*; Broom see it; the parson see it; old Frost see it; and lots more. Not one on 'em but 'ud take their Bible oath, if put to it, that it is Fred Massingbird's ghost."

"But it is not," said Tynn. "It can't be. Leastways I'll never believe it till I see it with my own eyes. There'd be no reason in its coming now. If it had wanted to come at all, why didn't it come when it was first buried, and not wait till over two years had gone by?"

"That's the point that I stuck at," was Roy's answer. "When my wife come home with the tales, day after day, that Fred Massingbird's spirit was walking,—that this person had seen it, and that person had seen it—'Yah! Rubbish!' I says to her. 'If his ghost had been a-coming, it 'ud have come afore now.' And so it would."

"Of course," answered Tynn. "*If* it had been coming. But I have not lived to these years to believe in ghosts at last."

"Then, what do you think of the parson, Mr. Tynn?" continued Roy, in a strangely significant tone. "And Broom,—he have got his senses about him ? How d'ye account for their believing it ? "

" I have not heard them say that they do believe it," responded Tynn, with a knowing nod. " Folks may go about and say that I believe it, perhaps : but that wouldn't make it any nearer the fact. And what has all this to do with Mr. Verner ? "

" I am coming to it," said Roy. He took a step backward, looked carefully up and down the road, lest listeners might be in ambush; stretched his neck forward, and in like manner surveyed the field on either side the hedge. Apparently it satisfied him, and he resumed his close proximity to Tynn and his meaning whisper. " Can't you guess the riddle, Mr. Tynn ? "

" I can't in the least guess what you mean, or what you are driving at," was Tynn's response. " I think you must have been having a drop of drink, Roy. I ask what this is to my master, Mr. Verner ? "

" Drink be bothered ! I've not had a sup inside my mouth since mid-day," was Roy's retort. " This secret has been enough drink for me, and meat, too. You'll keep counsel, if I tell it you, Mr. Tynn ? Not but what it must soon come out."

" Well ? " returned Tynn, in some surprise.

" It's Fred Massingbird fast enough. But it's not his ghost."

" What on earth do you mean ? " asked Tynn, never for a moment glancing at the fact of what Roy tried to imply.

"*He* is come back : Frederick Massingbird. He didn't die, over there."

A pause, devoted by Tynn to staring and thinking. When the full sense of the words broke upon him, he staggered a step or two away from the ex-bailiff.

" Heaven help us if it's true ! " he uttered. " Roy ! it *can't* be ! "

" It *is*," said Roy.

They stood looking at each other by starlight. Tynn's face had grown hot and wet, and he wiped it. " It can't be," he mechanically repeated.

" I tell you it *is*, Mr. Tynn. Now, never you mind asking me how I came to the bottom of it," went on Roy in a sort of defiant tone. " I did come to the bottom of it, and I do know it : and Mr. Fred, he knows that I know it. It's as sure that he is back, and in the neighbourhood, as that you and me is here at this gate. He is alive and he is among us—as certain as that you are Mr. Tynn, and I be Giles Roy."

There came flashing over Tynn's thoughts the scene of that very evening. His mistress's shrieks and agitation when she broke from Miss West ; the cries and sobs which had penetrated to their ears when she was shut afterwards in the study with her husband. The unusual scene had been productive of gossipping comment among the servants : and Tynn had believed something distressing must have occurred. Not this ; he had never glanced a suspicion at this. He remembered the lines of pain which shone out at the moment from his master's

pale face, in spite of its impassiveness: and somehow that very face brought conviction to Tynn now,
that Roy's news was true. Tynn let his arms fall
on the gate again with a groan.

" Whatever will become of my poor mistress ? "
he uttered.

" She ! " slightingly returned Roy. " She'll be
better off than him."

" Better off than who ? "

" Than Mr. Verner. She needn't leave Verner's
Pride. He must."

To expect any ideas but coarse ones from Roy,
Tynn could not. But his attention was caught by
the last suggestion.

" Leave Verner's Pride ? " slowly repeated Tynn.
" Must he ?—good heavens ! must my master be
turned from Verner's Pride ? "

" Where'll be the help for it ? " asked Roy, in a
confidential tone. " I tell you, Mr. Tynn, my
heart's been a-bleeding for him ever since I heard
it. *I* don't see no help for his turning out. I have
been a-weighing it over and over in my mind, and
I don't see none, Do you ? "

Tynn looked very blank. He was feeling so.
He made no answer, and Roy continued, blandly
confidential still.

" If that there codicil, that was so much talked
on, hadn't been lost, he'd have been all right, would
Mr. Verner. No come-to-life-again Fred Massingbird needn't have tried at turning him out.
Couldn't it be hunted for again, Mr. Tynn ? "

Roy turned the tail of his eye on Tynn. Would
his pumping take effect? Mrs. Tynn would have
told him that her husband might be pumped dry,
and never know it. She was not far wrong. Unsuspicious Tynn went headlong into the snare.

"Where would be the good of hunting for it
again—when every conceivable place was hunted
for it before?" he asked.

"Well, it was a curious thing, that codicil,"
remarked Roy. "Has it *never* been heered on?"

Tynn shook his head. "Never at all. What an
awful thing this is, if it's true!"

"It is true, I tell ye," said Roy. "You needn't
doubt it. There was a report a short while agone
that the codicil had been found, and Matiss had got
it in safe keeping. As I sat here, afore you come
up, I was thinking how well it 'ud have served Mr.
Verner's turn just now, if it *was* true."

"It is not true," said Tynn. "All sorts of
reports get about. The codicil has never been
found and never been heard of."

"What a pity!" groaned Roy, with a deep sigh.
"I'm glad I've told it you, Mr. Tynn! It's a heavy
secret for a man to carry about inside of him. I
must be going."

"So must I," said Tynn. "Roy, are you sure
there's no mistake?" he added. "It seems a tale
next to impossible.

"Well now," said Roy, "I see you don't half
believe me. You must wait a few days, and see
what them days 'll bring forth. That Mr. Massing-

bird's back from Australia, I'll take my oath to. *I*
didn't believe it at first : and when young Duff was
a-going on about the porkypine, I shook him, I did,
for a little lying rascal. I know better now."

" But how do you know it ? " debated Tynn.

" Now, never you mind. It's my business, I say,
and nobody else's. You just wait a day or two,
that's all, Mr. Tynn. I declare I am as glad to
have met with you to-night, and exchanged this
intercourse of opinions, as if anybody had counted
me out a bag o' gold."

" Well, good night, Roy," concluded Tynn,
turning his steps towards Verner's Pride. " I wish
I had been a hundred miles off, I know, before I
had heard it."

Roy slipped over the gate ; and there, out of
sight, he executed a kind of triumphant dance.

" Then there is no codicil !" cried he. "I thought
I could wile it out of him ! That Tynn's as easy to
be run out as is glass when it's hot."

And, putting his best leg forward, he made his
way as fast as he could make it towards his home.

Tynn made *his* way towards Verner's Pride. But
not fast. The information he had received filled
his mind with the saddest trouble, and reduced his
steps to slowness. When any great calamity falls
suddenly upon us, or the dread of any great calamity,
our first natural thought is, how it may be mitigated
or averted. It was the thought that occurred to
Tynn. The first shock over, digested, as may be
said, Tynn began to deliberate whether he could do

anything to help his master in the strait; and
he went along, turning all sorts of suggestions over
in his mind. Much as Sibylla was disliked by the
old servants—and she had contrived to make herself
very much disliked by them all—Tynn could not
help feeling warmly the blow that was about to
burst upon her head. Was there anything earthly
he could do to avert it?—to help her or his master?

He did not doubt the information. Roy was not
a particularly reliable person: but Tynn could not
doubt that this was true. It was the most feasible
solution of the ghost story agitating Deerham; the
only solution of it, Tynn grew to think. If Frederick
Massingbird—

Tynn's reflections came to a halt. Vaulting over
a gate on the other side the road—the very gate
through which poor Rachel Frost had glided the
night of her death, to avoid meeting Frederick Massingbird and Sibylla West—was a tall man. He
came straight across the road, in front of Tynn, and
passed through a gap of the hedge, on to the grounds
of Verner's Pride.

But what made Tynn stand transfixed, as if he
had been changed into a statue? What brought a
cold chill to his heart, a heat to his brow? ·Why,
as the man passed him, he turned his face full on
Tynn; disclosing the features, the white, whisker-
less cheek, with the black mark upon it, of Frederick
Massingbird. Recovering himself as he best could,
Tynn walked on, and gained the house.

Mrs. Verner had gone to her room. Mr. Verner

was mixing with his guests. Some of the gentlemen were on the terrace smoking, and Tynn made his way on to it, hoping he might get a minute's interview with his master. The impression upon Tynn's mind was, that Frederick Massingbird was coming there and then, to invade Verner's Pride : it appeared to Tynn to be his duty to impart what he had heard and seen at once to Mr. Verner.

Circumstances favoured him. Lionel had been talking with Mr. Gordon at the far end of the terrace, but the latter was called to from the drawing-room windows and departed in answer to it. Tynn seized the opportunity : his master was alone.

Quite alone. He was leaning over the outer balustrade of the terrace, apparently looking forth in the night obscurity on his own lands, stretched out before him. " Master ! " whispered Tynn, forgetting ceremony in the moment's absorbing agitation, in the terrible calamity that was about to fall, " I have had an awful secret made known to me to-night. I must tell it you, sir."

" I know it already, Tynn," was the quiet response of Lionel.

Then Tynn told—told all he had heard, and how he had heard it ; told how he had just *seen* Frederick Massingbird. Lionel started from the balustrade.

" Tynn ! You saw him ! Now ? "

" Not five minutes ago, sir. He came right on to these grounds through the gap in the hedge. Oh, master ! what will be done ? " and the man's voice rose to a wail in its anguish. " He may be coming

on now to put in his claim to Verner's Pride; to—
to—to—all that's in it!"

But that Lionel was nerved to self-control, he
might have answered with another wail of anguish.
His mind filled up the gap of words, that the delicacy
of Tynn would not speak. "He may be coming to
claim Sibylla."

END OF VOL. II.

BRADBURY AND EVANS, PRINTERS, WHITEFRIARS.

www.ingramcontent.com/pod-product-compliance
Lightning Source LLC
Chambersburg PA
CBHW021108270326
41929CB00009B/782